Biblical Mormonism

Biblical Mormonism

A Biblical Basis for LDS Theology

Richard R. Hopkins

ISBN 13: 978-0-88290-482-5
ISBN 10: 088290-482-5
HP Order #:1041

Published by CFI, an imprint of Cedar Fort, Inc., 925 N. Main, Springville, UT, 84663
Distributed by Cedar Fort, Inc. www.cedarfort.com
Cover design by Nicole Williams

Printed in the United States of America

10 9 8 7 6 5

Printed on acid-free paper

Contents

Part I
Mormon Theology

Preface

In recent years, Mormon writers have become prolific in their response to the charge of some Christian groups that Mormonism is a *cult*. That reproach was first aimed at Mormons by the late Dr. Walter Martin, founder of the Christian Research Institute (CRI), who included within his definition of the term many other Christian sects. Despite LDS reaction, the "cult" label has been widely accepted among those who identify themselves as *Evangelical*, largely because of CRI's nationally syndicated radio program, "The Bible Answerman."

Members of The Church of Jesus Christ of Latter-day Saints (Mormons, or Latter-day Saints) are deeply offended by this inappropriate characterization of their faith. However, few understand why their Church is thus defamed, or the theological significance of the "cult" label. This charge represents the most significant challenge the LDS Church has confronted in modern times.

Those who assert the claim that Mormonism is cultic are referred to in this book as *Evangelicals*. They include individuals from many denominations, both Protestant and Catholic. Despite their diversity, these devotees see themselves as part of the same Body, which they regard as the original, orthodox Church of Jesus Christ.

The tie that binds this group together, despite their many differences, is the acceptance of two fundamental doctrines they regard as central to historic Christianity. Any sect that does not accept these two tenets but claims to be Christian, is, by Dr. Martin's definition, a *cult* of Christianity—an apostate offshoot, disassociated from the true Body of Christ.

The two dogmas that identify this ecumenical movement are (1) the Trinity, and (2) the doctrine of salvation by grace without obedience. These tenets address the two most important subjects in religion—

theology, or the study of God, and *soteriology*, the study of God's plan for the salvation of Man.[1]

Unfortunately, by selecting these two teachings as their touchstone, Evangelicals have embraced the two most significant departures from the teachings of the Bible that have occurred in the two-thousand-year history of the Christian Church.

In the Mormon viewpoint, these two doctrines are the landmarks of the Great Apostasy prophesied by Christ and His Apostles. The first is a monument to the influence of Greek philosophy on the early Christian Church, and the second is a reflection of the moral decay that characterized the Dark Ages. The fact that Christendom has come to regard them as the fundamental characteristics of Christ's Church is a bit like finding the tenets of Nazism proclaimed as the cornerstones of Judaism two thousand years after World War II.

The difficulty of convincing Evangelicals of their error, however, cannot be underestimated. For over eighteen-hundred years "orthodox Christianity" has been so affected by Greek philosophy that its doctrines now include many concepts Evangelicals believe to be biblical that in reality have no scriptural basis whatever. Against the force of that belief system, it is necessary not only to show that Mormonism is biblical, but that many supposedly "orthodox" tenets are not. This is no easy task. Those who have been taught to regard the Hellenized version of Christianity as historic truth find biblical Christianity difficult to comprehend, much less accept.

Despite its dimensions, Latter-day Saints must not shrink from this task. They will need more than a mere defense of Mormon teachings, however, to accomplish it. This book provides an explanation and demonstration of how Latter-day Saints, through study and by acting in all humility and meekness, may be able to convince some Evangelicals that their position represents a departure from the Bible and that The Church of Jesus Christ of Latter-day Saints teaches biblical Christianity.

To accomplish that goal, Mormons will need to learn methods of reasoning and analysis that are familiar to Evangelical scholars. These methods include the biblical sciences of *textual criticism*, *apologetics*, and *hermeneutics*, to which Evangelicals give great deference. These subjects

1. Throughout this book, the terms Man and Men, when thus capitalized, designate both males and females, as in Genesis 1:27.

are introduced in this volume on a beginner's level. Greater scholarship in these areas is, of course, encouraged (but see 2 Nephi 9:28-29).

The first edition of this volume found few members of The Church of Jesus Christ of Latter-day Saints familiar with these philosophical techniques. That has changed in recent years, but more progress is needed, not only to improve understanding and advance missionary work among Evangelicals, but for personal growth and satisfaction. These principles provide an excellent basis for expanding one's own knowledge and understanding of the scriptures. Some will find them fascinating, others tedious, but any who wish to convince Evangelicals that Mormonism is true biblical Christianity must obtain at least a rudimentary grasp of these principles.

A lack of expertise in these study methods is considered by Evangelicals to be a lack of Bible scholarship. As a result, current efforts to evangelize Mormons have changed from the old tactics of criticizing LDS leaders and the Book of Mormon to a new approach in which Evangelicals attempt to place Latter-day Saints on the defensive about the biblical basis for their teachings.

In such circumstances, exposed for the first time to these techniques, many Mormon find themselves at a disadvantage, even those who have read and studied the Bible extensively. Evangelical scholars do not simply read the Word of God, they "*exegete* the scriptures with a satisfying *hermeneutic*." The nature of this approach and its scholarly mien can be quite intimidating. However, acquaintance with this new approach shows that many who wield the imposing sword of biblical scholarship do so inaccurately, even violating their own precepts.

Because the current Evangelical attack on Mormonism is directed at its biblical foundations, the sole authority relied upon in this book is the *Bible*. The other Standard Works of the Church—the *Book of Mormon, Doctrine and Covenants* (D&C) and *Pearl of Great Price* (sometimes referred to collectively as "Mormon Scripture")—are quoted only to substantiate LDS positions on specific issues and occasionally to provide insight.

Many points of Mormon doctrine expressed in this work will come as a surprise to Evangelicals. Some claim "that's not what your church *really* teaches," or "that's not what you used to teach." Such claims arise because Evangelicals have relied for their understanding of Mormonism primarily upon non-Mormons, who gleaned their limited understanding of

LDS theology from sources Latter-day Saints would call anti-Mormon. They quote material chosen from the statements of early Mormon leaders more for its susceptibility to misinterpretation and ridicule than from a desire to know what Mormons really teach.

To counter these quotations, Mormons should remember that there is a good reason the Church has accepted the four LDS Standard Works (the largest of which is the Bible) as its doctrinal canon. These works contain the Word of God, the most accurate statement of truth available to Man and *truth,essentially,* is Mormon doctrine.

Any Mormon attempting to discuss LDS theology with Evangelicals should not be diverted from a strictly biblical orientation by the use of such quotations. When confronted with them, the Latter-day Saint can say that the only statements of doctrine Mormons are required to accept as the Word of God are those contained in the Standard Works, including the Bible. Revelations pertaining to this day and age and statements by the First Presidency are occasionally added to the canon of scripture, but most remarks by Church leaders are intended to aid in understanding and applying the teachings Man has already received through these scriptures.

If a quotation from an LDS leader that seems to teach new and radical doctrine is nevertheless thrust upon a Mormon by an Evangelical antagonist, a number of responses would be appropriate. Writings by Mormon leaders that have not been added to the canon of scripture must be treated with care. They should be analyzed in much the same way as other inspired material that appears problematic or raises a scriptural contradiction. If necessary, they should be textually criticized, to ensure that they accurately reflect the author's original statements; the author's audience, usage and idiom should be given due consideration; and great care should be taken to ensure that the quotations are not taken out of context. A general understanding of biblical truth must also be established, for comments by LDS prophets, like those of ancient prophets, can only be interpreted accurately if biblical teaching as a whole is understood.

The Latter-day Saint can point out that such studies take time—time that is at a premium in theological discussions. Is it worth the time to make such an analysis when one can simply use the Bible as the fundamental authority upon which both Mormons and Evangelicals agree? Usually the discussion can be returned to a biblical basis in this way. Only if the Bible can be made the focus of the discussion will it be possible to show that Mormonism is biblical.

The need for Evangelicals to reconsider their teachings on the points examined in this book is critical. If their misconceptions about the Gospel, for example, are not corrected, many well-meaning Christians will find themselves swallowed by the tide of evildoing that inexorably engulfs all who embrace the notion that Man can be saved without obedience to God's commandments. Some of the best and brightest among Evangelical leaders have fallen prey to serious sin because of such false teaching.

This book was not written in a spirit of enmity. No offense to any Evangelical believer or scholar is intended by anything said in this work, nor should any Mormon give such offense. Every individual's interpretation of the Bible should be respected (though not necessarily accepted), and while Mormons should know that they subscribe to the most accurate interpretation, they should always be agreeable when disagreeing. Discussions of faith and belief must be conducted pleasantly and with the Spirit of the Lord (even when that Spirit is not displayed by the other party to the discussion).

The diversity of religious opinion on the fundamentals of Christianity has led some to say that the truth cannot be demonstrated from the Bible. That assertion is not entirely true. The other Standard Works assure accurate understanding of the truths taught in the Bible through cross-reference, and to Latter-day Saints there is no question that truth is taught in the Bible! In fact, there has been a progressive improvement in the accuracy of non-LDS commentary by good Bible scholars during the last century. Some still turn a blind eye to their own analytical techniques in a determined effort to avoid accepting what Mormons teach, but good bible scholarship can bring many to the realization that Mormonism encompasses the best understanding of the Bible.

This book was written in hope of paving the way for meaningful exchange on the central issues that separate The Church of Jesus Christ of Latter-day Saints from other Christian denominations. While LDS missionaries should not mistake Bible discussions for proselyting, an exchange of beliefs is often essential as a preamble to effective missionary work, especially among Evangelicals. Many who would not otherwise accept the message of Christ from the representatives of His Church, will have their minds opened by hearing biblical reasons for LDS teachings phrased in a form with which they are familiar.

The Evangelical reader is asked to be open-minded about the issues and arguments presented in this book, and to refrain from rejecting them simply because they come from Mormons. One should not resist the truth because it has been mislabeled by its adversaries. Those who seek to identify the Body of Christ through a study of His teachings, will find that the biblical principles taught in The Church of Jesus Christ of Latter-day Saints identify it as the true historic and orthodox Christian Church.

1

How Firm a Foundation! An Introduction to the Biblical Sciences

The Bible bears a special position of importance to all Christians. It is a source of history, doctrine, wisdom, comfort and truth. It is an ensign of morality to all nations, a standard against which individual beliefs and ethical systems can be measured. It also creates a bond between all Christians throughout the world who revere it as the Word of God.

Yet reverence for the Bible has not led to doctrinal unity among Christian religions in nearly two thousand years. This simple fact attests to one incontrovertible conclusion—without the assistance of the Holy Ghost, the words written on its pages, which communicate a knowledge of spiritual truths, include some degree of misunderstanding. This situation results from the faults and frailties of Men, who from the beginning, have been the major source of error in God's eternal plan.

Revelations from God have been given to Man (John 17:8, 14), but simply delivering these revelations exposes them to the very errors they were meant to correct. One source of error is Man's language. Since the Tower of Babel, Men have had problems *transcribing* God's message. Another source of error is Man's intellect, emotions and predilections. These present problems in *receiving* the message. Other errors arise when Men attempt to *transmit* the revelations of God to their fellows, or *preserve* that message for their posterity.

Transcribing God's Word generates errors not only because Men are not Xerox machines, but because Man's tongue is imperfect. His language varies from country to country, and even within countries. Idiom and context also affect the meaning of the message, and the mode of expression may have an impact as well. In some languages, the meaning of words can vary with the pitch of the tone at which they are spoken.[1]

1. This is true of the Thai language, for example.

Adding to the various problems of transcription are variations in the ability of Men to accept and comprehend written revelations. Errors arise because of the educational and intellectual level of the receiver. Men often err in their understanding of God's message because they do not wish to hear what He wants to tell them.

As if the problems of communicating with each other now were not enough, Men face the problem of transmitting God's messages to, and translating them for, people who live thousands of years apart, who speak different languages and have different customs. All these factors contribute to the difficulty of understanding the truths taught in the Bible today.

Biblical Inerrancy. Despite these problems, Evangelicals are wont to refer to the Bible as *inerrant.* That label describes the original message transmitted by God, but it draws a deceptive veil over errors that are unavoidable in the subsequent human communication of that message. It distorts the character of the writings Men have today, no matter how inspired their source. Any reluctance to call the Bible "inerrant" should be without criticism if it is accompanied by a reverence for the textual integrity and original inspiration of that worthy Scripture.

All Bible scholars acknowledge that the texts of the Bible, as they are now preserved, contain some error. Mormons are committed to the principle that despite such errors, biblical texts contain *the Word of God* to the fullest extent flawed human language can convey that message to an imperfect humanity.

The Eighth Article of Faith expresses the official view of The Church of Jesus Christ of Latter-day Saints regarding the inerrancy of the Bible. It reads as follows:

> We believe the Bible to be the word of God as far as it is translated correctly; . . .

This simple statement speaks worlds about acceptance of the biblical texts. It acknowledges that the currently accepted texts, transmitted over the ages from the original *autographa* (the original pages written by the prophets and apostles, or their scribes), are sufficiently accurate that Men need only be concerned with the accuracy of their *translation* in order to receive an understanding of God's message.

It has always been the position of The Church of Jesus Christ of Latter-day Saints to accept and staunchly defend the Bible. So strongly has that position been asserted from the beginning that a frustrated Joseph Smith, rebuking the Christian sects of his day, once gave the following answers to the two questions most frequently asked of him by his detractors:

> First "Do you believe the Bible?"
>
> If we do, we are the only people under heaven that does, for there are none of the religious sects of the day that do.
>
> Second "Wherein do you differ from other sects?"
>
> In that we believe the Bible, and all other sects profess to believe their interpretations of the Bible, and their creeds.[2]

The extent to which Mormons criticize the Bible has been grossly exaggerated among Evangelicals. Some have the impression that Mormons do not use or rely on the Bible at all. Others falsely claim that "[Mormon apostles] have been teaching us that the Bible has been corrupted through the centuries and as a result, cannot be trusted,"[3] or that "the LDS Church is teaching that English Bibles lack correct translation."[4]

Those who level such criticisms at the Mormon Church and its leaders have little or no practical experience with LDS teaching. For example, at the direction of the very apostles maligned in these quotations, two years out of every four are spent in the study of the Old and New Testaments at weekly Sunday School classes attended by all adult Mormons. LDS leaders constantly teach *from* the Bible, *about* the Bible, and that every Mormon should *study* the Bible.

Nor are Mormons more suspicious of errors in translation than are Evangelicals. Mormons have very few problems with biblical translation, and certainly none that are not shared by most Bible scholars. Evangelicals are just as familiar with the problems in the English translation of the Bible as are Mormons, and if anything, are more concerned about errors that may have arisen due to transcription and transmission of the original texts.

---

2. Joseph Smith, Jr, from *Teachings of the Prophet Joseph Smith,* comp. Joseph Fielding Smith (1970 reprint, Salt Lake City: Deseret Book Company, 1938), 119.

3. Cary Trivanovich, *"Speaking the Truth in Love" (Ephesians 4:15): What Every Mormon Should Know* (Orange: Promise Publishing Company, 1988), 10. Though Trivanovich is not a Bible scholar, his pamphlet, cited frequently in this work, summarizes the positions of several Evangelical scholars, making it a convenient resource.

4. Trivanovich, *Speaking the Truth in Love,* 14.

Of course, Mormons are not without some concern about the texts of the Bible. In 1830, Joseph Smith undertook to obtain from the Lord, by direct revelation, an accurate English translation of the original *autographa* of the Bible.[5] This work is referred to as the Joseph Smith Translation (JST). But the Church has not chosen to replace the King James Version (KJV) with the JST. Rather, the Church's official publication of the KJV is footnoted with occasional excerpts from it. This reflects a general satisfaction with the text upon which the KJV is based.

In light of their own concerns, Evangelical criticism of Mormon teachings about errors in the Bible borders on hypocrisy. The entire subject of biblical analysis known as *textual criticism,* recognized and accepted by Evangelicals, attests to the disingenuous nature of such allegations. The following introduction to textual criticism is provided to put this type of criticism into proper focus.

An Introduction to *Textual Criticism*

Textual criticism is the field of biblical study that deals with the morass lying between the original *autographa* of the Old and New Testaments and the existing texts available today. It is a sad fact that **Bible scholars have no original manuscripts of any of the books of the Bible**. The most ancient manuscripts they now have derive from the originals through an unknown number of intermediate copies. (In light of this, the complaint that Mormons do not have the original plates of the Book of Mormon also smacks of hypocrisy.)

The goal of textual critics is to derive a text as close as possible to the original *autographa* by using all available copies, fragments of copies, ancient versions and translations and quotations by other early writers, and by examining the internal evidence for the accuracy of those sources.[6] Fortunately, in the case of the Bible, a very large number of copies (referred to by scholars as "mss." for manuscripts, "ms." being the singular form) are available today from a variety of locales.

Old Testatment Texts. The number of mss. of the Old Testament is a lesser concern to scholars than the number of mss. of the New Testament.

5. Joseph Smith, Jr., *The Holy Scriptures: Inspired Version* (Independence: Herald Publishing House, 1974).

6. Paul Maas, *Textual Criticism*, trans. Barbara Flower (Oxford: University Press, 1967), 1.

The Masoretes, a guild of specially trained Jewish scholars, have maintained the text of the Old Testament for milennia with such painstaking care that the mss. currently in existence show little divergence from the most ancient texts, even the recently discovered Dead Sea Scrolls of a much earlier origin.

However, even in the most well preserved texts from ancient times, there are slight variations and deviations. In addition, translators have added words to provide clarity and improve the syntax of their translation. In the KJV and most English translations, these words are printed in italics. The same format is followed here, so that, unless otherwise indicated (by the words "emphasis added"), italics are used to identify words that do *not* appear in the original Greek or Hebrew texts.

Despite *textual variations* between the various ancient texts, there are few instances where a difference in the text changes the meaning of the passage. For example, one can compare the text of Isaiah contained in the Book of Mormon (2 Nephi ch.12-24), which dates from before the Babylonian captivity (approx. 600 B.C.), to the texts of Isaiah 2-14 in the KJV and the New American Standard Bible (NASB– considered by many scholars to be a more accurate translation. Numerous textual variations can be found, but the meaning of the verses is unaffected.

This can be demonstrated using a commonly criticized excerpt from the Book of Mormon text of Isaiah. The specific passage is Isaiah 4:5-6 (KJV and NASB), which appears in the Book of Mormon as 2 Nephi 14:5-6. The three versions read as follows shown in the box on the next page.

The words capitalized in each version raise what some see as an important issue. The word, "DEFENSE" (now commonly spelled "defense"), is thought to be a mistranslation in the KJV. "CANOPY" (or "covering"), found in the NASB, is closer to the literal translation of the Hebrew. But the word "defense" is also used in the Book of Mormon. Critics ask why the incorrect translation from the KJV appears in the Book of Mormon if it is earlier in origin and was translated by the power of God. One critic claims these words represent "irreconcilable errors which deny any possibility that the Book of Mormon was inspired of God."[7]

The answer to this criticism requires an introduction to the concept of thought-for-thought translation, as opposed to word-for-word (or "literal") translation. Reading each verse in context, it is obvious that the KJV and

---

7. Trivanovich, *Speaking the Truth in Love*, 6. If Trivanovich is serious about this, he must reject all inspired writing. There are textual variations in all Bible texts.

King James Version	Book of Mormon	New American Standard
And the Lord will create upon every dwelling place of mount Zion, and upon her assemblies, a cloud and smoke by day, and the shining of a flaming fire by night: for upon all the glory *shall be* a DEFENSE. And there shall be a tabernacle for a shadow in the daytime from the heat, and for a place of refuge, and for a covert from storm and from rain.	And the Lord will create upon every dwelling-place of mount Zion, and upon her assemblies, a cloud and smoke by day and the shining of a flaming fire by night; for upon all the glory [of Zion] shall be a DEFENSE. And there shall be a tabernacle for a shadow in the daytime from the heat, and for a place of refuge, and a covert from storm and from rain.	then the Lord will create over the whole area of Mount Zion and over her assemblies a cloud by day, even smoke, and the brightness of a flaming fire by night; for over all the glory will be a CANOPY. And there will be a shelter to give shade from the heat by day, and refuge and protection from the storm and the rain.

the Book of Mormon versions have the same meaning as the NASB. Even if the word "canopy" is a better word-for-word translation, the word "defense" conveys the protective nature of the canopy or covering that the Lord promised Israel. Thus, it imparts the meaning of the passage more clearly. It is an excellent thought-for-thought translation.

Such translations are difficult because they attempt to translate God's thoughts apart from His words (see Isa. 55:8-9). Still, where they are accurate, they are preferable. The thought-for-thought translation that appears in the KJV was obviously retained in the Book of Mormon because Joseph Smith was inspired to give the best translation possible. In this instance, that translation is the one given by the King James translators.

Note, however, that the words "of Zion," bracketed in the Book of Mormon text, do not appear in the KJV or the NASB. These words give greater clarity to the passage, without changing its meaning. This and many other slight variations suggest that the Book of Mormon was not copied from the KJV, but was translated (by a person familiar with KJV language) from a text of ancient origin, as professed in the Book of Mormon.

New Testament Texts. Problems with divergence between texts in New Testament mss. are considerably more extreme and abundant than those in the Old Testament. There is no authoritative revision of the New Testament comparable to the Masoretic Text. In addition to the problems of divergence between mss., there are many spurious compositions that were passed around in the early Church under the names of the Apostles, making it difficult to determine the inspired canon.[8]

As a result, the best authorities estimate that the extent of certainty regarding the original *autographa* is substantially less for the New Testament than for the Old. However, about seven-eights of the words in the original *autographa* are known for certain, and of the questions that affect the remaining one eighth, most relate only to order and form, so that "serious doubt does not appear to touch more than one-sixtieth [1/60th] part of the whole text."[9] While this is reassuring, the reader should know that **there are approximately 150,000 variant readings among the Greek texts of the New Testament.**[10]

The techniques of early textual critics are illustrated in the writings of Origen (182-251 A.D.), an Alexandrian scholar whose comments on Matthew 19:17-21 (the reply of Christ to the rich young man) demonstrate his approach.

Origen reasoned that Jesus could not have concluded his list of commandments with the all-inclusive requirement, "Thou shalt love thy neighbor as thyself" because the rich young man had replied, "All these things have I kept from my youth up." Jesus evidently accepted this statement as true, but if the rich young man had loved his neighbor as himself from his youth up, he would certainly have been perfect. But Christ answered him "*If* thou wilt be perfect, . . ." implying that he was not yet perfect. Hence, Origen concluded that the commandment "Thou shalt love thy neighbour

8. For more about the canon of the New Testament, see Bruce M. Metzger, *The Canon of the New Testament* (Oxford: Clarendon Press, 1987).

9. Joseph Angus, *The Bible Handbook: An Introduction to the Study of Sacred Scripture*, rev. by Samuel G. Green (New York: Fleming H. Revel Company, n.d.), 76.

10. Josh McDowell, *Evidence That Demands a Verdict* (San Bernadino: Here's Life Publishers, 1979), 43-46. This is substantialy fever than critics fo the Book of Mormon have come up with.

as thyself" was not spoken by Christ on this occasion and deleted it from his copy of Matthew's text.

Fortunately, this kind of thinking found acceptance in only one group of mss., the Western texts, popular in Rome. The texts ultimately accepted by the Protestant Reformation were derived primarily from the Byzantine group, which were much better preserved (see Appendix A). The final version is called the *Textus Receptus* (the Received Text) and was edited by Erasmus. The *Textus Receptus* was the first printed edition of the Greek New Testament (1516).

A second edition, also edited by Erasmus, formed the basis for Luther's German version, which was hailed by Joseph Smith as the most accurate translation available in his day.[11] The fifth edition, by Beza (1598), is the one on which the KJV is based. All the editions agree so closely they are sometimes referred to collectively as the *Reformation Text*. The New American Standard Bible (NASB) is based upon a slightly different text that employs two much older mss. of the Alexandrian group (see Appendix A). These texts were discovered in the nineteenth century.

All the texts of the Greek New Testament were assembled using principles of textual criticism that are applied to other ancient documents, with some variations appropriate to inspired scripture. The process of textual criticism is essentially twofold. First, the text as it existed in the original mss. is pieced together as far as possible from the external evidence (the available copies). Next, the contents of the text is examined with reference to its composition, authorship, date, and historical value, to determine whether the internal evidence supports the conclusions derived from the external evidence. This process is called *higher criticism*.

These two processes employ a variety of common-sense rules and a great deal of painstaking study to arrive at a text that will contain the smallest possible deviation from the original. (For a more extensive review of the texts of the Bible and their history, see Appendix A.) Mormons may have confidence that the texts currently used by scholars convey the messages originally intended by God with a high degree of accuracy. Examination of these Greek and Hebrew texts can provide insight into the correct translation.

---

11. Joseph Smith, Jr, *History of The Church of Jesus Christ of Latter-day Saints*, 2d ed. rev., 7 vols. (Salt Lake City: Deseret Book Company, 1978), 6:364.

Known Errors in the Biblical Texts

There are a few instances where differences between texts are known to have made a difference in the meaning of the passage. For example, in the Textus Receptus, 1 John 5:7-8 reads as follows:

> For there are three that bear witness [in heaven, the Father, the word, and the Holy Spirit: and these three are one. And there are three that bear witness in earth,] the spirit, and the water, and the blood: and these three agree in one.[12]

The bracketed words comprise what scholars call the *Johannine comma.* They are found only in ancient Latin versions, and there are no Greek texts that contain it, except two later texts that appear to have been translated into Greek from the older Latin versions. The Johannine comma is considered by most scholars today to have been an apocryphal addition to the original text even though its message is consistent with other scripture, including many passages from the Book of Mormon. It is not included in the NASB, but it is in the JST. Hence, Mormons could conclude that the addition was inspired.

Scholarly criticism has also been focused on the last twelve verses of the Gospel of Mark (Mark 16:9-20). But in this instance, there is substantial evidence that these verses were in the original *autographa.* They are found in all the Greek mss., except *B* (Vaticanus) and *Aleph* (Sinaiticus) (see Appendix A), and appear in all the Latin mss., except one. They were quoted as scripture by Justin Martyr (c.150) and Tatian (c.175),[13] and verses 9-16 are quoted by Irenaeus (c.180) and Hippolytus (c.200). Mark 16:9-16 appears in the NASB in brackets, but verses 17 through 20 are *not* included in that version. The entire passage is found in the JST.

Evangelicals claim that the errors found in scriptural texts "are all variations in spelling and a small number of paraphrased renderings."[14] That is not an accurate description of the situation, especially in the case of the two passages cited above. But such errors rarely affect doctrinal analysis or apologetic interpretation. They are not without controversy, though.

12. Edward F. Hills, *The King James Version Defended!: A Christian View of the New Testament Manuscripts* (Des Moines: The Christian Research Press, 1956), 127.

13. Hills, *The King James Version Defended!*, 109.

14. Trivanovich, *Speaking the Truth in Love*, 12.

Mark 16:16, for example, is quoted by Mormons and others who believe in the necessity of baptism for salvation. It is a proof-text some, Evangelicals would prefer to see deleted from the canon.

Translating the Texts

As noted in the Eighth Article of Faith, the challenge for biblical science today is to get an accurate translation of the accepted texts. A perfect thought-for-thought translation would be ideal. Such a translation has been attempted. It is found in the popular New International Version (NIV) of the Bible. The problem with such translations, however, is they are too easily influenced by the theology of their translators. This problem makes the NIV of little value in resolving doctrinal conflicts. For that purpose, a good word-for-word translation is best. The KJV and NASB are both considered superior to the NIV in this regard.

One problem in translating New Testament Greek is that the scriptures were not written by Greeks, but by Jews who spoke Greek. Their modes of thought were formed in Hebrew roots and their minds were steeped in the language of the Septuagint version of the Old Testament. Therefore, a prime source for interpretation of New Testament Greek is the Septuagint, referred to by scholars as "the LXX."

The LXX was translated into Greek by a group of approximately seventy Jewish scholars living in Alexandria, Egypt, two to three hundred years before Christ. (Hence the name "Septuagent," which means "Seventy.") The Greek they spoke was modified to embody Hebrew thought and idiom. It could be characterized as Hebrew-Greek.[15] There are even words and phrases from non-Greek sources, e.g., Aramaic, Latin, Persian, Egyptian, and others peculiarly Jewish. The word "paradise," for example, which is so important in understanding the story of the thief on the cross (Luke 23:43), is a Persian word meaning "a garden of beautiful trees."[16]

It is not enough simply to know Greek in order to translate the Greek New Testament. One must have a knowledge of *New Testament Greek* and of the LXX. Therefore, in selecting a lexicon for research, one must distinguish between those written for interpretation of the New Testament and those written for translating classical Greek.

---

15. Angus, *The Bible Handbook*, 43.
16. Angus, *The Bible Handbook*, 44.

Except where specifically noted, the Greek translations that appear in this book were taken from the lexicon in Robert Young's *Analytical Concordance to the Bible*, 21st American ed., rev. Wm. B. Stevenson (New York: Funk & Wagnalls, n.d.). *Handbook to the Grammar of the Greek Testament* by S. G. Green, and *Language of the New Testament,* and *Writers of the New Testament* both by W. H. Simcox, are also recommended.[17] But the lexicon most commonly used by scholars today is Walter Bauer's *A Greek-English Lexicon of the New Testament and Other Early Christian Literature*, 4th Ed., trans. William F. Arndt and F. Wilbur Gingrich (Chicago: University of Chicago Press, 1957).

Mormons will find footnotes to the KJV published by The Church of Jesus Christ of Latter-day Saints that give alternate meanings of the Greek and Hebrew where they are important to understanding the translation. The footnotes also contain explanations of idioms and of rare and archaic words. The LDS publication of the KJV also contains the most extensive topical index available.

To avoid arguments over translation, the NASB has been used in this book. That version is considered by many Evangelical scholars to be the best word-for-word translation of the original *autographa* available today. Quotations from the NASB are designated as such wherever they appear in this work. If a citation does not designate the version from which it is quoted, it is from the KJV. Unless the designation "emphasis added" appears before or after a quotation, the words in italics were added by the translators for clarity and do not appear in the original Greek or Hebrew text.[18]

This book is based on the premise that an accurate understanding of God's message is contained in the Bible. It would be useless to demonstrate that Mormonism is biblical without a belief in this axiom. Anyone who does not share this view will not be aided by this book, for it is necessary to accept the Bible's authority as the word of God before men will form their beliefs based on its teachings.

17. Angus, *The Bible Handbook*, 44.

18. In passages marked "some emphasis added," some of the words that appear in italics are in the original text and some are not.

Inerrancy Versus Completeness

Evangelical theology regarding the Bible goes beyond inerrancy, and beyond issues associated with human communication to a belief that the written Word of God is *complete*.

This view denies that God could have more instruction to give Man. It also rejects the distinct possibility that Men have lost some of the precious Word of God revealed to them through the ages. Finally, it rejects the possibility that God revealed Himself to groups outside the Middle East who also made a record of His communications. Evangelicals assert that everything God has ever said, or will ever say, is contained within the current canon accepted as the Protestant Bible.

Evangelicals would probably have rejected this view had they lived in the time of Christ and been told by the scribes that the Old Testament contains all God had revealed or ever will reveal to Man. It is incongruous, therefore, for them to accept it now. If inerrancy includes completeness, one must ask *when* the scriptures became complete. Was not the Pentateuch complete when it was revealed to Moses? What about the writings of the other Old Testament prophets? Were they not complete, e.i., inerrant before the time of Christ?

To be inerrant, God's word need not contain everything He ever said, or ever will say. It is complete only in the sense that it contains the entire message He intended for the audience to whom it was revealed at the time. The Bible is not a single work. It was not combined into one book until 367 A.D., long after the original *autographa* were gone. The word "Bible" derives from the Greek *biblia*, a plural word meaning "little books." The word itself implies an anthology of inspired works.

Protestant Bibles published today (e.g., the KJV) are a collection of the available sacred writings considered accurate and reliable by the majority of early Church scholars. Vast schisms have arisen based on disagreements over the correct canon. Even Mormons have a point of disagreement in this area given Joseph Smith's statement that "the Songs of Solomon are not inspired writings."[19] The very nature of the Bible implies it is not complete.

The Evangelical notion of completeness is also undermined by the fact that some books, originally part of inspired literature, appear to have been

19. *The Holy Bible*, Authorized King James Version (Salt Lake City: The Church of Jesus Christ of Latter-day Saints, 1979), 856 (footnote to Song of Sol. 1:1).

lost (see Appendix B). What if the lost Book of Enoch were found today, not the apocryphal version common in many libraries, but the one from which Jude quotes in Jude 14-15? What about the first epistle of Jude (Jude 3), or the epistle to the Laodiceans (Col. 4:16)? What about the book of the prophet from whom Matthew quotes in Matthew 2:23? Would these texts be excluded from the canon if they were found today? Achaeological research is unearthing new texts every day. What does this do to Evangelical notions of biblical completeness?

If the canon of Scripture is not complete in the sense Evangelicals assert, it follows that additional works could be added, if satisfactorily authenticated. This is why Mormons accept certain additional volumes as scripture. Their reverence for these works does not and should not distract in any way from their reverence for the Bible. (Further information on this subject is provided in Appendix B.)

As to the *accuracy* of the Bible, no implication arises from an assumption that the canon is not complete. Lost scripture merely proves that God has revealed some things that Man has unwittingly failed to preserve. It should come as no surprise that Men have been so fallible. The addition of new scripture, on the other hand, only shows that Men continue to need revelation from God, a conclusion that will shock no one familiar with Man's intemperate tendencies.

But despite the occasional failure of Men to safeguard sacred writings and their need for additional guidance on a continuing basis, Mormons are confident God has preserved in the existing text of the Bible the important truths, the good tidings He published to the Jews and the early Church.[20] That confidence can be held without also embracing the unbiblical notion that the canon of scripture is full or that inerrancy demands an end to revelation from God.

Interpreting the Bible

How does one prove that Mormon theology is biblical? Mormons may think this goal has already been accomplished in numerous works citing Bible quotations that support Mormon doctrine. Indeed, many wonder

20. Strictly speaking, the Bible contains only the words God intended to make *public*. There are references therein to more esoteric information, the revelation of which God has restricted (see, e.g., 2 Cor. 12:34; Deut. 29:29).

why Evangelicals ignore these citations if they really believe in the Bible. They ask why *Evangelicals* teach doctrine that is contrary to the Bible.

This view highlights a fundamental distinction between the way in which Mormons interpret the Bible and the Evangelical approach to that effort. Though most Mormons recognize this distinction in theory, few appreciate its practical effect. The contrast is largely a matter of degree, but in extreme terms, the two approaches are described in 1 Corinthians 2:12-14 as follows:

> Now we have received, not the spirit of the world, but the spirit which is of God; that we might know the things that are freely given to us of God.
>
> Which things also we speak, not in the words which man's wisdom teacheth, but which the Holy Ghost teacheth; comparing spiritual things with spiritual.
>
> But the natural man receiveth not the things of the Spirit of God: for they are foolishness unto him: neither can he know *them*, because they are spiritually discerned.

This passage explains that spiritual things are communicated through the Holy Ghost to spiritual Men. The natural or worldly Man does not understand them. But between the totally spiritual Man and the totally worldly Man are many individuals who strive to understand biblical language but find great difficulty in doing so. They struggle for those gifts of the Spirit known as interpretation, discernment, knowledge and wisdom (1 Cor. 12:7-10), but find them difficult to obtain.

The power of the Holy Ghost in interpreting and understanding scripture is illustrated by a story from the life of the author's father, Robert C. Hopkins, who tells of his conversion to Mormonism after many years in the Midwest as an assistant and student minister with his parents, both of whom were ordained ministers in the Christian Church.

As a result of his background, Robert was very familiar with the Bible before he heard of The Church of Jesus Christ of Latter-day Saints. After his baptism as a Latter-day Saint, he received the gift of the Holy Ghost through the administration of men duly authorized to perform that sacred ordinance. He then reread the Bible. So greatly was his understanding of scripture enlarged by the inspiration of the Holy Spirit, he related that "it was like reading a new book."

Sadly, some Mormons fail to use this gift to the extent they could in scripture study. Some even lose it through disobedience unrepented of, and finding themselves like those who never experienced the gifts of the Holy Ghost (or worse), they struggle for understanding or lose interest in the scriptures altogether.

Most Mormons, however, come to take the Holy Ghost's enlightenment for granted. They read the Bible, and without the aid of the biblical sciences, find in it great light and knowledge, which they prize highly. Unfortunately, when they seek to share that light and knowledge with others, they assume the meaning, so obvious to them because of the Spirit they enjoy, is also apparent to their audience. Unfortunately, the passages that Mormons think are powerful to the convincing of Men frequently fall upon unreceptive ears.

Until Mormons understand how to use techniques of biblical analysis to communicate the truths of God contained in the Bible, they will have difficulty convincing Evangelicals that Mormonism is biblical. Thus, the techniques developed by earnest men over the ages to aid in understanding the scriptures must also be learned by Mormons.

An Introduction to Apologetic Analysis

Apologetics, according to Webster, is the "branch of theology devoted to the defense of the divine origin and authority of Christianity."[21] This branch of theology appears to have been inspired by the Apostle Peter in 1 Peter 3:15. He admonished the early saints to "sanctify the Lord God in your hearts: and *be* ready always to give an answer [NASB: defense] to every man that asketh you a reason of the hope that is in you with meekness and fear."

Guidelines for presenting answers (or defenses) in support of the Christian faith were given by Peter in the next verse: "Having a good conscience; that, whereas they speak evil of you, as of evildoers, they may be ashamed that falsely accuse your good conversation in Christ."

From these instructions it appears that Christians should be prepared to defend their beliefs when they are questioned, but their defense should be made with such gentleness and meekness that the teachings of Christ are exemplified in their good behavior.[22] The term "apologetics" is an appropriate word for this form of defense.

---

21. A. Merriam-Webster, ed., *Webster's Ninth New Collegiate Dictionary*, (Springfield: Merriam-Webster, Inc., 1987), s.v. "apologetics."

22. The Doctrine and Covenants reiterates these guidelines in D&C 19:30 ("And thou shalt do it with all humility, trusting in me, reviling not against revilers").

An Early Loss of Understanding. Those asking for reasons or attacking the faith of early Christians were not believers endowed with the gift of the Holy Ghost. Those in power were, however, accomplished students of philosophy. Hence, there arose a need to defend the truths of God using popular techniques of philosophical analysis.

Unfortunately, the Greek thinking of the time was not based upon the wisdom of God. The Greeks accepted, without adequate evaluation, what appeared obvious to them, and frequently neglected to scrutinize the basis or accuracy of their assumptions.[23] As a result, the early Church became infiltrated with Greek notions of philosophy that had no basis in the Bible or in truth.

This was especially unfortunate because the early Church lost its most inspired leaders to lethal persecution. By 117 A.D. only two men remained alive who ever had any contact with an Apostle (Polycarp of Smyrna and Papias of Heiropolis), and of their writings only one letter survived the third century.[24]

Employing principles of logic, philosophy and scientific reasoning, those, church leaders who remained in the second century could not reliably determine the truth, and significant conflicts arose. As demonstrated by the textual criticism of Origen described above, the biblical science of that era was more often a hindrance than a help.

In the intervening centuries there have been improvements, but one must always exercise caution. Not everything that appears logical is true, and that which is true doesn't, always appear logical to everyone. Nevertheless, there is much value in the branch of apologetics that analyzes passages from the Bible to support theological beliefs. This branch is called *exegesis* or *exposition*, and is performed using the rules of *hermeneutics.*

Hermeneutics. The study of theories for the interpretation of meaning is known as hermeneutics.[25] Lawyers apply hermeneutic principles to determine the meaning of contracts and statutes in real-life situations. For

---

23. E.g., early Greek reasoning on the principles of physics made numerous false assumptions and lacked a careful and quantitative observation of reality (see "History" in *Encyclopaedia Britannica*, 1960 ed., s.v. "Physics: General Survey").
24. See, Richard R. Hopkins, *How Greek Philosophy Corrupted the Christian Concept of God* (Bountiful: Horizon Publishers, 1998).
25. Josef Bleicher, *Contemporary Hermeneutics: Hermeneutics as Method, Philosophy and Critique* (London: Routledge & Kegan Paul Ltd, 1980), 1.

lawyers, these principles are called the rules of construction. This is a well-developed science in other fields as well.

Evangelicals place great emphasis on hermeneutics as the means for correctly interpreting biblical texts. However, although the rules of hermeneutics aid in the understanding and interpretation of scripture, there is no absolute method that will ensure accuracy. This is apparent from the array of opinions derived by different scholars using the same rules.

Despite the failings of this area of apologetics, Evangelicals decry the lack of familiarity with hermeneutic principles among Mormons. Latter-day Saints may be right, but don't always know how to explain why they are right. Evangelicals use this deficiency to justify their rejection of Mormon arguments based on the Bible.

When one uses hermeneutics to analyze a passage of scripture, the result is called an *exegesis*, and the person performing such an analysis is an *exegete* (a word that is also a verb—*to exegete*). Exegesis is the application of hermeneutic principles in "the actual bringing out into formal statement, and by other means, the meaning of the author's words."[26]

This is to be contrasted with a deceptively similar, and highly improper, form of analysis called *eisegesis*. In eisegesis, the apologist imposes upon the language of the text his interpretation of its meaning, rather than drawing from it the meaning intended by the author. In practice, it is often difficult to distinguish between eisegesis and exegesis, or to avoid the one in performing the other.

Generally, an apologist will use exegesis in *exposition*. "Exposition denotes a more extended development and illustration of the sense, dealing more largely with other scriptures by comparison and contrast."[27] Much of what follows in this book is exposition. Before undertaking that analysis, however, it is necessary to review the rules most commonly employed in biblical hermeneutics.

A summary of the rules of hermeneutics is set forth in detail in Table 1 at the end of this chapter. In reviewing them, the reader will note that they are based on common sense. But common sense is often forgotten or misconstrued in biblical interpretation. So it is useful to have these rules presented in a systematic form.

---

26. Milton S. Terry, *Biblical Hermeneutics: A Treatise on the Interpretation of the Old and New Testaments* (Grand Rapids: Zondervan, n.d.), 19.
27. *Ibid.*

The principle techniques include the following: **(1) review all passages in their proper context; (2) consider passages from the point of view of the audience to which they were delivered; (3) compare the wording with similarly worded passages and passages dealing with the same subject, especially those written by the same author, to determine how key words are used; (4) determine whether a passage should be interpreted literally or figuratively; and (5) interpret literal and figurative passages appropriately** (e.g., through contrast, comparison, metaphor, simile, and type/antitype). To this should be added another important rule, **(6) get an understanding of key words in their original language**.

Literal interpretation is always preferred. However, **poetic language and language that could not have a literal meaning should be analyzed figuratively**. Not infrequently, Hebrew literary forms are employed in the Bible to bring multiple levels of meaning to passages, and types are used in contrast with antitypes to put across important spiritual messages.

The rules of hermeneutics are employed (without specific reference) throughout this book. Though Mormons are accused of bad hermeneutics, their common sense, spiritual insight and respect for the plain language usually produces a satisfactory hermeneutic. On the other hand, when attempting to contradict Mormon theology, Evangelicals often violate their own rules. This tendency can be noted to advantage by Latter-day Saints in an appropriate discussion, but only if the rules are known and understood.

The rules of biblical hermeneutics can also prove useful to those who find themselves struggling with Bible texts, or want to obtain a deeper understanding of the scriptures. Some rules (e.g., those of Hasel in Table 1) can be used to explain why Mormon Scripture should not be cited out of context.

There is no certainty that a correct interpretation will result from the rules of hermeneutics. It is always easier to eisegete than to exegete a passage. What usually results from exegesis is a number of reasonable alternatives. Without inspiration, it is difficult to ascertain which is the true interpretation. So, on many points, Mormons and Evangelicals must simply agree to disagree. But with sufficient correlation between groups of scriptures, the kind of study characteristic of an exposition, the truth usually becomes apparent.

Hermeneutics are used in this book to demonstrate that Mormonism represents, at the very least, a set of reasonable alternative interpretations of the Bible. Evangelical theology, to the extent it differs from Mormon doctrine, is also examined to show its flaws. Actual acceptance of any interpretation requires the reader to seek spiritual confirmation from the Holy Ghost through prayer. Mormons reading this book should not expect to argue their Evangelical friends or acquaintences into conversion through the use of good hermeneutics. That is, at best, a preamble to spiritual conversion.

It should also be noted that a clear understanding of the meaning of Bible passages will sometimes result in a surprise for Mormons. It may be that an individual or group within the Church has held a misunderstanding or misinterpretation regarding a particular passage. This is not something to be feared, but a portal to greater understanding and enlightenment. The Church is true! All its doctrines are biblical. That will always be the conclusion of a careful and scholarly look at the scriptures. Rare indeed are the occasions when Mormons need to say, "this passage represents an error in the text." When that happens, be aware that most such passages are already known to scholars.

False Hermeneutics. There is, however, a more dangerous side to hermeneutic analysis. When confronted with Bible passages that contradict strongly held Evangelical beliefs, the temptation to adjust the rules of hermeneutics grows in proportion to the importance of the subject matter. Over the years, this tension has resulted in some adulteration of the rules of hermeneutics. Mormon apologists should be careful to note and avoid improper variations on these rules.

One such variation is the claim that "statements in the Old Testament must be interpreted in light of passages in the New Testament."[28] This mock rule is deceptively similar to some stated in Table 1. The difference is that legitimate biblical hermeneutics recognizes a continuity of truth between the Old and New Testaments. Proponents of the mock rule invariably use it as an excuse to dismiss any doctrine taught in the Old Testament that contradicts their interpretation of passages in the New.

This and another false rule of hermeneutics have developed into an entire school of biblical interpretation—*Dispensationalism*, the brainchild

28. As thus worded, this adulteration of the rules of hermeneutics is often heard on "The Bible Answerman" radio broadcast.

of Lewis Sperry Chafer.[29] The view of those subscribing to his school is that there have been changes in God's laws relating to salvation during the different divisions, or dispensations, of time. While Mormons recognize different dispensations of the Gospel over the earth's history from Adam to the present, Dispensationalists believe the Gospel, the means for salvation, actually changed after the death and resurrection of Christ. They dismiss, as inapplicable to Christians today, the teachings and commandments of Christ Himself, during His earthly ministry, including many crucial lessons contained in the Sermon on the Mount.

Most Evangelicals reject this school of interpretation, and agree that the truth did not change at the resurrection of Christ, but they still regard with some suspicion any authority quoted from the Old Testament unless it appears to support their own theology.

It is true that a greater understanding of the mysteries of God is provided in the New Testament than was had among the people in Old Testament times, but this in no way discredits the teachings of the Old Testament. Unless a change has been specifically noted in the New Testament, such as the fulfillment and abrogation of the Law of Moses, the unequivocal position of Mormonism is that Old Testament authority carries the same weight as New Testament authority, and passages from both Testaments should be interpreted so they agree.

Two Examples of Exegesis

Two examples of hermeneutic exegesis are given below. The first is quite simple and demonstrates that an enriched understanding of New Testament Greek can resolve many apparent contradictions between Bible texts. The second is somewhat more difficult, and will lead into the first area of analysis in this work—the Mormon understanding of God.

Textual Contradictions *(Acts 9:7 and 22:9).* Two texts commonly cited by Mormons as a contradiction in the Bible are Acts 9:7 and 22:9 in the KJV. Both of these passages relate to the story of Paul's vision on the road to Damascus. Acts 9:7 (emphasis added) reads, "And the men which journeyed with him stood speechless, *hearing a voice*, but seeing no man." Acts 22:9 (emphasis added) reads: "And they that were with me saw

29. Lewis Sperry Chafer, *Dispensationalism*, rev. ed. (Dallas: Dallas Seminary Press, 1951).

indeed the light, and were afraid; but they *heard not the voice* of him that spake to me."

In the KJV translation, these two passages seem to contradict. In the first, Paul says the men with him heard the voice, while in the second, he says they did not. These two passages are mentioned under "Bible Errors" in Keith Marston's *Missionary Pal: Reference Guide for Missionaries & Teachers* (Salt Lake City: Publishers Press, 1991), a popular work among LDS missionaries.

A study of the words used in these passages, however, reveals that different forms of the Greek word "to hear" are used in the two texts. The difference is not reflected in the KJV translation. The form of the Greek word translated "heard" in Acts 22:9 actually means "to hear *with comprehension,*" "to understand." Acts 9:7 however, uses a form best translated "hearing," which means only *to hear.* Thus, the men with Paul heard the voice but did not *understand* what was said.

Evangelicals often accuse Mormons of ignorance for citing these verses as an example of error.[30] That is not generally true, except for the inclusion of these verses in Keith Marston's work. The official position of the Church is reflected in the LDS edition of the KJV, which cites the JST translation of Acts 9:7. That translation is consistent with Acts 22:9, and is provided in the footnotes to Acts 9:7.

Doctrinal Contradictions *(Colossians 1:15).* Colossians 1:15 contains the statement that Christ is "the firstborn of every creature." Though the language of this statement seems clear, the theology it implies is in conflict with Evangelical doctrine. Hence, this passage is interpreted by Evangelicals in a way that goes beyond the plain meaning of the words. A typical example is as follows:

> LDS teaching suggests that this means He was "born first" in God's creation. "Firstborn," however, does not mean born first nor even imply birth. The Greek word used is prototokos, and means "priority and pre-eminence."[31]

The first error in this exegesis is its mistranslation of the word *pr¯ototokos. Pr¯ototokos* comes from two root words that mean "first" and "born." The word implies "priority and pre-eminence," of course, but literal

30. Trivanovich, *Speaking the Truth in Love*, 16.
31 *Ibid.*

translation renders this term "priority or pre-eminence." The NASB, for example, translates the phrase: "the first-born of all creation."

Second, it is clear that the word "first-born" implies not only birth, but the fact of being born first. That is the exact meaning of the Greek roots. While Mormons would certainly agree that Christ has priority and preeminence over all creation, the word *prōtotokos* implies that His pre-eminence is associated with His being first in birth order. The concept is of Hebrew origin and, in its Hebrew equivalent, refers to one holding the special rights of inheritance conferred upon the Hebrew male who is born first.[32]

The Evangelical exegesis expressed above is supported by the following note to Colossians 1:15 by C. I. Scofield, a respected turn-of-the-century Bible scholar:

> As used of our Lord here, this term (Gr. *prōtotokos*) refers to priority of position rather than of origin. This meaning is clear in Ps. 89:27: "I also shall make him My first-born, / The highest of the kings of the earth." The assertion in 1:15, therefore, is that Christ, as the eternal Son, holds the position of priority in relation to all creation, in that He was before all things (v. 17), He created all things (v. 16), and by Him all things hold together (v. 17).[33]

Scofield's limiting exegesis is based on Psalms 89:27, which he quotes as follows: "I also shall make him My first-born." The key word in this phrase is "make." If this is an expression of the Father's intent to *make* Christ his first-born at some point in the future (note the use of the future tense, "shall"), Scofield's interpretation makes some sense. Stating an intention to make an existent Being (Christ) God's firstborn does not neccesarily imply anything about birth or birth order (though it does raise havoc with trinitarian theology).

The problem with his analysis is this: In Psalms 89:27 the word trans-

32. There are two semi-exceptions ("semi" because they both involve firstborn twins). Between Jacob and Esau, and Ephraim and Manasseh, God designated one as "firstborn" (in each case the second to exit the womb) See, e.g., Jer. 31:9.

33. C.I. Scofield, ed., *New Scofield Study Bible: New American Standard*, rev. 1967, consultants Paul S. Karleen and Glenn R. Goss (New York: Oxford University Press, 1988), 1681 (footnote to Col. 1:15).

lated "make" is the Hebrew word, *nathan*, which usually means *to give.*[34] If the preferred translation were used, the verse would be rendered "I also shall *give* him My first-born, The highest of the kings of the earth." (Emphasis added.)

This translation provides no support for Scofield's interpretation. If the promise of Psalms 89:27 is that God will *give* Man a Savior, His first-born, Jesus the Christ, who is "the highest of the kings of the earth" (i.e., preeminent over all earthly authority), one is forced to acknowledge that Christ was born first, as Colossians 1:15 says.

A review of other relevant passages reveals that the latter exegesis of Colossians 1:15 is without contradiction in the Bible. It is consistent with the proclamation that Jesus Christ is the Son of God, and emphasizes that Christ ("the image of the invisible God"[35]) is preeminent over Man because of His character which perfectly reflects the character of His Father.

Colossians 1:15 (NASB) also declares that Christ was part "*of* all creation." This is just as antithetical to Evangelical doctrine as the notion of Christ being born first. They interpret this portion of Colossians 1:15 to mean "*in relation to* all creation," as Scofield insinuated above, or "*over* all creation," as some argue. These interpretations are nothing but eisegesis of the passage. The word "of" here is part of the Greek word *pases*, which is the *genitive* case of the word "all." The genitive case in Greek is similar to the English possessive, charaterized by use of the word "of" but conveys the concept of *origin*, indicating that Christ *belonged to* and *was part of* "all creation."[36]

As indicated by this simplified example of exegesis, it is best to start by confirming the accuracy of the translation, then study the use of key words by other authors. In doing so, it is important to confirm the translation of cross-referenced passages. The grammatical construction of key

---

34. *Nathan* is translated "make" 108 times in the KJV. It is rendered "give" 1023 times. "Give" is clearly the preferred translation.

35. The word "invisible" in Colossians 1:15 does not mean that God fails to reflect or emanate light in the visible range. It is translated from the Greek word *aoratos*, meaning "unseen." Man is not privileged to see God the Father (John 6:46). Rather, Christ is His visible type (Heb. 1:3; 1 Pet. 2:21).

36. *Standard Dictionary of the English Language: Combined with Britannica World Language Dictionary*, international ed. (New York: Funk & Wagnals Company, 1960), s.v. "genitive"; see, also, *Reader's Digest Illustrated Encyclopedia Dictionary* (Pleasantville: The Reader's Digest Assn., 1987), s.v. "genitive."

words is also important. Even small words, like "of," can affect interpretation. Preconceived theological notions should not be indulged to avoid the plain meaning of a passage. In this instance, honest scholarship would decline the argument that being "first-born" has nothing to do with being born first.[37]

The Value of Exposition. Before accepting an exegesis, the scriptures as a whole should be examined to determine if other passages confirm the proposed interpretation, i.e., to see if it fits into the teachings of the Bible as a whole. This is the role of exposition. For Colossians 1:15, Part I of this book constitutes that exposition.

The most important step however, is to consult the Lord in humble prayer. All who read this book are encouraged to do so in respect to any question examined here. For LDS readers, a review of Mormon Scripture should also be conducted. So clearly are the truths of the Gospel taught in the Book of Mormon, for example, it is like having the answers at the back of the textbook available during the test. If an exegesis is not consistent with the truths taught elsewhere in the Standard Works, that exegesis should be re-examined.

Conclusion

In what follows, the reader may find it useful to refer to the historical material and rules of hermeneutics discussed in this chapter. Further study in the biblical sciences using the reference works cited herein is also recommended. Bible commentaries by non-LDS writers can be useful in giving the reader an understanding of the thinking that has come from centuries of study on specific passages.[38] The reader should have a Bible convenient at all times and look up references rather than relying upon the author's research.

---

37. Exo. 4:22 speaks of "Israel," the nation, being God's "firstborn," even though Israel, the man, was in fact born after his brother Esau. This passage uses the term in a slightly broader sense, but one that is still related to birth order, as verse 23 demonstrates (the "firstborn" of Pharoah will be slain if he refuses to release God's "firstborn").

38. Scholarly non-LDS Bible commentaries explain individual passages in a manner surprisingly similar to LDS doctrine. However, they often include unsupported disclaimers of the interpretation they acknowledge, accompanied by attempts to give an alternative meaning (see, e.g., discussions of Matt. 5:48 and Cor.15:29 in many non-LDS commentaries).

This undertaking has been arranged in three Parts. Since the first and most fundamental concept in any system of theology is its teachings about God, *Part I* begins with an examination of Mormon Theology. *Part II*, Mormon Soteriology, addresses the next most significant subject—the salvation of Man. Because it is inextricably connected to the issues of salvation, *Part III* discusses Mormon Eschatology,[39] the final judgment of Mankind.

The purpose of this arrangement, and of this book as a whole, is to aid Mormons in their effort to convince a growing Evangelical community of the biblical basis of Mormonism. Persuasion and reason are used here. All who use this book are encouraged to follow the same formula, "reviling not against revilers" (D&C 19:30). Only through a scholarly approach will the Church make significant progress in proselyting Evangelicals, who may one day recognize the truths of biblical Mormonism.

39. "The branch of theology that is concerned with the ultimate or last things, such as death, judgment, heaven, and hell." *Reader's Digest Illustrated Encyclopedic Dictionary*, s.v. "eschatology."

Table 1
Rules of Biblical Hermeneutics

The following rules (in italics) are quoted with permission from Prof. D. R. Dungan, *Hermeneutics: a Text-Book*, 3d ed. (Cincinnati: The Standard Publishing Company, n.d.) Chap. VII and VIII. The material that follows each rule is drawn from Prof. Dungan's treatise. Additional rules and advice are extrapolated from Milton S. Terry, *Biblical Hermeneutics* (Grand Rapids: Zondervan Publishing House, n.d.); Gerhard F. Hasel, "Principles of Biblical Interpretation" in *A Symposium on Biblical Hermeneutics*, Gordon M. Hyde, ed. (Washington: The Review and Herald Publishing Association, 1974); and Walter M. Dunnett, *The Interpretation of Holy Scripture* (Nashville: Thomas Nelson Publishers, 1984).

Rules for the Interpretation of Sentences

Rule 1. *Always interpret according to the known purpose of the author.* Exception: not applicable where the author is making an incidental remark.

How May We Know the Purpose of the Author?

Rule 1. *The speaker or writer sometimes states just what he wanted to accomplish by speaking.* The first place to look is the text itself.

Rule 2. *Carefully consider the immediate context.* What was done and said at the time may throw light on the meaning of the words used.

Rule 3. *The Bible, being the truth of God, must harmonize with itself.* The Bible should never be interpreted so its statements are in conflict.

Rule 4. *Light may be thrown upon a doubtful or difficult passage by comparing it with other statements of the author on the same subject.* By gathering all that can be found from the same writer, one can better understand his view on the subject.

Rule 5. *Help may be had in the interpretation of sentences by examining the statements of other writers on the same subject who are of equal authority.* Statements by one apostle should agree with those of the Savior and other apostles on the same subject.

Rule 6. *The use of common sense respecting the things which we know, of ourselves.* Common sense is the basic tool men use to interpret the scriptures, but the exegete cannot array his whims against the word of God in the name of common sense. He is not at liberty to assert his own opinion as the standard.

Rule 7. *That which is figurative must be interpreted according to the laws that govern figurative speech.* Literal language is not to be interpreted by figures. Rather, figures are to be interpreted by that which is literal.

Rules by Which the Meaning of Words Shall Be Ascertained

Rule 1. *All words are to be understood in their literal sense, unless the evident meaning of the context forbids.* Figures are the exception, literal language is the rule.

Rule 2. *Commands generally, and ordinances always, are to be understood in a literal sense.* If an order is not meant to be literal, the author will usually take precautions to assure that the figurative language cannot be misinterpreted.

Rule 3. *The literal meaning of a word is that meaning which is given it by those to whom it is addressed.* An author will use a word in the sense that he knows will be understood by his audience.

How shall we know what the words meant, or in what sense the people understood them? By the use of the same word by the same author in addressing the same people elsewhere; by the use of the same word by other authors among the same people; or by an indication from the audience to whom the language was addressed of the meaning they gave it. If none of the foregoing establishes any special meaning for the word, the classic use may be assumed.

Rule 4. *The Scriptures are supposed to give to some words meanings which they do not have in the classics, and therefore the Bible becomes a dictionary of itself.* (See, e.g., the word *elder.*) Caution: no word in the Scriptures is used in a sense contrary to its classical use.

Rule 5. *Words of definite action can have but one meaning.* Examples: jump, walk, run, shoot, hang, strike. The meaning relates to the action. When action is ordered by any such word, it cannot be obeyed by doing anything other than that which is the meaning of the word.

Rule 6. *The writer's explanation is the best definition that can be found.* If the writer has stated the meaning he wished to put into the word, in words that admit of no doubt, that is the sense in which it must be taken.

Rule 7. *The proper definition of a word may be used in the place of the word.* If the definition of the word is substituted in the passage for the word itself, a true definition will give the same sense that the word itself gives. If the definition is wrong, the sense of the passage will be so altered as to make it readily apparent that the definition is incorrect.

Rule 8. *By antithesis.* When two positions are matched against each other, the antithesis may define the thesis. By substituting the antithesis for the thesis, one can often see the meaning of the word.

Rule 9. *By the general and special scope.* The main purpose (general scope) of the author must be kept in mind when interpreting words used in connection with any sub-purpose of the writer (the special scope).

Rule 10. *Etymological construction will many times tell the meaning of the word.* (Etymology is the analysis of roots or component parts of words.) Caution: Words frequently take on meanings entirely different from the parts of which they were originally composed. Example: *sincere,* from two Latin words that refer to honey, and mean "without bee's wax."

Rule 11. *The meaning of a word is frequently known by the words used in the construction with it.* The grammatical and syntactic setting should be considered. If it is determined what part of speech the word is, whether it indicates action or transition, the meaning of the word may be made clearer.

Rule 12. *We may have to sometimes study the history of a word in order to get its meaning at any particular time.* Some words have changed their meanings since they were used by the author or the translator. Example: the word *let* in old English meant "to hinder." It has that meaning in the KJV.

Rule 13. *Illustrations or parables may give the peculiar sense in which a word is to be understood in the Scriptures.* E.g., the parable of the Good Samaritan defines the special sense in which the Lord used the word "neighbor." And the parallelisms of Hebrew poetry may provide a greater understanding of the writer's use of certain words.

Rule 14. *In defining a definition, nothing but primary meanings are to be used.* Example: *To eat* means literally "to chew and swallow." If this word is translated into any other language, the word containing that thought must be used and no other. If a secondary meaning is used (such as *to consume*), a subsequent translation could result in error (e.g., use of the word to *burn*, instead of the word to eat, since a fire may also *consume,* and to be consumed by fire is *to burn*).

How Can We Know Figurative Language?

Rule 1. *The sense of the context will indicate it.* Nothing should be regarded as figurative unless the immediate context or the meaning of the passage as a whole demands it.

Rule 2. *A word or sentence is figurative when the literal meaning involves an impossibility.* Caution: What is possible to God is often impossible to Man. One must know that impossibilities are confronting them before they assume the passage is figurative.

Rule 3. *The language of Scripture may be regarded as figurative if the literal interpretation will cause one passage to contradict another.* If there are two passages, and the literal interpretation of both make them contradict each other, the language of one, at least, may be regarded as figurative.

Rule 4. *When the Scriptures are made to demand actions that are wrong, or forbid those that are good, they are supposed to be figurative.* Example: It is not right for a man to dissect himself, so when Christ says, "And if thy hand or thy foot causeth thee to stumble, cut it off, and cast it from thee," He is speaking figuratively.

Rule 5. *When it is said to be figurative.* When the author says that the language is figurative, it is figurative.

Rule 6. *When the definite is put for the indefinite.* When a definite amount/number/thing is substituted for an indefinite concept, the definite is figurative. Example: The command to forgive "seventy times seven" does not mean that after 490 times, forgiveness may be denied.

Rule 7. *When said in mockery.* Men have the habit of using words in mockery to convey a thought quite different from what a literal interpretation would indicate.

Rule 8. *Common sense. Figures of speech sometimes occur when we have to depend on the things we know in order to decide if the language is figurative or literal.* Statements made for emphasis or intensification, which are in excess of the facts, may be recognized, through common sense, to be figurative.

Rules for the Interpretation of Figurative Language

Rule 1. *Let the author give his own interpretation.* When speaking figuratively, the author will often recognize the need for explanation. The exegete should not think to correct the blunders of the author by making out of the figure things that the writer never intended.

Rule 2. *The interpretation should be according to the general and special scope.* The rule is the same as when interpreting literal language.

Rule 3. *Compare the figurative with literal accounts or statements of the same things.* The figurative does not contradict the literal, but adds beauty and strength.

Rule 4. *By the resemblance of things compared.* A diligent search should be made for the features of likeness between the symbols (the figurative) and the facts (the literal). Caution: Be careful not to compare accidental qualities the figure was not intended to illuminate.

Rule 5. *The facts of history and biography may be made to assist in the interpretation of figurative language.* If the person or thing referred to is known for certain, the point and the power of the figure can be better ascertained. Also, if the fulfillment of a prophecy is known, the language of the prophecy that was dark because of the imagery becomes plain in light of the history.

Rule 6. *Any inspired interpretation, or use of the figure in an argument or teaching, will decide its meaning.* If an inspired writer has exegeted a figurative passage, his interpretation may be accepted as the meaning of the figure.

Rule 7. *We must be careful not to demand too many points of analogy. Too* many exegetes interpret figures by inventing as many features of similarity as they can and demanding a literal thought or purpose for each. The purpose for which God intended the figure is often lost in this effort.

Rule 8. *It must be remembered that figures are not always used with the same meaning.* Usually, the figurative meaning of words cannot be compared between texts. However, if two writers are describing the same thing and employing the same figure for that purpose, it is possible that one of them has been clearer in his use of the figure than the other.

Rule 9. *Parables may explain parables.* One figure of speech may be used in the interpretation of another. Christ often gave more than one parable to illustrate a single teaching. Each parable may have different ends in view, but be similar in several features. If so, one may be used to interpret the other.

Rule 10. *The type and the antitype are frequently both in view at the same time.* A spiritual thought or fact (the antitype) becomes apparent through figurative use of words, descriptions, events, institutions, and persons (the type). The type brings out the fuller import and deeper meaning of the antitype. However, several types may be employed to represent the same antitype, and the writer may have several antitypes in mind when using one type.

Rules for Interpreting Rare Words

(from Terry)

To ascertain the meaning of rare words, words that occur only once, and words of doubtful import, ancient versions of scripture are useful. The LXX is preferred, but other ancient versions should also be consulted. Caution: Sometimes the rules of interpretation will have greater weight than the usage of the word in ancient versions, especially where the versions conflict.

In cases where it is still difficult to determine the meaning of the word, ancient lexicons and glossaries may be useful. It may be necessary to study the word in non-biblical literature. But the timing of that literature must be noted. Words were sometimes used in a different sense in sacred writ than they conveyed in secular writing centuries later or earlier.

Interpreting Scripture as a Whole

(from Hasel)

The individual word is properly understood within the sentence and the sentence by means of its words. This reciprocal relationship is called the "hermeneutical circle." It spirals out from individual words to the entire Bible. There is mutual dependence of general knowledge on the particular and the particular on the general.

Interpreting the Old Testament in Light of the New

(from Hasel)

It is apparent from the New Testament that Old Testament writers themselves recognized that their words had a deeper level of meaning and a fuller import which they sensed but may not have fully comprehended themselves. This fuller import and deeper meaning must be homogeneous with the literal meaning and sense, and is merely an outgrowth of what the original author put into words. The interpreter may gain a more comprehensive understanding than the author may have had, based upon the context of the entirety of inspired revelation, if he allows all the inspired scriptures to illuminate the meaning of a particular text. This is the hermeneutic function of the canon of scripture as a whole.

Interpreting the Scriptures

(from Dunnett)

In any effort to understand the scriptures, one must (a) cultivate an awareness of the similarities and differences between the biblical world and the modern world; (b) be alert to the diversity of history and culture within the scope of biblical writings; (c) look for evidence within the writings that defines specific cultural expressions or historical events, persons, institutions, or customs; (d) relate Old Testament backgrounds to New Testament texts, and do the same within each Testament (e.g., the book of Acts can be related to the epistles with great benefit); and (e) keep in mind that there may be more to the text than the cultural situation suggests—the author may be saying something that transcends his own cultural situation.

Part I

Mormon Theology

2

The Nature and Characteristics of God

While Mormons occasionally disagree on obscure points of doctrine, the diversity of beliefs among other religions calling themselves Christian is staggering. Evangelicals are comfortable with this diversity to varying degrees, but there is a growing effort amongst them to present a more united doctrinal front. That effort is led by the Christian Research Institute (CRI), founded by the late Dr. Walter Martin.

That organization sponsors the nationally syndicated Christian radio program, "The Bible Answerman," through which a daily effort to stabilize Evangelical opinion is made by refuting contrary views. CRI subscribes to the position that there are two major doctrines on which all must agree if they wish to bear the name "Christian." The first of these will be examined in this Part. It is a belief in the Trinity as the historically orthodox concept of God.

Mormons do not accept this concept, though it has been taught for over eighteen hundred years in most Christian denominations. For this reason, Dr. Martin, CRI, and a large portion of the Christian community accuse Mormonism of being a "cult." Such name-calling does nothing to aid in the discernment of truth. The fact that Mormon teachings about God do not comport with these ideas is entirely irrelevant to any reasoned inquiry about which theology is biblical.

Most Evangelicals treat the "orthodox" concept of God as though it were part of the Bible itself. It is, however, nothing more than an interpretation of biblical texts. Mormons believe in those texts as much as do Evangelicals. They simply have a different interpretation of them.

Instead of exploring their interpretation, Evangelicals assume the Mormon interpretation is wrong and accuse them of teaching "another Jesus." The passage cited to support this accusation is 2 Corinthians 11:34 (NASB):

> But I am afraid, lest as the serpent deceived Eve by his craftiness, your minds should be led astray from the simplicity and purity *of devotion* to Christ.
>
> For if one comes and preaches another Jesus whom we have not preached, or you receive a different spirit which you have not received, or a different gospel which you have not accepted, you bear *this* beautifully.

Paul's criticism of the Corinthian saints in this passage is a reminder that, though open-mindedness can be a virtue, it is possible to be so broad-minded that everything falls out. The failure to discern correct principles and hold fast to the truth can lead to acceptance of teachings so foreign to Christ that one, in effect, accepts "another Jesus." But the question is: Who has done this, the Mormons, or the early Christians to whom Paul was writing?

Evangelicals point to the Mormons as the culpable party because of a statement in verse 3 ("lest as the serpent deceived Eve by his craftiness"). Wrongly exegeting the Genesis account of Eve's deception, they say Mormons lead their followers to "another Jesus" by teaching that Men can become like God. Such teaching, they assert, is what Satan taught Eve when he tempted her with the promise that she and Adam would be "as gods" if they partook of the forbidden fruit (Gen. 3:5).[1]

But their exegesis on this point is grossly flawed. It takes a single verse out of context without analyzing the passage as a whole. The entire passage, Genesis 3:1-7 (NASB) reads as follows:

> Now the serpent was more crafty than any beast of the field which the LORD God had made. And he said to the woman, "Indeed, has God said, 'You shall not eat from any tree of the garden'?"
>
> And the woman said to the serpent, "From the fruit of the trees of the garden we may eat;
>
> but from the fruit of the tree which is in the middle of the garden, God has said, 'You shall not eat from it or touch it, lest you die.'"
>
> And the serpent said to the woman, "You surely shall not die!

1. See, e.g., Robert Morey, *Battle of the Gods: The Gathering Storm in Modern Evangelicalism* (Southbridge: Crown Publications, 1989), 18, *et seq.*

> "For God knows that in the day you eat from it your eyes will be opened, and you will be like God, knowing good and evil."
>
> When the woman saw that the tree was good for food, and that it was a delight to the eyes, and that the tree was desirable to make *one* wise, she took from its fruit and ate; and she gave also to her husband with her, and he ate.
>
> Then the eyes of both of them were opened, and they knew that they were naked; and they sewed fig leaves together and made themselves loin coverings.

The subtlety of Satan is shown in this passage by the fact that he told Eve both a lie and a truth. He told her (1) that she would not die, and (2) that she would become like God in the sense that she would obtain a knowledge of good and evil. It is clear from verse 7 that Satan's second statement (verse 5) was the truth! Adam and Eve did, in fact, obtain the promised knowledge, and God, Himself, attested to that fact in verse 22 (NASB: "Behold, the man has become like one of Us, knowing good and evil").

Satan frequently mixes truth with error in this manner. The challenge is to discern which statements are the truth and which are the lies. Only by using inspired discernment can the maze laid out by Satan's deception be traversed correctly. The critics of Mormonism have failed to meet that challenge in this instance.

Satan's lie to Eve is found in his first statement, "You surely shall not die! " In that statement he directly contradicts God's declaration of the consequences that would follow disobedience to His commandments (Gen. 2:17). Contrary to Satan's promise, and true to the word of God, Adam and Eve died as a result of eating the forbidden fruit. Their death was both spiritual-they were cast out of the Garden of Eden (Gen. 3:23), where they lived in the presence of God—and physical. Man and all creation became subject to corruption and death (cf., Gen. 3:16-19) in what is now referred to as the Great Fall.[2] Mormons teach only the true portion of Satan's message to Eve.

The problem Paul addressed in 2 Corinthians 11 was the readiness of the Corinthian saints to accept false doctrine. Unfortunately, they did not repent of that propensity. For nineteen-hundred years the influence of

---

2. Adam literally died "in the day" he partook of the fruit. A day to the Lord is as a thousand years (2 Pet. 3:8), and Adam lived only 930 years (Gen. 5:5). Thus, God's word was fulfilled to the letter.

Greek philosophy, in which the Corinthians were steeped, so permeated the historic Christian Church that those who embrace orthodoxy today do not even realize how many of their concepts about God have come from Hellenism rather than the Bible.[3]

The truths about God taught in the Bible differ significantly from the concepts of Greek philosophy. Thus, to Evangelicals whose theology is influenced extensively by Hellenism, the truth can actually sound blasphemous. They often react to Mormon teaching in the same way the ancient Pharisees reacted to Christ (John 10:31). They want to take up stones.

This poses an enormous barrier in the effort to show that Mormon teachings are biblical. Since much of what Evangelicals believe about God is actually *unbiblical*, their greatest challenge is to put aside preconceived notions based on Greek thinking, and acknowledge what the Bible *really* teaches. Only then will they learn the true nature and characteristics of God.

For example, a Bible question-answerer on Evangelical radio once claimed that Men are so different from God, it is as impossible for a man to become like God as it is for a dog to become like a human.[4] The same person also taught, consonant with Bible passages, that men and women are the children of God, made in His image. Resolving the contradictory nature of these two statements is a herculean task for Evangelical expositors.

The strain of such exposition disappears when one realizes that the first premise, the notion that God is utterly different from Man, is pure Hellenism. The Bible teaches that God differs from Man in degree, not in kind. Many other contributions from Greek culture and philosophy have infiltrated historic orthodoxy, and remain part of the theology of most Christian churches today. The object of this book is to separate such adulterationns from the true concept of God taught in the Bible.

---

3. "Platonism After Plato: Influence on Christian Thought" in *Encyclopaedia Britannica,* 1960 ed. (Chicago: Encyclopaedia Britannica, Inc., 1960), s.v., "Plato;" Hopkins, How greek Philosophy Corrupted the Christian Concept of God.

God the Father Has a Body of Flesh and Bones

The Image of God. The true physiological nature of God was made clear in entirely unambiguous terms at the beginning of the first book of the Old Testament. Genesis 1:26-27 (NASB, brackets added) reads as follows:

> Then God [Heb: *elohim*, a plural noun] said, "Let Us make man in Our image, according to Our likeness; and let them rule over the fish of the sea and over the birds of the sky and over the cattle and over all the earth, and over every creeping thing that creeps on the earth."
>
> And God [*elohim*] created man in His own image, in the image of God [*elohim*] He created him; male and female He created them.

The words "image" and "likeness" in this passage have been the subject of extensive exegesis by those unwilling to accept their plain meaning. Evangelicals treat this passage figuratively, acknowledging a similarity between Man and God that includes selected characteristics—e.g., free will, and the capacity to exercise reason and discernment.

A figurative interpretation, however, is not appropriate for this passage. An examination of the author's other writings reveals that he used these words literally. Just four chapters later, in Genesis 5:1-3 (NASB, brackets added), Moses states:

> This is the book of the generations of Adam. In the day when God [*elohim*] created man, He made him in the likeness of God [*elohim*].
>
> He created them male and female, and He blessed them and named them Man [Heb: *Adam*] in the day when they were created.
>
> When Adam had lived one hundred and thirty years, he became the father of [literally *begot*] *a son* in his own likeness, according to his image, and named him Seth.

The words "likeness" and "image" in verse 3 above come from the same Hebrew words used in verse 1 and in Genesis 1:26-27. Seth was the literal son of Adam, and clearly inherited Adam's appearance and characteristics through the laws of genetics as well as Adam's teachings. Adam is known to have had other sons before Seth, e.g., Cain and Abel (Gen. 4), but only of Seth is it said that he was in the image and likeness of his father. Thus, it is clear that the words "image" and "likeness" were used by Moses to convey a concept that is both physical (i.e., genetic) and spiritual. To claim that the terms "image" and "likeness" in Genesis 1:26-27 refer only to a figurative resemblance is to introduce a limitation not reflected in Moses' use of those terms.

Further evidence of the physical dimension inherent in the words "image" and "likeness" is found in Genesis 1:26-27, itself. The physical characteristic of *gender* is specifically mentioned in verse 27 as one way in which Man resembles *elohim.* Thus, "image" and "likeness" convey more than a figurative dimension of similarity. There is a literal physiological connection between *elohim* and Man.

Since Adam was a Man, it must be concluded that God is a Man, though not a *mortal* man since Adam was not mortal—that is, subject to Physical death—when God spoke the words recorded in Gen. 1:26-27. The reference in this passage to a *female* image supports Mormon speculation that there is a Mother in Heaven just as the reference to the male gender denotes the existence of a Father. That may be one reason for the use of the plural noun *elohim* to designate God in these passages.

From the beginning, the Bible teaches the concept of an anthropomorphic God, (see, Gen. 32:30; Exod. 33:18-23; and Num. 12:5-8). These verses are eyewitness accounts, *not* figurative descriptions. Any other idea of God's nature is not biblical in origin, but the result of Greek philosophy popular among the Jews and the early Church at the time of Christ.

God is the Father of the Human Race (speaking genetically and without reference to gender). He has a body like that of Man in its basic genetic structure, though unimaginably superior "glorified" and not subject to death. References to different physiologies can be explained by context. For example, reference is made to God's "wings" in Ruth 2:12, Psalms 17:8, and Psalms 91:4. That the language in these passages is figurative appears from their context (see, e.g., Christ's use of similar language in Matthew 23:37 while referring to himself).

Mormons are not forced to believe God has wings to be consistent in their interpretation of the Bible. Following the simple rules of hermeneutics requires that one set of passages be interpreted figuratively and the other literally.

Lessons from the Resurrection of Christ. The resurrection of Christ is taught by all Christians as the heart of the Gospel (1 Cor. 15:14).

Nevertheless, there is great confusion among Evangelicals about the physical nature of Christ's resurrection and its implications. CRI has attempted to resolve this confusion in favor of a belief in the physical resurrection, but it refuses to acknowledge the implications of that truth.[5] In fact, a well-known Christian radio teacher, speaking of the resurrection, once candidly admitted that he did not really understand why Man would want his "grubby flesh" back in the resurrection.[6]

This remark evidences the continuing influence of Greek philosophy on Evangelical theology today. The idea that Man's flesh is "grubby," and less desirable than his spirit, comes from the philosophy of Plato.[7] The fallen state of Man's physiology, "the flesh," is recognized by inspired writers as a source of evil habits, and on one occasion was associated by Paul with Man's current sinful condition (Rom. 8:3), but flesh itself is never characterized as evil in the Bible.

Nevertheless, so ingrained in orthodoxy is the Platonic deprecation of the flesh that some have gone so far as to claim the resurrection is not a raising of the flesh, but of the *spirit*.[8] To reconcile that claim with the implications of the word "resurrect," those who teach this doctrine claim that, upon death, the spirit becomes unconscious and is only raised from that state by the resurrection.

Under this theory, the state of the spirit after death is called "soul sleep." The proof-text used to support this belief is Ecclesiastes 9:5 (NASB: "but the dead do not know anything, nor have they any longer a reward, for their memory is forgotten"; see also Eccles. 9:10). Their reliance on this passage, however, is misplaced. It is part of a discourse examining the viewpoint of Men "under the sun" (Eccles. 9:3), and reflects the attitude of the natural world that knows nothing of God. It is a description of death from the viewpoint of the worldly man. It does not reflect the true state of the dead.

Paul has said that "to be absent from the body" is to be "at home with the Lord" (2 Cor. 5:6-9, NASB; see, also, Phil. 1:21-24). This implies a

---

5. Norman Geisler, "The Battle for the Resurrection," *Christian Research Newsletter* 5, no. 1 (1992).

6. Pastor Raoul Reiss, of Calvary Chapel Golden Springs and Diamond Bar, on "Manna For Today," KKLA, late 1991.

7. Plato, *Phaedo,* trans. R.S. Bluck (London, 1955).

8. Dr. Walter Martin complains of people making this error in *Essential Christianity* (Ventura: Regal Books, 1980), 64.

conscious state after death. The story of the rich man and Lazarus told by Christ in Luke 16:19-31 clearly supports that position.

The resurrection is not a raising of the spirit but of the body in a restoration of flesh and bone to spirit. As Job triumphantly declared: "And *though* after my skin *worms* destroy this *body*, yet in my flesh shall I see God: Whom I shall see for myself, and mine eyes shall behold, and not another; *though* my reins be consumed within me" (Job 19:26-27; see, also, Ezek. 37:1-14[9]).

Note, however, that it is flesh and *bone* that are restored, not flesh and blood. Paul refers to "flesh and *blood*" as "mortal" and "corruption" (1 Cor. 15:49-55[10]).

The reality of the physical resurrection was graphically demonstrated by Christ when He appeared before His apostles who were assembled in an upper room on the first Easter Sunday. The account is provided in Luke 24:36-43 (NASB) with the clinical objectivity typical of Luke who is believed to have been a medical doctor:

> And while they were telling these things, He Himself stood in their midst.
>
> But they were startled and frightened and thought that they were seeing a spirit.
>
> And He said to them, "Why are you troubled, and why do doubts arise in your hearts?
>
> "See My hands and My feet, that it is I Myself; touch Me and see, for a spirit does not have flesh and bones as you see that I have."
>
> [And when He had said this, He showed them His hands and His feet.]
>
> And while they still could not believe *it* for joy and were marveling, He said to them, "Have you anything here to eat?"
>
> And they gave Him a piece of a broiled fish;
>
> and He took it and ate *it* before them.

From this account, there is no mistaking that Christ's resurrection involved the restoration of His spirit to His body. He was not merely a spirit when he appeared, though He was mistaken for one (which shows that

9. This reference is also a type of the return of Israel to its native land in the last days.

10. Evangelicals concur in this distinction. See, Martin, *Essential Christianity*, 67.

the appearance of the body and that of the spirit are the same). He had "flesh and bones"; He demonstrated His material nature by eating solid food; He was recognizable to those who had known Him during His mortal life; and He retained the prints of the nails in His hands and feet as evidence of His sacrifice for mankind.

Of course, His resurrected body and Man's mortal body exhibit significant differences. Christ appeared out of nowhere in the closed upper room where the disciples met; another passage indicates He could disappear at will just as easily (Luke 24:25-32); and He could keep his identity hidden from those to whom He appeared until He chose to reveal Himself (Luke 24:16; see also verse 31).

While Evangelicals may endorse the bodily resurrection,[11] they refuse to accept its implications. If Christ's spirit were again to be separated from His resurrected body, that new and glorious body would die (James 2:26). Paul testified that this would will never occur. In Romans 6:9 (NASB), he assured the Church: "knowing that Christ, having been raised from the dead, is never to die again; death no longer is master over Him."

Being raised from the dead with a body of flesh and bones, a body from which His spirit will never separate, it is clear that "flesh and bone" is Christ's permanent physiological nature. The testimony of those who saw Him after His resurrection is that the form of His body of flesh and bone was definitely human (Luke 24). To put it in biological terms, Jesus the Christ is the same species as Man, though resurrected, and He will remain so forever.

In light of this conclusion, consider the significance of passages that compare Christ with the Father. Paul told the Colossians that Christ "is the image of the invisible God" (Col. 1:15). Paul made this statement in approximately 60 A.D., well *after* Christ's resurrection. It was also *after* His resurrection when Paul told the Philippians that Christ is in the "form of God" (Phil. 2:6, c. 60 A.D.). The author of Hebrews[12] makes the same point, also *after* Christ's resurrection, proclaiming that Christ is "the *express* image of his [the Father's] person" (Heb. 1:3, c. 68 A.D., emphasis added).

---

11. Martin, "The Gospel of Resurrection," Chapter 6 in *Essential Christianity*, 63-69.

12. Tradition holds that Paul was the author of Hebrews, but some scholars disagree, noting differences in literary style between Hebrews and other writings by Paul. Since the concepts presented in Hebrews are typically Pauline, some believe the book may have been written by Barnabus, Paul's frequent missionary companion.

By examining the image, the original may be known. That is the point of identifying the image, and a major reason for Christ's appearance in the flesh. He came, in part, that Man might know the Father through Him (John 14:1-14; especially verses 7-9). After His resurrection Christ was an immortal human being with a glorified body of flesh and bones. Inescapable logic requires the conclusion that God the Father is also an immortal human being with a glorified body of flesh and bones. If the Son came to show the Father, he who would know the Father must turn an open mind to the physical characteristics of the Son.

Lessons from the Sonhood of Christ. The biblical conclusion that God the Father has a body of flesh and bones as tangible as Man's is consistent with the scriptural declaration that Christ be the literal, *begotten* Son of God (John 1:14, Luke 1:30-35). As a begotten Son, the laws of genetics require that the physical nature of Christ be identical to that of His Father. There is nothing contrary to this message anywhere in the Bible. Not only is the Father human, like Christ, He is literally the Father of the human race.

Christ taught this principle in John 20:17 (NASB): "but go to My brethren, and say to them, 'I ascend to My Father and your Father, and to My God and your God.'" Brethren, sons and fathers are *always* of the same race. The words used in this passage cannot be interpreted to ignore that truth under any sound hermeneutic. A figurative interpretation of this passage is not reasonable, nor would it detract from this exegesis of the passage. The message is clear. Men have a relationship to God that is like that of Christ in at least two respects. God is the "Father" of both Christ and Men, and He is the "God" of both Christ and Men. Men are human, and Christ is human, as He demonstrated after His resurrection. If God is the Father of humans, and if His "only begotten" is human, God too must be human.

Answers to Counter-arguments. Despite the foregoing, Evangelicals claim that the Bible teaches God is only a spirit and has no physical body. Most commonly cited for this proposition is John 4:24, which reads in the NASB as follows: "God is spirit, and those who worship Him must worship in spirit and truth." Because this passage says "God is spirit," Evangelical exegetes jump to the conclusion that He is *only* spirit. The possibility that He is spirit *and* has a physical body is denied by them without a valid reason in either scripture or logic.

If John 4:24 is interpreted in the restrictive manner endorsed by Evangelicals, it must also be construed as a requirement that Men shed their physical bodies in order to worship God. If God is *only* spirit and this passage requires Men to worship Him "in spirit," then Men must worship God *only* in spirit. Thus, to cite John 4:24 against the teachings of Mormon theology is to claim that Men cannot worship God as mortal beings.

That conclusion is obviously contrary to the Bible, which commands all Men to worship God (*present tense*, see, e.g., 1 Chron. 16:29). The idea that John 4:24 describes God exclusively as Spirit must be rejected for it relates also to Men. That verse merely tells of God's spirituality and requires the same of Men. It does not describe God's physiological nature—any more than it does Man's. Men must communicate with God spiritually, that is, spirit to spirit, and to do that they must develop a spiritual nature.

Of course, God *is* spirit (as well as Body), and so is Man. Both Man and God have a spirit *and* a body. Man's spirit is now clothed with a fallen, mortal body of flesh and blood. The Father's spirit is clothed with a glorified body of flesh and bone like that of Christ after His resurrection. (Notably, if Man did not have a spirit-and some sects teach that he does not-he could never worship God "*in spirit* and in truth"; see, also, Numbers 16:22, Ecclesiastes 12:7, and Isaiah 42:5.)

If this is not the case, all the passages describing God's anthropomorphic characteristics would have to be taken figuratively. Such interpretation would not be hermeneutically sound. There is nothing in any passage from Genesis through Revelation that suggests all of the anthropomorphic descriptions of God contained in the Bible should be interpreted figuratively. To do so, regardless of context, would be poor hermeneutics.

In every way God is truly "Our Father which art in heaven" (Matt. 6:9). Through the resurrection of Jesus Christ, all Men can be like Him and, correspondingly, like their Father (or Mother) in Heaven (Rev. 3:21). They can obtain bodies of flesh and bone that are incorruptible and glorious (1 Cor. 15:51-57).

Yet another passage quoted to support the Evangelical concept of God is Numbers 23:19 (NASB): "God is not a man that He should lie, Nor a son of man, that He should repent." Like John 4:24, this passage focuses on the spiritual characteristics of God. But in the original Hebrew, it includes a subtle assumption Evangelicals routinely miss.

The word "man" in the phrase "God is not a man," is not the usual Hebrew word for Man (*adam*). It is *ish*, which is used in verses like this to contrast one type of human with another; a young man as compared to an old man, a man as compared to a woman, a husband compared to a wife.[13] Here it contrasts an honest Man (God) with dishonest Men. This implies that God is physiologically a Man, but He is not a dishonest man. (Note a similar statement using the same Hebrew word in Hos. 11:9.) The point of Numbers 23:19 is not to deny the physiological nature of God, but to proclaim His integrity as compared to that of mortal Men.

The fact is that God, as taught in the Old and New Testament, is a Man, more precisely, a perfect and glorified Human Being. Though the apostate Jews of Christ's day also thought this concept was blasphemous (John 10:31), it is not. It is a simple, biblical truth. To recognize this truth, however, one must reject yet another doctrine born in Greek philosophy—the notion that being human limits God to finite characteristics.

The Father of Man Is Infinite

Mormons deny that the physiological nature of God, as taught in the Bible, is an inhibiting characteristic. Even those Evangelicals who acknowledge the physical resurrection of Jesus Christ declare that physical existence in space-time limits one to a "finite" existence, while the nature of God is infinite.[14] Evangelicals rarely deal with the implications of this belief as it affects Christ. Is Christ's physiological nature as a resurrected human being somehow incompatible with His infinite nature? Orthodox Christians say Christ has a divine as well as a human nature. Why can't His Father have the same?

Evangelicals draw a dichotomy between what exists in real space-time and what they consider to be infinite, and they assume there actually is such a dichotomy in the real universe. Hence, they assume that anyone who believes God has a physical body cannot believe He is also infinite.

Mormons reject these notions as fabrications of the Hellenism popular at the time of Christ. They aver that God exists in real space-time and has a resurrected body of flesh and bones, *and* infinite in the ways He is described as such in scripture. This is not a contradiction, but a recognition of a reality that is more complex than the Greek philosophers imagined.

---

13. *Gesenius' Hebrew and Chaldee Lexicon*, Samuel Tregelles, trans. (Grand Rapids: Baker Books, 1979).

14. Morey, "Invisible and Incorporeal," Chapter 17 in *Battle of the Gods*, 189-190.

Though a description of God's characteristics as infinite occurs only once in the Bible (Ps. 147:5, referring to His understanding), other characteristics of God are described as infinite in Mormon Scripture (2 Ne. 1:10; Mosiah 5:3; and Hel. 12:1;—His goodness; Moro. 8:3—His goodness and grace; Mosiah 28:4—his mercy); God Himself is described as infinite in Alma 34:14; D&C 20:17 and 28; and His atonement is described as infinite in four additional passages (2 Ne. 9:7, 25:16; Alma 34:10, 12). One of the most profound discussions of God's infinite nature found in inspired writ is Alma 34:8-16 in the Book of Mormon. Thus, Mormons acknowledge and accept the biblical truth about God's physical nature, and at the same time proclaim His infinite glory.

Critics of Mormonism cling to the idea that a Being with a physical body cannot have the characteristics attributed to God in the Bible.[15] Those characteristics are associated in the minds of "orthodox" thinkers with an incomprehensible being who doesn't exist in space or time.[16] That these assumptions, adopted from Greek philosophy, are neither logical, realistic, nor biblical can be demonstrated by a review of the Bible's teachings about God's infinite characteristics.

Omnipresence. The issue of God's omnipresence is perhaps the most obvious point on which Greek thinking requires a distinction between the finite and the infinite. The Hellenist argues that only an infinite being, one without finite bodily restrictions, can be omnipresent. If the Bible taught that being omnipresent means being present at every point in the universe *simultaneously*, this Hellenistic assumption might make sense, but the Bible contains no such doctrine.

The definition of omnipresence assumed by Hellenists is barely removed from the pagan notion of *pantheism* (the belief that God is, or is in, everything). If God is present at every point in the Universe simultaneously, one can conclude that God is in everything and that everything is God. Suddenly the worship of idols can be justified. If God is in everything, God is in the idol and the idol becomes a symbol on which to focus one's worship. This form of omnipresence is contrary to biblical teaching.

---

15. Morey, *Battle of the Gods,* 192-193. Note that Morey's philosophical conclusions are asserted without a single biblical citation.
16. Morey, *Battle of the Gods,* 189.

The Bible teaches that, though God is bodily in one place at any one moment in real space-time (see, e.g., Rev. 7:10), His glory, influence, and power fill the universe (Jer. 23:24). He is continually aware of everything that is happening everywhere in the universe, and can communicate with, and travel to, any spot instantaneously (Ps. 139:7-12). The combination of these abilities could be described as "omnipresence," though the Bible nowhere uses that word.

Jeremiah 23:24 states: "Can any hide himself in secret places that I shall not see him? saith the Lord. Do not I fill heaven and earth? saith the Lord." The language of the second question in this passage must be interpreted in context with the first. The assertion is not that God is of such enormous size that He takes up all available space in the universe. Rather, there is no place hidden from Him and no place from which He is excluded. His perception fills heaven and earth; an awareness of Him permeates all creation. This is biblical omnipresence.

The Bible nowhere supports the notion that God is literally present at every point in the universe simultaneously. Were that notion accurate, it would make no sense for Paul to tell the Greeks on Mars Hill, "he be not far from every one of us" (Acts 17:27). The phrase, "not far from," is hardly descriptive of the physical distance between Man and a god who is simultaneously present at every point in the universe. Paul's statement describes God as a person who, though He may not be in Man's presence, He is aware of all that transpires and can beat any point in the universe instantaneously. In that way, He is "not far from every one of us."

Omniscience. That God is omniscient, yet still a man, is another problem for Greek thinkers. The Bible teaches both that God is a Man and that His mental capacity is unlimited (Ps. 139:6). Of course, mortal Men do not know what God knows (Isa. 55:8-9), but the human brain has unlimited capacity to learn. Some researchers have determined that "the brain's memory storage capacity is effectively unlimited."[17] Thus, a glorified and perfected human body provides the preeminent tool for an omniscient God to function on an infinite basis in real space-time. The contrary assumption of Hellenists is nothing but philosophical conjecture based on a limited knowledge of both reality and biblical truth.

---

17. Steve Emmons, "The Mystery of Memory," *Los Angeles Times,* Tuesday, January 11, 1994, Section E (citing the work of Dr. Gary Lynch, UC Irvine, Center for the Neurobiology of Learning and Memory).

That God *is* omniscient is unquestioned by Mormons. They teach that God is constantly aware of all that transpires throughout His creations, and is in possession of all knowledge. Seond Nephi 9:20 in the Book of Mormon is incontrovertible on this point: "O how great the holiness of our God! For he knoweth all things, and there is not anything save he knows it." Such knowledge constitutes omniscience, and Evangelicals cannot deny that a glorified Man is the possessor of such knowledge on the basis of any passage in the Bible.

Some Mormons postulate that God's omniscience with respect to future events arises from His ability to plan for any possible contingency. (Blake Ostler, "The Mormon Concept of God," *Dialogue: A Journal of Mormon Thought* 7 (Summer 1984), 76-78.) There is biblical authority for this view (Isa. 46:10-11), but Men must be careful not to image finite limitations on such omniscience. It is difficult for man to comprehend the perfection of God's knowledge regarding every possible contingency and its exact probability, or the subtle means by which He, having such knowledge, can act to ensure, with absolute certainty, the occurence of any predicted outcome without interferring in the free agency of a single human being. This is infinite omniscience, not finite guesswork.

Perfection. Mormon theology teaches that God is infinitely perfect. This is not a characteristic that is incompatible with humanity, for Men are made perfect through the blood of Christ. (Mormon theology does not teach that God the Father required the benefits of an atonement—cf., John 5:19.) The Bible records that some men were perfected during their mortal lives (e.g., Noah: Gen. 6:9; and Job: Job 1:8). All Men have been called to this standard of perfection (Matt. 5:48). Evangelicals typically claim it is not a possibility for Man. But it makes sense that the children of a perfect Being would be capable of achieving the same goal. Otherwise it was an intentional insult for Christ to say: "Be ye therefore perfect, even as your Father which is in heaven is perfect" (Matt. 5:48). The fact that Christ pointed to the Father as Man's example in their struggle for perfection is yet another indication that the Father *is* a Man.

Omnipotence. That God could be a Man and still be omnipotent is another difficult concept for Hellenist thinkers. However, there is nothing in the Bible that suggests physical existence is incompatible with infinite power. In fact, it is logical to conclude that both physical and spiritual existence is necessary for omnipotence in both realms.[18]

Man is incapable of understanding God's power at this time, and often leaps to erroneous conclusions about it. Is God all-powerful in the sense that He has every power that exists in a real universe, or does His infinite power include the ability to act in ways that contradict the very fabric of the universe? Does God have the ability to act paradoxically, such as creating a rock so large He cannot lift it, or causing something to exist and not exist at the same time?

The Bible does not make distinctions in this regard (see, e.g., 1 Sam. 14:6; Jer. 32:17; Matt. 19:26). However, it appears from observation of the universe God created that He does not allow the existence of paradoxes. One could assert that paradoxical power, by definition, does not exist, and therefore is not a dimension of omnipotence, or one could argue that God simply refrains from exercising paradoxical power for good reasons of His own (e.g., because paradoxes violate principles of perfect justice). Either way, Mormons believe paradoxes are not a part of the real universe.

Knowing that God does not act paradoxically despite His omnipotence is important in responding to the challenge of skeptics who point to the Problem of Evil and claim that a God who is All Good and All Powerful would not allow Evil to exist. The truth is Evil exists because God has opted to give Men free agency. To do this requires that Men be allowed to make *real* choices between good and evil. Evil choices invariably bring evil consequences. To prevent evil consequences while granting Men true free agency would involve a paradox, and God does not work in paradoxes.

Thus, evil will always be part of a universe in which free agency is allowed. God's infinite power deals with Evil (Rom. 8:28), but it does so without eliminating its existence. Thus, God is omnipotent and the epitome of love (1 John 4:8), but He allows the existence of a real universe in which His plan of salvation is designed to compensate for problems stemming from the gift of free agency that Men have been given.

Eternal, Immutable, and Uncreate. There are many passages in the Bible, and even more definitive statements in uniquely Mormon Scripture,

18. It should *not* be assumed, however, that Christ, before He came to earth and obtained a mortal body, was less than omnipotent. There is no basis in scripture for such a conclusion. Christ has always acted in oneness with His Father, who *did* have a physical body. It is possible, therefore, that the omnipotence of the Father was exercised by the Son.That would be consistent with Paul's teachings in 1 Cor. 8:6, and Christ's statements in John 5:17-20, 30; and 8:28-29.

that say God is eternal, immutable, and unchangeable (see e.g., Heb. 13:8). D&C 76:4 states, "From eternity to eternity he is the same." Moses 1:3, in the Pearl of Great Price, reads: "And God spake unto Moses, saying: Behold, I am the Lord God Almighty, and Endless is my name; for I am without beginning of days or end of years; and is not this endless?"

Yet there have been changes in the way God has dealt with Man, and in His own physical form. The priesthood and the Law of Moses were changed following Christ's sacrifice on the cross (Heb. 7:12). Jehovah, who spoke to Moses and identified Himself as "the Lord God Almighty" (Moses 1:3), became flesh and dwelt among Men as Jesus the Christ (Phil. 2:6-8). How then is God's immutability and eternal nature to be understood from a biblical perspective?

Clearly, God is not static. He causes, permits, and participates in change.[19] The Creation is doubtless the most extraordinary of God's changes. Understood in that sense, it is easier to accept the biblical teaching that Christ, Himself, experienced changes in connection with the Creation, while at the same time He remained, in the most fundamental sense, eternal and immutable.

Evangelicals view the Creation in a purely Hellenistic way. Two axioms of the Greek-influenced creeds of early Christendom are that God is *uncreate*, meaning, not created,[20] and that He created the space-time universe out of nothing.[21] In the Hellenist's view, nothing that was created existed before the Creation. Hence, only the Creator can be called *eternal*. This view is without biblical support. From the perspective of an Eternal Being, the Creation was a *change*, not a *start*.

Of events before the creation of this earth the Bible gives little information (but see, Prov. 8:22-23). However, it does *not* teach that time began with the Creation, as Evangelicals claim.[22] Nor is there anything in the Bible to suggest that there was no material in existence before the Creation, or that God formed the heavens and the earth out of nothing.

---

19. On this point Evangelicals concur (Morey, *Battle of the Gods*, 212).

20. See, e.g., "The Athanasian Creed" (A.D. 490) in Philip Schaff, *The Creeds of Christendom,* 6th ed., 3 vols. (Grand Rapids: Baker Book House, 1983), 2:66-70.

21. Morey, *Battle of the Gods*..156

22. Morey, *Battle of the Gods,* 203-208. Morey argues that to say God is eternal, means He does not exist in time but that time was created by Him and did not exist before "the beginning" (205-207). This argument is made on the basis of Genesis 1:1, but no cognizable semantic principle can stretch that passage to support Morey's interpretation of it.

The word *create*, used in the Bible, does *not* mean to make something out of nothing (Latin: *ex nihil*). Indeed, the phrase "out of nothing" appears nowhere in the Bible. The only use of the word "nothing" in connection with the Creation appears in Job 26:7 (NASB, emphasis added) which states that God "*hangs* the earth on nothing." Modern astronomy would attest to the accuracy of that statement.

The Hebrew word translated "create" in the first chapters of Genesis is *bara*, which means, literally, "to cut prepare, form, or fashion." Thus, it distinctly implies the impressing of *information* upon *existing* material. The Greek word for create, *ktizo*, found in the New Testament, has the same meaning. It refers to a "making" or a "thing made." The concepts communicated by these words do not require the assumption that no material was used to fashion the final product.

The Greek word *ginomai*, from which the word "made" is translated in John 1:3, means "to become" or "begin to be." This comes closest to supporting the "out of nothing" concept, but only if one assumes that a thing that "becomes" must be fashioned out of nothing, or that it did not exist as formless matter before it "began to be." Clay will begin to be a pot when it is formed in the potter's hand, but before it becomes the pot it exists as formless clay.[23]

Consistent with these principles, Mormons teach that God created the heavens and the earth by forming the planets, the sun, and the stars out of formless matter. Even the spirits of Men were formed out of existing components. Before being formed into spirits, Men existed as *intelligences* (Abraham 3:22-23 in the Pearl of Great Price). Even intelligences were *not created out of nothing* but are *eternal* in nature (D&C 93:29)

Thus, it is a distinctive precept of Mormon theology that, before His creation as the firstborn of the Father, Christ existed from all eternity, His form being that of a perfect intelligence. In a very real and significant way, He was, therefore, "uncreate." His "creation" as the Son of God only meant His eternal nature as an intelligence took on the form of the spirit Son of God. The Bible attests that Christ is *immutable*, or unchanging, but it only makes such statements in relation to His *basic character*. This is a reassuring and powerful testimony of Christ, and one that does not force Him into immobile stasis.

---

23. For an indepth analysis of Heb 11:3 and Rom 4:17, cited by Evangelicals in support of the *ex nihilo* doctrine, see Hopkins, *Greek Philosophy Corrupted the Christian Concept of God*, 292-294.

While Mormons believe all Men have an eternal element in their nature (their intelligences have also existed from all eternity), they believe that all Men, save Christ alone, have to change their basic character to some degree in order to be in the perfect image of God. No such change appears to have been necessary for Christ. Though He learned from the Father (John 5:20), He has *always* been the perfect example of the Father's Love (cf. John 5:19). Thus, only the *form* of His existence has changed (Phil. 2:6-8). God revealed to Men in the flesh, He has remained perfect and unchanged in that perfection throughout all eternity.

The idea that Christ was created, even in the sense indicated above is soundly rejected by Hellenists. But, as will be demonstrated later, the Bible clearly teaches that Christ was formed by God the Father as His first creation—His firstborn spirit child. It is only Greek thinking that prevents Evangelicals from accepting this biblical truth.

Dr. Robert Morey, a noted Evangelical philosopher, claims "it is the addition of the concept of 'infinity' that makes God the Creator instead of a creature."[24] The God he imagines is a philosophical fiction based on non-biblical assumptions. In Morey's view all that is created is finite, or limited, because it was created out of nothing and exists in real space-time. In this view, if Christ was created, He is a "creature," and must be finite, not the infinite Creator.

But only the Aristotelian logic of a philosopher could assume that everything God creates is finite. The Bible specifically refutes that view. Ecclesiastes 3:14 states: "I know that, whatsoever God doeth, it shall be for ever: nothing can be put to it, nor any thing taken from it: and God doeth it, that men should fear before him." Thus, God's creations are exactly the opposite of Dr. Morey's assumptions about them. They are infinite, they "shall be for ever."

Do Evangelicals suppose that God, although omnipotent, has no power to reproduce Himself? The Bible teaches that He did exactly that in Christ (Col. 1:15; Heb. 1:3). The change Christ experienced at the creation of His spirit form did not make an infinite nature impossible. Exactly the opposite. It was the beginning of an increasing empowerment, part of a plan that included incarnation in the flesh (Phil. 2:6-8), and later, resurrection. Since God did it, it was intended from the beginning to be infinite.[25]

24. Morey, *Battle of the Gods,* 192.

25. A thorough review of these issues and the Hellenistic basis for modern othrodox Christianity can be found in Hopkins, *How Greek Philosophy Corrupted the Christian Concept of God.*

The Creation of God the Son

John 1:1-3 (NASB) teaches of Christ's creation as follows:

> In the beginning was the Word, and the Word was with God, and the Word was God.
>
> He [literally, *This one*] was in the beginning with God.
>
> All things came into being by [*through*] Him, and apart from Him nothing came into being that has come into being.

Evangelicals note that this passage says Christ ("the Word,"see John 1:14) existed (i.e., "was"), "in the beginning . . . *with God*." They interpret this to mean that Christ existed in triunity with God the Father at the time of Creation. From this they conclude that Christ could not have been created because He existed *before* the Creation and participated in it. According to this logic, He existed, He was with God, and He was God, creating "all things" out of nothing.

Not only is this interpretation based on ignorance of Christ's eternal existence as an "intelligence" *before* the Creation, it ignores the construction of verse[1] , running its three separate clauses into a single incomprehensible jumble. The first clause in verse[1] says, "in the beginning was the Word." This clause states that Christ existed at the beginning of the creative acts described in Genesis. In fact, it will be shown later that the first thing God did in creating the heavens and the earth was to create, or form, the Word (In His spirit form).

The second clause states that the Word was "with God." This is John's testimony that, after His creation or formation, Christ was with the Father and assisted Him in the creation, as indicated in verse 3. The third clause proclaims a change in Christ " He was God." This does not mean Christ was the Father. Even Trinitarians do not make that claim. What then does it mean? Based on passages to be explored in the next Chapter, it appears that this is a reference to a change in Christ's pre-mortal status. Prior to the creation of the heavens and the earth, He was elevated to a status equal with the Father. These three events, or stages in Christ's pre-mortal life, are described separately by Isaiah (see, Isa. 9:6), as well as by John.

The second verse in this passage is transitional. John, who details Christ's progression in verse 1, here states that He acted jointly with the Father in the Creation, the scope of which he describes in verse 3. This sequence of events provides the context for the phrase, "all things" in verse 3 ("*all things* came into being by him").

"All things" is translated from *pas* (or one of its derivatives), a single Greek word that literally means, "all [*blank*]." The word "things" is not in the text. What is included within the scope of [*blank*] depends entirely on the context in which the author uses *pas* or one of its derivatives. (The derivatives relate to how inclusive "all" is intended to be.) Thus, if the context of the passage were men, *pas* would refer to "all men"; if the author were talking about animals, the scope of the word would be "all animals."

Similarly, the word "nothing" in the second half of verse 3 is translated from the single Greek word *oude*, meaning, "not even." Like *pas*, its opposite, *oude* takes its scope from the context of the passage.

To understand this verse, therefore, the context must be fully and accurately established. Temporally, the context of John 1:3 is a point in time *after* Christ's creation. Thus, when verse 3 says "*all things* came into being by Him," it includes all things created *after* His spirit was formed. Verse 3 testifies of Christ's participation in the creation of the heavens and the earth. It does not discuss His own creation, nor the creation of God's other spirit children. The scope of "all things" in this passage would not embrace those aspects of God's work.

This understanding is corroborated by another statement about the creative work of Christ—as indicated in Colossians 1:15-17. Colossians 1:15 was analyzed briefly in Chapter 1. A more thorough analysis is appropriate here. That passage reads in the NASB as follows:

> And He is the image of the invisible God, the first-born of all creation.
>
> For by Him all things were created, both in the heavens and on earth, visible and invisible, whether thrones or dominions or rulers or authorities —all things have been created by Him and for Him.
>
> And He is before all things, and in Him all things hold together.

Understanding this passage also begins with an exegesis of the term "all things" (Greek: *pas*) used in verses 16 and 17. Does "all things" in this context mean "everything," as most Evangelicals say? If so, it teaches some very strange doctrine. Verse 16 mentions "the visible and the *invisible*," and verse 15 refers to God the Father as the "*invisible* God." If the phrase "all things" really refers to "everything," it would require the conclusion that Christ created God the Father! Such an interpretation is patently erroneous. Therefore, it is certain that the term "all things" in this passage does not include *everything*, but must be narrowed to the scope originally intended by the writer.

The scope of *pas* in Colossians 1:16-17 is determined by Colossians 1:15, which states that Christ was "the first-born of all creation." Assuming this means that Christ was created *first*, the scope of *pas* in verse 16 is exactly the same as in John 1:3. It is limited to all things created *after* Christ was formed as the first-born spirit Son of God. That which was created after Christ is expressly described in the balance of the verse, thus confirming this hermeneutic. Colossians 1:16-17 refers to the creation of the earth and the heavens surrounding it, which Moses described in Genesis. It does not refer to the creation of spirits in the abode of God.

The word "by" in the first phrase of verse 16 ("for by Him all things were created") is from the Greek word *en*, which may be translated either "by," "in" or "with." The latter ("with") is the choice that appears the most accurate in this context. Combined with the appropriate limitation on the word *pas*, the first phrase in verse 16 may be rendered: "For *with* Him [that is, with His assistance] all *the things that were formed after He was born the first of God's spirit children* were created."

The word "by" in the last phrase of verse 16 ("all things have been created by Him and for Him") is from the Greek word *dia* which also means "through" or "by means of." This confirms the interpretation that Christ *assisted* the Father in the creation.

That understanding is implied in Proverbs 30:4, which reads in the NASB (emphasis added) as folows:

> Who has ascended into heaven and descended?
> Who has gathered the wind in His fists?
> Who has wrapped the waters in His garment?
> Who has established all the ends of the earth?
> What is *His* name or *His son's* name?
> Surely you know!

The Jews knew, or should have known. *His* name was Elohim.[26] He was the Father, and *His son's* name was Jehovah. His Son was created or

26. However, the word elohim is used throughout the Old Testament in contexts where it obviously does not refer to God the Father. The same is occacionally true of the name Jehovah.
27. New Scofield Study Bible,1681 (footnote to Col.1:17)

formed first, then the Father and the Son "established all the ends of the earth."

The Greek wording translated, "And He *is before* all things" in verse 17 may also be rendered "And He *has existed prior to* all things."[27] Again, "all things" has the same context and scope in this verse as it does in verse 16. It also refers to all things created after Christ was formed as the firstborn of the Father. Thus, verse 17 may be translated: "And He has existed prior to the Creation of all things that were formed after He was born the first of God's spirit children." This affirms, consistent with Mormon doctrine, that Christ existed eternally as an intelligence before He was formed as the first spirit Son of God.

The testimony of Paul in Colossians 1:15-17 is identical to that of John in John 1:1-3. These two testimonies are confirmed by yet another source, the author of Hebrews (Heb. 1:2). In no way do any of these passages conflict and none of them contradict the LDS teaching that Christ was created first, the firstborn spirit Son of God, and that God the Father had other spirit children before the heavens and the earth were created by Him and the Savior acting together. (See also Job 38:4-7.) Each passage confirms that the Creation was initiated *after* Christ's creation as a spirit, and after He was exalted to God's right hand.

That Christ's spirit birth marks the true beginning of God's creation is taught in Colossians 1:18 (NASB, emphasis added) which states: "He is also head of the body, the church; and *He is the beginning*, the firstborn from the dead; so that He Himself might come to have first place in everything." Christ is first in the Church, He was the firstborn spirit child of God, and He was the first to be resurrected from the dead. Truly, as this passage indicates, He has "first place in everything."

That Christ's spirit birth was the first creative act of God is unequivocally taught in Revelation 3 which contains Christ's message to the Church at Laodicea. At the outset of His message (Rev. 3:14, NASB, emphasis added), Christ identifies Himself as follows: "And to the angel of the church in Laodicea write: The Amen, the faithful and true Witness, *the Beginning of the creation of God*, says this."

Truly, Christ's birth as the firstborn of God's spirit children was "the beginning" of Creation, so that He is personally addressed here as "*the Beginning of the creation of God*." The word translated "Beginning" in this phrase is *archē*, the same word used in John 1:1. At some point after Christ's creation, the heavens and the earth were created with and through Christ, so that He is the Creator of the ends of the earth (Isa. 40:28); He laid its foundations (Job 38:4); He created the heavens, and stretched them out (Isa. 42:5); and mortal Men are the work of His hands, as the clay is the work of the potter (Isa. 64:8; see also, John 1:10; Acts 17:24; Eph. 3:9; Heb. 1:2, 11:3; 2 Pet. 3:5; and Rev. 4:11). All these acts were carried out *after* He was first created or formed as the first spirit Son of God. Thus, the Bible teaches that He is literally the Son of God, both physically and spiritually.

Conclusion

There is nothing in the infinite nature of God or Christ that is incompatible with the anthropomorphic characteristics of God described in the Bible. Nor is the infinite nature of Christ inconsistent with His birth as the first spirit Son of God the Father. The reluctance of Evangelicals to accept these principles stems solely from their indoctrination in the notions of Greek philosophy that infiltrated the early Church and influenced the basic creeds of historic orthodoxy.

The Bible teaches that both the Father and the Son are Men. Mortal Men were literally created in their image and likeness. They have His appearance in a spiritual sense ("image") and are genetically like Him ("likeness"). That God is a glorified, omniscient, omnipotent, omnipresent, perfect, and infinite *Human Being* is entirely consistent with the teachings of the Bible, and observations of the real space-time universe. God's physiological nature, as a Man, is not only compatible with His infinite nature, as God, it is a perfect part of that reality.

This is the Mormon understanding of the nature of God. It is also what the Bible teaches about Him. That the current Evangelical concept of God differs from it is not the result of any hermeneutic analysis of Bible passages. It is the result of Greek thinking, so influential in the early Church, which became memorialized in early creeds and continues to bias mainline theological opinion to this day.

3

The Number of God

Mormons believe the Father and the Son are separate *individuals* and that there is a literal father-son relationship between them. They also believe in the Holy Ghost as the third individual identified by the title "God" in the New Testament. Because of this, Mormons have been labeled *polytheists* (believers in more than one God) by the Evangelical community.[1]

Some claim that Mormons believe in many gods and are worthy of the polytheist label on that account. This accusation arises because most Evangelicals do not understand the relationship between Man's worship of God and the Mormon teaching that Men can become like God. With Paul, Mormons declare, "to us *there is but* one God (1 Cor. 8:6). Mormons do not now, and have never, taught that Men (speaking of the children of God who did, do, and will, inhabit this planet) were, are, or ever will be, subject to any God other than the Father, the Son, and the Holy Ghost.

If Mormons are to be accused of polytheism, let the record be clear as to the true basis for that criticism. It is their refusal to accept the merger of these three, whom the Bible refers to both individually and collectively as God, into a literal singularity, one Being, the Trinity. All who believe in the Father, the Son, and the Holy Ghost, must face the same criticism if they cannot explain, as this chapter will, why a belief in three separate persons, each of whom is called God, can rightly be termed *monotheism* (a belief in *one* God).

---

1. Walter Martin, *The Maze of Mormonism* (Ventura: Regal Books, 1978), 74.

God Is One

A declaration of the number of God first appears in the Bible in the Old Testament at Deuteronomy 6:4 (NASB): "Hear, O Israel! The LORD is our God, the LORD is one!" The word translated "Lord" appears in the original Hebrew mss. as "YHWH" without vowels, as was the practice in the Hebrew text of the Old Testament, and was not expressed by the Jews. The exact pronunciation is unknown. Though it is sometimes vocalized as "Yahweh," the traditional transliteration is "Jehovah." Mormons believe this is the name most commonly used to designate the pre-mortal spirit Son of God known on earth as Jesus the Christ.

The word translated "God" in Deuteronomy 6:4 is the Hebrew *elohim*[2] (the plural of *eloah*), commonly translated in the singular as "God." The term is not a proper name, but is often used as a title meaning "God," and is plural in construction. Used over 2,500 times in the Old Testament, it isn't used consistantly to identify a specific member of the Godhead. In fact, it is often used in reference to heathen gods. However, in colloquial usage, Mormons equate the term *Elohim* with God the Father, distinguishing Him from *Jehovah*, whom then equate with God the Son. *Elohim* is often used in the Old Testament in conjunction with YHWH to designate the position or authority of Jehovah, and occasionally it is used as the equivalent of the term *Godhead*, introduced in the New Testament (Acts 17:29).

Deuteronomy 6:4 literally reads "YHWH is our elohim, YHWH is one!" This passage can be interpreted as a statement that Jehovah occupies the position of Elohim (God) over Israel, and is the one God Israel is commanded to worship, the God of Israel. The passage is clear in its message: Jehovah, who is *our* God, is one. The passage can be used to prove that the Father, Son, and Holy Ghost are not New Testament fabrications.[3] *Elohim*, a *plural* word, is used to describe God instead of the singular *eloah*. There are many passages in the Old Testament that are consistent with the New Testament's teachings about God. Genesis is filled with them (see, e.g., Gen. 3:22, NASB, emphasis added: "Behold, the man has become like one of *Us*, knowing good and evil"; see, also, Prov. 30:4).

---

2. It was not uncommon in early 19th Century America to spell this word "Eloheim" consonant with the rules of English pronunciation at that time ("ei" being pronounced "e").

3. Evangelicals concur on this point. See Edward Bickersteth, *The Trinity* (Grand Rapids: Kregel Publications, 1957), 144-146 (footnote).

The New Testament introduced Israel to a great deal of new information about God. That knowledge, however, caused an element of confusion in the Hellenistic world of the time. The Godhead was identified at the baptism of Jesus as consisting of three separate, distinct individuals located in three separate places (Matt.3:13-17; Mark 1:9-11; Luke 3:21-22). Each is separately declared in various passages of the New Testament to be "God" (see, e.g., Acts 5:3-4, which implies that the Holy Ghost bears that title). Showing how these passages are to be understood, in light of the Old Testament's teachings of monotheism, has been a challenge to Christianity for centuries.

The Johannine Comma directly addresses this issue. 1 John 5:7 states, "For there are three that bear record in heaven, the Father, the Word, and the Holy Ghost: and these three are one." As indicated in Chapter One, however, this language is not accepted by most scholars as part of the original text of 1 John. But the Bible generally, and the uniquely Mormon Scriptures specifically, are consistent with its message. The Book of Mormon for example, teaches (2 Nephi 31:21):

> And now, behold, my beloved brethren, this is the way; and there is none other way nor name given under heaven whereby man can be saved in the kingdom of God. And now, behold, this is the doctrine of Christ, and the only and true doctrine of the Father, and of the Son, and of the Holy Ghost, which is one God, without end. Amen. (See also, Alma 11:44, and D&C 20:27-28.[4])

In light of these teachings, it is natural to ask, "How can Three persons be One God?" That question racked the early Church during the second through fourth centuries, A.D. It was used by Marcus Aurelius in the late second century to indict Christians and send them to their deaths. The answer that became historical Christian orthodoxy was the seminal step into an Apostasy that has influenced Christian churches to the present era. The Trinity, a conglomeration of the Three into one being, one substance, essence, or nature—co-substantial, co-equal and

4. Another interesting passage on this subject is Mosiah 15:1-5. The prophet Abinadi there refers to Christ's flesh as "the Son" and His spirit as "the Father," declaring that Christ was the Son of God in the flesh and the "Eternal Father [or Creator] of heaven and earth" (Mosiah 15 :4) as a pre-mortal spirit being, consistent with John 1:1-3, Col. 1:16-17, and Heb. 1:1-3.

5. Walter Martin taught that the Three are "coequal in power, nature, and eternity." Martin, *Essential Christianity,* 27.

co-eternal,[5] and comprehensible only in the metaphysical construct assumed by the Philosophers of at the time, remains one of the two most telling legacies of that Apostasy in Christianity today. Mormons reject this concept as an early heresy, and insist that references to God's oneness were not meant to be interpreted in the sense demanded by a culture permeated with Greek philosophy, but in a figurative sense consistent with all relevant passages in the Bible.

The Triune God of Historic Orthodoxy

The formulation of the Trinity as an explanation for Bible passages about the number of God reflects a need in Man as ancient and deep-rooted as idol worship. Without the guidance of prophets, the Greek philosophers sought to embody in their theology a psychological need for the characteristic of inscrutability in the Being they choose to worship.

The ancient Greek ego, which lies at the heart of rationalism and humanism today, found it hard to worship a real Father in Heaven as the true and living God. The anthropomorphic God of Abraham, Isaac and Jacob was too mundane, and too familiar in nature to be GOD. To find a GOD worthy of his submission, Man invented false deities, including idols, who appeared transcendently different and far more wonderful than themselves.

Early idol worship incorporated many elements of mystery in common with the later-adopted Trinity. For example, the spirit, or essence, of the false god was supposedly embodied in the object of worship.[6] The paradoxical mysticism associated with idols provided a level of comfort not found in the simple Hebrew worship of a God who lives in some remote place called Heaven.

In the second century AD, as Greeks joined the Christian church in droves and Roman persecution threatened to destroy the non-conforming cult, Man's intellect generated the ultimate idol. A completely inscrutable paradox, the false concept of god known as the Trinity transcends both substance and comprehension. According to Dr. Robert Morey, the Trinity is a singular Spirit Being, who manifests Himself (Itself?) in "three centers of consciousness" which are only *metaphorically* referred to as the

6. *Encyclopaedia Britannica,* 1960 ed., s.v. "idolatry."

7. Dr. Robert Morey from *Mormonism: The Mormon Concept of Gods,* a debate between Robert Morey and Richard Hopkins, 4 audiotapes (Irvine: Christian Research Institute, 1992), 1st hour.

Father, the Son, and the Holy Spirit.[7] This is the god of current Evangelical theology, whom Mormons are expected to worship if they want to be called "Christian" by the Evangelical community.

Initially, it may be noted that Dr. Morey's explanation of God does not satisfy certain logical objections. One can imagine lessons to be learned from the appearance of a god in *two* centers of consciousness metaphorically referred to as the Father and the Son. The imagery would show that Man's obedience to God should be like a child's obedience to his father, and that the love of God for Man is like the love of a father for his children.

Problems arise, however, in finding a reason for the metaphoric reference to a third person. Why did God chose to reveal Himself as *three* centers of consciousness, and why is the third center of consciousness metaphorically referred to as the Holy Ghost (or Holy Spirit)? This aspect of the metaphor is unintelligible, and hence the message to Man is clouded. A satisfying answer is not provided in Trinitarian theology. (The real reason for calling the third member of the Godhead the Holy *Ghost* or Holy *Spirit* is that this name distinguishes His nature from that of the Father and the Son, both of whom have *bodies* of flesh and bone.)

Still, the Mormon scriptures cited above state the number of God in a way that, at first, appears compatible with the Trinity. For that reason, some Evangelicals claim that the Book of Mormon, which clearly teaches the Three are "one God," contradicts the later teachings of Joseph Smith, who said that the Father, the Son, and the Holy Ghost are three separate individuals.[8]

Of course, Evangelicals also teach (1) the Father, the Son, and the Holy Ghost are "three separate persons," and (2) "these three persons eternally co-exist as the one God."[9] The difference between Mormons and Evangelicals on this point arises from the following unusual distinction draw by Evangelical theologians: While Evangelicals believe that the Father, Son, and Holy Ghost are three separate *persons*, they emphatically deny that they are three separate *individuals*. The distinction is neither biblical, nor consistent with semantics or common sense. It was developed during the second century AD, and strictly enforced after the Arian Controversy of the fourth century resulted in the Nicene and Athanasian Creeds and the Council of Constantinople. Yet

---

8. Trivanovich, *Speaking the Truth in Love,* 19-20.
9. Trivanovich, *Speaking the Truth in Love,* 20-21.

Evangelicals call Mormons polytheists (or *tritheists*—believers in three Gods) on the basis of this bewildering differentiation, while they justify labeling themselves monotheists.

On this point, Elwell's *The Concise Evangelical Dictionary of Theology* states:

> While the term "person" in relation to the Trinity does not signify the limited individuality of human persons, it does affirm the I-thou of; personal relationship, particularly of love, within the triune Godhead.[10]

This attempt to explain the distinction between "persons" and "individuals" is so illogical it requires the abandonment of all common sense simply to express it. And describing the "individuality of human persons" as "limited" is unsupported by any scriptural reference, being nothing but pure Hellenism. Nor is Elwell able to explain how "the I-thou of personal relationship" within the "triune Godhead" differs from the "individuality of human persons" (limited or otherwise).

Another attempt to distinguish the indistinguishable is made by Donald Bloesch in his *Essentials of Evangelical Theology*. He states: "It should be recognized that *persons* in the early church did not mean personalities in the modern sense (which indicates autonomy) but objective modes of being."[11]

It's not clear what Bloesch means by "Objective modes of being," but the word "persona" (Latin) was made popular in the late second century by Tertulian, a lawyer, who used it in a legal sense It is not found in the Bible, and Bloesch gives no citations therefrom in its defense.

Bloesch at least recognizes some of the problems inherent in his distinction. A footnote to the sentence quoted above reads:

> Barth rightly recognizes that the modern concept of personality includes the attributes of self-consciousness and this, therefore, creates problems for the doctrine of the Trinity. To hold that there

10. Walter Elwell, ed. *The Concise Evangelical Dictionary of Theology,* abridged by Peter Toon (Grand Rapids: Baker Book House, 1991), s.v. "God, Doctrine of: *The Trinity.*"
11. Donald Bloesch, *Essentials of Evangelical Theology: Volume 1, God, Authority, and Salvation* (San Francisco: Harper & Row, Publishers, 1978), 35.
12. *Ibid.*

> are three distinct centers of consciousness, three self-conscious personal beings, comes close to tritheism.[12]

Is Bloesch suggesting that the three centers of consciousness making up the Trinity are not conscious of their separateness, or is he contradicting Morey's explanation of the Trinity? Wasn't Christ self-conscious while here on earth? How can a triune Being use personal pronouns ("I," "Thou," "My,' etc.) as God the Father and Jesus Christ do (see, e.g., Matt. 3:13-17), if there is no individual self-consciousness. Bloesch does not answer these questions, nor can he because his doctrine is Greek, *not* biblical.

The theology Evangelicals have embraced to explain how the Three are One simply does not make sense. Mormons should not be criticized for rejecting such nonsense. Nor can anyone claim that, by rejecting the Trinity Mormons reject biblical truth, for the Trinity is not in the Bible. It is Evangelicals, not Mormons, who should be called cultists for accepting such false creeds, rather than using the Bible to learn about God

The Nicene Creed

Mormons accept the Bible's teachings that (1) God the Father, His Son, Jesus Christ, and the Holy Ghost are three separate persons, each of whom is referred to in the Scriptures as "God"; and (2) these Three are One God. However, unlike Evangelicals, Mormons do not resolve these two seemingly contradictory statements by adopting the doctrine known as the Trinity.[13]

The Trinity is based on heresy embraced by the Council at Nicaea in 325 A.D. The transmutation of God into an incomprehensible Being was an irresistible temptation for the early Church. Greek philosophy was the only acceptable mode of thinking for intellectuals at that time. Intense Roman persecution had caused the death of knowledgeable Christians (e.g., the Apostles) before new leaders could be adequately trained, and the Romans threatened to destroy all Christians if they did not explain their theology in Greek terms.[14]

---

13. See, Martin, *Maze of Mormonism,* 75.
14. For details on this crucial period of early Church history, see Hopkins, (*How Greek Phylosophy Corrupted the Christian Concept of God).*

Councils, such as that held at Nicaea, were unprecedented as means for learning the truth about God. Historically, God revealed His truth through prophets (Amos 3:7). Of course, if a prophet had convened the Council at Nicaea, it is conceivable that an illuminating Creed revealing God's true nature might have resulted. Instead, the early Church confirmed a formula that added more error than truth to the prevailing theories of the age, for this Council was convened, not by a prophet, but by Constantine, the heathen emperor of Rome. To make matters worse, he was not seeking the truth, but to resolve a controversy that threatened to split his kingdom.[15]

Constantine had chosen the Christian religion to unify the warring factions of the Roman Empire, only to find that there were deep schisms within the Church itself. The Arian Controversy, which the Council convened to resolve, was the most divisive of its time. Arius was a subordinate to Alexander, bishop of Alexandria. Though Mormons would disagree with many of Arius' theories about God, he correctly identified many problems in the *trinity in unity* concept then accepted by a large segment of the early Church. Many sided with Arius, and the resulting conflict was bitter.

While the Nicene Council was arrayed to sit in judgment of Arius, the attendant bishops found it difficult to refute the arguments he raised. Finally, Constantine interceded, suggesting that the Greek word *homoousios* (*homo* meaning "same," and *ousios* meaning "substance, being, or essence") be incorporated in the Creed that would silence Arius and his followers.

While the word *ousia* is found in the Bible (only once—Luke 15:13), *homoousios* (or *homoousia*, a rendering advanced by another faction) appears nowhere. It has never been associated with the relationship between the Father, the Son, and the Holy Ghost in any inspired writ. For that reason, the Nicene concept was viewed as a major theological change by many bishops of the time, and initially it resulted in even more dissension than it quelled.[16] Constantine was forced to replace dissenting bishops with ones willing to support the new Creed.[17] By this means, and with the aid of such proponents as Athanasius, the new doctrine ultimately found universal acceptance in the Roman Church.

---

15. *Encyclopaedia Britannica,* 1960 ed., s.v. "Nicene Creed."

16. *Ibid.*

17. *Encyclopaedia Britannica,* 1960 ed., s.v. "Athanasius 'The Great'."

The Creed itself is an ancient eastern baptismal confession into which the heretical wording was inserted. Mormons agree with the original confession (quoted below), but firmly reject the additions made at Nicaea. Those additions are indicated by brackets in the following translation of the revised baptismal confession that became the Nicene Creed:

> We believe in one God, the Almighty Father, creator of all things visible and invisible.
>
> And in one Lord Jesus Christ, the son of God, who alone was begotten of the Father [that is of the substance of the Father] God of God, Light of Light [very God of very God, begotten, not made, of one substance with the Father], through whom all was made that is in heaven and on earth, who for us men and for our salvation came down and became flesh, became man, suffered and rose on the third day, is ascended to heaven and will come to judge the living and the dead.
>
> And in the Holy Spirit.[18]

Note that, among other things, the idea of Christ being "*begotten*, [meaning to be born] *not made*" appears here but not in the earlier confession. These later additions demonstrate the progression of the early Church from its original understanding of the true God to the philosophy-laden concept of the Trinity.

The most popular restatement of the Nicene Creed is named after Athanasius. The widely accepted Athanasian Creed (written later than Athanasius—c. 490 A.D.) expresses the inscrutability of the Trinity in its classic form as follows:

> We worship one God in Trinity and Trinity in Unity. Neither confounding the Persons, nor dividing the Substance. For there is one Person of the Father, another of the Son, and another of the Holy Ghost. But the Godhead of the Father, of the Son and of the Holy Ghost is all One, the Glory Equal, the Majesty Co-Eternal. Such as the Father is, such is the Son, and such is the Holy Ghost. The Father Uncreate, the Son Uncreate, and the Holy Ghost Uncreate. The Father Incomprehensible, the Son Incomprehensible, and the Holy Ghost Incomprehensible. The Father Eternal, the Son Eternal, and the Holy Ghost Eternal and yet they are not

18. *Encyclopaedia Britannica,* 1960 ed., s.v. "Creeds."

> Three Eternals but One Eternal. As also there are not Three Uncreated, nor Three Incomprehensibles, but One Uncreated, and One Incomprehensible. So likewise the Father is Almighty, the Son Almighty, and the Holy Ghost Almighty. And yet they are not Three Almighties but One Almighty. So the Father is God, the Son is God, and the Holy Ghost is God. And yet they are not Three Gods, but One God. So likewise the Father is Lord, the Son Lord, and the Holy Ghost Lord. And yet not Three Lords but One Lord.[19]

(The word "incomprehensible" in this Creed is believed by some to be translated from a word that literally means "infinite."[20] However, all who accept the Athanasian Creed also teach that God is incomprehensible.[21])

No matter how it is expressed, this represents what appears to be a statement of contradictions, and its proponents intended it to be nothing less. Early post-Nicene theologians taught the notion of the Trinity, or Triune God, by claiming that the Father, the Son, and the Holy Ghost are a "generical" and "numerical" unity of substance, and hence a paradox.[22]

The Trinity, a man-made incongruity, is a monument to Aristotelian thinking. The concept, as it is commonly taught by Evangelicals, is that, "within the nature of the one true God, there are three separate persons: the Father, the Son, and the Holy Spirit, and these three persons eternally coexist as the one God."[23] The key word here is "co-exist." It appears nowhere in the Bible, but to Evangelicals it means something much different than "peaceful co-existence." They believe all Three persons exist in one Being. As, Bloesch puts it:

> Barth is correct when he affirms that God exists in three modes of being, but these are distinctions, as he acknowledges, that pertain to the inner life of God himself and not merely to dimensions of his activity (as in the heresy of Modalism). This is why orthodox theology speaks of the ontological or essential

19. Bruce R. McConkie, *Mormon Doctrine,* 2nd ed. (Salt Lake City: Bookcraft, 1966), s.v. "Athanasian Creed" (citing, Catholic Encyclopedia, 2:33-34). See, also, Schaff, *The Creeds of Christendom,* 2:66-70
20. Morey, *Battle of the Gods,* 273.
21. Morey, "The Incomprehensibility of God," Chapter 12 in *Battle of the Gods,* 161-171.
22. *Encyclopaedia Britannica,* 1960 ed., s.v. "Trinity."
23. Trivanovich, *Speaking the Truth in Love,* 20-21.

> trinity and not just the economical trinity, which refers to the way in which God relates himself to the world. The Trinity must be thought of neither as one God in three manifestations nor as a symmetrical triad of persons with separable functions; instead the Trinity signifies one God in three modes of existence—Father, Son, and Spirit, and each of these participates in the activity of the other.[24]

To the extent any explanation of an incomprehensible god can itself be comprehensible, the god described here is a being whose nature defies Man's God-given common sense. Evangelicals acknowledge this, but claim their formula for God is the only biblical alternative to the heresy of Arianism. But where is their effort shown to be biblical? There is not a single citation to any Bible passage in Bloesch's explanation of the Trinity quoted above.

Old Testament Arguments for a Triune God

While the Bible speaks pluralistically of God in both the Old and New Testaments, and it also refers to God as one, such passages do not support the Trinity as the correct explanation of the number of God. To do that, Evangelicals must find texts that prove the Three are one in *substance* or *essence*—co-existent, co-substantial, and co-eternal, as described in the Nicene and Athanasian Creeds.

Evangelicals acknowledge that the Father, Son, and Holy Ghost did not come into existence as three separate persons (or centers of consciousness) at the birth of Christ.[25] While the identification of three separate persons reflects the greater understanding of God provided in the New Testament, that new understanding did not reflect a change in God's basic nature.

The Jews, working from the Old Testament alone, accuse *both* Evangelicals and Mormons of being polytheists. Therefore, when Evangelicals use Old Testament passages to contend with Mormons on this issue, they hoist themselves on their own petard. Both Evangelicals and Mormons must put Old Testament passages in context to show that they are consistent with New Testament teachings. To rebut Jewish accusations of polytheism,

24. Bloesch, *Essentials of Evangelical Theology,* 35.
25. Martin, *Essential Christianity,* 27-28.

Evangelicals must use the same explanation of Old Testament passages that Mormons use in replying to Evangelical criticism.

Two Old Testament passages frequently quoted by Evangelicals to discredit Mormon theology are Isaiah 44:8 ("Is there a God beside me? yea, *there is* no God; I know not *any*"), and Isaiah 43:10 ("before me there was no God formed, neither shall there be after me"). The context of both is a message from God to the ancient Israelites spanning chapters 41 through 46 that contains frequent reference to the practice of idol worship so rampant in that day. That context indicates these verses were meant to uphold the sovereignty of Jehovah, the God of Israel, in the face of popular idolatry, not to rebut the doctrine of deification.

Referring to Isaiah 43:10, Evangelicals claim: "Mormon missionaries nearly always teach that this passage is referring to idol-gods. It can't be though, because idols were formed after Him!"[26] This response uses the fact that idols were constructed after Jehovah to argues that the passage could not refer to idolatry because it says no God will be formed "after me."

This exegesis is grossly flawed, but it does, at least, acknowledge that the phrase, "neither shall there be after me" refers to a specific point in time, when Jehovah was "formed." The Hebrew word from which "formed" was translated is *yatsar*, which may also be rendered "constitute." Men have *constructed* idols after Jehovah was *constituted* (i.e., appointed as God over Man), but in so doing they never formed a God over Man. An idol is not God, no matter what those who form it intend.

The only one who can form, or *constitute*, a God over Man is God Himself. No matter how many idol-gods Men have formed through the ages, they are, and have always been, nothing (1 Cor. 8:4). The scriptures record the constitution of only one God over Man, namely Jesus the Christ, who was known in the Old Testament as Jehovah (see Isa. 9:6; John 1:1; and other passages to be discussed below).

Isaiah 43:10 and 44:8 must be interpreted so they do not contradict the New Testament teaching that there are three separate persons who constitute the Godhead. These passages condemn the efforts of Men to establish false gods, idols. That is their context and the setting in which they must be construed. The verses immediately following Isaiah 44:8 (Isa. 44:9-20) clearly confirm this analysis.

---

26. Trivanovich, *Speaking the Truth in Love,* 20.
27. Trivanovich, *Speaking the Truth in Love,* 23.

None of these passages can be used to support the Greek concept of the Trinity because that dogma also teaches that God is three separate persons.Therefore, in seeking Biblical support for the Nicene god, Evangelicals attempt to demonstrate that there are two Jehovahs. Their argument is based on Isaiah 44:6, which they quote in the following form: "Thus saith the LORD the King of Israel, and His Redeemer the LORD of Hosts; I am the first, and I am the last; and beside Me there is no God."[27]

The Evangelical criticism of Mormonism based on this passage is as follows:

> In Mormon theology, Jesus is Jehovah. However, two persons are called Jehovah (translated "LORD") in this verse. The first Jehovah is called "the King of Israel." The second Jehovah ("LORD of Hosts") is called "His Redeemer," namely the One who belongs to the King of Israel. This presents another serious problem in the Mormon doctrine of God, because if Jesus is the only Jehovah in Mormon theology, then who is His Redeemer? The Bible tells us here that two separate persons are Jehovah. Also notice that the two persons exclaim as one Jehovah, "I am the First, and I am the Last; and beside Me there is no God."[28]

This interpretation presents far more problems for Evangelicals than it does for Mormons. For example, it postulates the heretical notion that Jehovah needs a Redeemer. Mormons reject that concept and this exegesis with it. Surprisingly, the error in this analysis arises from nothing more than a grammatical mistake-capitalizing the word "His" in the phrase "*His* Redeemer, the LORD of hosts." That mistake makes it appear that the pronoun "His" refers to deity. That is contrary to both the KJV and the NASB (which is very careful about capitalization). In the NASB, the passage reads as follows:

> Thus says the LORD, the King of Israel
> "And his Redeemer, the LORD of hosts:
> "I am the first and I am the last,
> "And there is no God besides Me."

Note that the word *his* before "Redeemer" in the second line is *not* capitalized. That is because it does *not* refer to deity. The pronoun *his*

28. *Ibid.* This argument was also made by David Hocking on "Solid Rock Radio," KKLA, c. early 1992.

modifies the nearest noun—Israel. Thus, the LORD, the King of Israel, is also the Redeemer of Israel. Jehovah (the one and only Jehovah) is *Israel's* Redeemer *and* the LORD of Hosts. There are not two Jehovahs, but only one, who is given two titles in this passage. The phrase calling Jehovah both a King and a Redeemer is a typical example of parallelism—a common form of Hebrew writing found hundreds of times in the Old Testament.

Evangelicals make the same error analyzing Matthew 28:19. In that passage, Christ commanded baptism "in the name of the Father, and of the Son, and of the Holy Ghost." A typical Evangelical exegesis of this phraseology says: "Notice that it says 'name,' not 'names.' In the original Greek, this suggests the meaning: 'in the One Whose name is Father-Son-Holy Ghost.'"[29]

This analysis is also flawed. The singular form of the word "name" is used to shorten the passage from "*in the name* of the Father, and *in the name* of the Son, and *in the name* of the Holy Ghost" to "*in the name* of the Father, and of the Son, and of the Holy Ghost." If the plural form were used, it would suggest that the passage had been shortened from "*in the names* of the Father, and *in the names* of the Son, and *in the names* of the Holy Ghost." The use of the singular (*name*, rather than *names*) is proper where each person designated in the phrase has His *own name*, as when one is speaking of three separate individuals. Thus, this passage militates against the Nicene theory, not in its favor.

The New Testament always treats the Father, Son, and Holy Ghost as separate persons in what way are they one Being? How could Christ be one in being with God the Father, if He **prayed** to God the Father? Surely He was not a ventriloquist at His own baptism, where the Father said, "This is my beloved Son, in whom I am well pleased" (Matt. 3:17). When the Father said Jesus was the **Son** of God, was He lying? Could Jesus really be one in being with his own Father? If He were His own Father, why did He describe Himself as the Son?

One Evangelical response to these questions is especially revealing. It holds that "He was not both God the Father and God the Son at the same time."[30] This claim requires that Christ, as God the Son, was materially separated from Christ as God the Father at some point in time. Philippians

29. Trivanovich, *Speaking the Truth in Love,* 22.
30. Trivanovich, *Speaking the Truth in Love,* 24.

2:6-8 is sometimes offered to prove that this separation occurred when Christ was born on earth.

Unfortunately, this notion that the "center of consciousness" metaphorically referred to as the Son separated from the "center of consciousness" metaphorically referred to as the Father at the birth of the former is contrary to the Nicene creed. Note also that it was *during* Christ's life on earth that He taught of His oneness with the Father (John 10:30). Whatever the nature of Their oneness while Christ was on earth is the nature of Their oneness throughout all eternity (John 17:20-23). Since this explanation admits that the oneness of God did not include co-substantiality while Christ was on earth (and see Matt. 3:16-17; Mark 1:10-11; and Matt. 27:46), Evangelicals who believe this explanation should admit that the oneness of the Father and of the Son does not include co-substantiality at any time.

Beings that aren't *always* co-substantial, cannot be defined as co-existent, since they would lack the essential element of continuity in their co-substantial existence. If they are ever separate, they cannot be defined as both co-existent and co-substantial. Either They always have the same substance, or They do not co-exist eternally as co-substantial beings.[31]

In the final analysis, all arguments in favor of the Nicene concept reach a paradox. Thus, the doctrine of the Trinity frustrates all the principles of apologetics and *solo scriptura* (reliance solely upon scriptural authority, not tradition, for divine truth). This makes the only support for the Nicene Creed a position of non-argument. As Dr. Walter Martin put it, "the Trinity is a-logical, or beyond logic. It, therefore, cannot be made subject to human reason or logic."[32] Elsewhere, he explains:

> There can be no doubt that the New Testament sets forth the thesis that there are three separate Persons in the Deity, known as the Father, the Son, and the Holy Spirit, and each of these is affirmed to be the Eternal God (2 Peter 1:17; John 1:1;

---

31. Some Evangelical scholars lose sight of the original meaning of the term "substance" as it was used in the trinitarian formula. While the word *ousia* (substance, or essence) was "used by Aristotle as "the definition of a species"—a list of characteristics that describes one type of thing and no other—applying that usage to God was considered heretical in the early Church. See C.L. Feltoe, *The Letters of Dionysius of Alexandria* (Cambridge, 1904).

32. Martin, *Essential Christianity,* 25.

33. Martin, *Maze of Mormonism,* 75.

> Acts 5:3,4). At the same time, the New Testament declares that there is only one God (1 Timothy 2:5). We are led inexorably to the conclusion that the three distinct Persons are the one God, though the finite mind of man may not be able to grasp the depth of this revelation of the divine character.[33]

(Notably, 1 Timothy 2:5 does not support Dr. Martin's thesis. It mentions one God, the Father, *and* one mediator between God and Man, Christ).

Thus, according to the best Evangelical authorities, Man's inability to understand the Trinity (which Man, himself, invented) is the result of Man's finite intellect. "The concept of the Trinity is difficult to comprehend because we have nothing to relate it to in our limited, three-dimensional thinking."[34] This is a poor excuse indeed. Today's mathematicians are quite capable of analyzing n-dimensional space. The Trinity, however, is a mathematical contradition in any dimension.

Bible commentators from the Christian Research Institute have been heard to say, "God is three persons in one 'What?',"[35] referring to God as an unknown. This expression aptly describes the attitude of many Evangelical scholars toward God. To them, God is a question mark, an unknowable, an unfathomable mystery—a paradox. Because they cannot understand Him, they label Him a "What? The real problem in comprehending the Trinity is not "the finite mind of man" or "three-dimensional thinking," but the erroneous adoption of Greek philosophical concepts as biblical truth.

Ignorance about the nature of God is, itself, contrary to biblical precept, and a sign of apostasy. That was the teaching of Christ, when He spoke to the Samaritan woman at the well. In John 4:22, He chided the apostate Samaritans for a lack of knowledge about the nature of God, saying: "Ye worship ye know not what: we know what we worship: for salvation is of the Jews."

The Jews did not consider God an unknown "what." This passage specifically states that they knew the "what" of God's nature. That is because He was revealed in the Old Testament-as an individual, in form like a man (Gen. 32:30; Exod. 33:18-23; Num. 12:5-8). John 4:22 identifies as false any system of theology that leaves God a "what" (cf., John 17:3). The Nicene and Athanasian Creeds teach that God is a "what,"

34. Trivanovich, *Speaking the Truth in Love,* 21.
35. Craig Hawkins, "The Bible Answerman," KKLA, 1989-90.

fundamentally incomprehensible. In so doing, they evidence the same apostate condition Christ found in the ancient Samaritans.

Of course the depth of God's ways, thoughts, knowledge, and love, are unknown to Man (Job 38; Ps. 139:6; 145:3; Isa. 40:27-28; 55:8-9; Rom. 11:33-36; see also Moses 1:5 in the Pearl of Great Price). But not one passage in the Bible suggests there is anything incomprehensible about God's *nature*. Instead, the Bible teaches that He is a glorified, perfected Human Being endowed with the infinite capabilities displayed in His Son, Jesus Christ. It is impossible to believe that Christ is "the image of the invisible [or *unseen*] God" (Col. 1:15), and still conclude that God is a "what."

The Nicene Creed Contradicts the Bible

Though the Nicene Creed speaks of the Father, Son, and Holy Ghost separately, its mechanical interpretation of Their oneness doesn't allow for true separation at all. The Creeds say the Three are separate, but they go on to state that They are *not* separate. Which is true? Trinitarians are required to believe both. This is a classic paradox.

Not only does this paradox make God a "What," it eliminates any rational resolution of the conflict between the large number of Bible teachings that imply a literal separation between the Three and the concept of oneness taught in the Trinity.

For example, how can the Father and the Son be the same in the triune sense when one was the **teacher** of the other (John 5:19-20, 8:28)? If the Father and the Son were the same in the way the Nicene Creed describes them, why did one **raise** the other from the dead (Gal. 1:1; Eph. 1:20)? How could the Son have been "**sent**" by the Father (John 5:24)? How could the Son be the **firstborn** of the Father (Col.1:15; Ps. 89:27; Rom. 8:29; Heb.1:6; 12:23)?

Further, if the Father and the Son were one Being, as the trinity teaches, They would **share the same knowledge**. Yet the Bible teaches that they do not. Matthew 24:36 reads in the NASB (emphasis added): "But of that day and hour no one knows, not even the angels of heaven, *nor the Son*, but the Father alone."

The Son was seen standing on the right hand of the Father by Stephen the martyr in his vision of God (Acts 7:55-56). Evangelicals try to explain this vision by pointing out that Stephen saw "the glory of God," as if that means he didn't actually see God at all. That is not the implication of the passage. In both verses 55 and 56 (NASB), Stephen states that he saw

"Jesus [v. 56: the Son of Man] standing at the right hand of God." Clearly, both Jesus and God the Father were seen by Stephen, separately and in juxtaposition to each other.

Evangelicals also argue that Stephen didn't see God because no man can see Him (John l:18: "no man hath seen God at any time"). But in John 6:46 (emphasis added) John the Beloved clarifies his earlier statement as follows: "Not that any man hath seen the Father, *save he which is of God, he **hath** seen the Father.*" Evangelicals claim that Christ is the only one to whom this passage refers, the only one who is "**of God**," and hence the only one who has seen the Father. But there is no rational basis for so limiting John's statement. In fact, this phrase is specifically defined by John in John 8:47, where he explains that "He which is **of God**" is he who heed Christ's teachings.[36]

In John 10:30, Christ referred to God as "Father." Indeed, He consistently testified of a literal father-son relationship between Himself and God (see, e.g., John 5:17-18). The Nicene dogma mandates that such references be taken figuratively, for a literal father-son relationship between them is impossible in the Trinitarian view. (A son can hardly be his own father, or a father his own son.) Thus, the Trinity doctrine denies the real Fatherhood of God. This is doubtless the saddest contradiction of biblical truth embraced in the early Church.

---

36. A key word in these passages is the preposition "of" that appears in the phrase "of God." John 6:46 uses the Greek preposition *para*, which the KJV translates "of" and the NASB translates "from." John 8:47 uses the Greek preposition *ek*, which both versions render "of." *Para* indicates close proximity, and in the context of verbs of origination, it means "to be from someone." *Ek* indicates origin from something with which there has been a close connection. It can be translated "from, of or by." There is no valid reason, outside of theological preference, to give these prepositions a different meaning in this context. *Para Theou*, for example, is used in John 1:6 in reference to John the Baptist.

Another key word is "he," translated "the One" in the NASB as if it were intended to refer only to Christ. But the subject ("he" or "the One") doesn't appear in the Greek text of John 6:46 at all. It must be assumed from the construction of the phrase, *o hon para tou Theou*. *O* and *tou* are forms of the definite article "the." *Hon* is comparative, and means "as, like as, even as, according as, in the same manner as, etc." The subject of the clause is left to be assumed by the reader. This suggests a broad designation, one that would incorporate the reader as well as all Men. There is no valid reason to assume the clause refers exclusively to Christ. Thus, the KJV is truer to the Greek, where "he" could be translated "he, she or it." Even if one were to assume that Christ is the subject of the clause, the Greek word *hon* broadens its application to all who are "like as" Christ.

The One God of the Bible

Historically, critics of trinitarianism, while correct in their rejection of that heresy, have provided no biblical alternative to Arianism to explain the oneness of God taught in the scriptures. It would be unfair to so scathingly critique this ancient doctrine without also offering a biblical explanation of LDS theology that will distinguish its teaching from both Arius and Nicaea. That explanation lies in a thorough understanding of the Bible's teachings about God the Father and his relationship to the Son.

The scriptures make no effort to explain their seemingly contradictory teaching that three Persons are one God. Yet, in light of John 4:22, one must assume that the information available to the Jews of Christ's day was sufficient for anyone, not in a state of apostasy, to know exactly *what* they worshiped.

Knowing that the essence of eternal life is to know God (John 17:3), and that God wants all Men to be like Him (1 John 3:2), there is only one conclusion that can be drawn from the failure of biblical authors to provide an explanation of what, to those trained in Greek methods of thought, seems a mysterious contradiction. It is that, in fact, there is no mystery at all. The fundamental nature of God, and the relationship of the Father, the Son, and the Holy Ghost, is neither complex nor unfathomable, and may be perceived through simple concepts familiar to all.

Bible authors obviously intended their references to the oneness of God to be taken figuratively-in the sense of composite unity. The early Church fathers erred in assuming that the term "one God" refers to one Being. Thinking metaphysically, rather than as ancient Hebrews, they forced three entirely separate Persons into a single entity. The Jewish scriptures require no such feats of consolidation. They teach only that the Three are one ***God***, *not* that they are one ***person***. The question is not "How can three persons be one Person?" but, "How can three Persons be one *God*?" In that context, passages that treat the Three as one can be understood in terms comprehendable by all.

The word *God* in the New Testament comes from the Greek word *theos*, which designates an "object of worship." No Biblical text demands that this word refer to a singular *Person or Being* except when the word is used to identify a specific individual who bears that title. Thus, the Bible teaches that there are three entirely separate *individuals* who are so perfectly organized and aligned in will, purpose and thought that they may be referred to as "One." They constitute a single, universal authority over all things, a single "God."

The term "God," used of the Three collectively in this manner, is best rendered *Godhead.* That term is derived from Paul's writings. He referred to *theios* ("the *godhead,*" or "that which is divine") in Acts 17:29, *theiotes* ("divinity") in Rom. 1:20, and *theotes* ("Deity") in Col. 2:9. The KJV translators wisely rendered all three of these words "Godhead," and thereby correctly captured the sense of composite unity comprised in the Bible's teachings about the oneness of God.

All of the concepts necessary to understand this sense of oneness are used in other contexts in the Bible and are common to human experience. For example, in Ephesians 5:31 (emphasis added) Paul taught: "For this cause shall a man leave his father and mother, and shall be joined unto his wife, and they *two* shall be *one* flesh." This verse does not mean that a man and his wife will cease to be separate individuals and become metaphysically joined in a paradoxical form of co-substantial flesh. The perfect unity of husband and wife, like that of the Godhead, is one of authority, will, character, thought, direction and goals, not literal substance or *homoousios.*

Husbands and wives are often treated as one in the modern legal system also (see e.g., *California Corporations Code*, § 158(d)). In community property states, either the husband or the wife are authorized to act as the sole administrator or manager of jointly owned property for "the community," a singular term used to refer to the married partners collectively (*California Civil Code*, § 5125).

Similar concepts of composite oneness, or unity, appear in business law and other applications. A group of individuals are treated as one in a corporation, and in some ways even in a partnership. A Board of Directors, which may comprise any number of individuals, is often referred to in the singular as *the Board.* A military group acting jointly is called a *unit.* None of these concepts is mysterious. Likewise, there is nothing mysterious or incomprehensible about the Father, Son, and Holy Ghost being "one." The depth of that oneness is shown in many statements made by Christ, which not only teach of His relationship with the Father, but provide guidance for those seeking to follow His lead. See, e.g., John 5:19-20, 22-23; 6:37-38; 8:19, 26, 28-29, 42.

In yet another effort to explain what he claims is unexplainable, Dr. Martin comes very close to the Mormon view in the following:

> But what does the word "one" mean? Does it always indicate solitary existence? Genesis 2:24 recounts that God spoke of Adam and Eve becoming: "one flesh" (*bosor echod*). God did not mean that Adam became Eve, or vice-versa; rather, He meant that in the marriage union the two persons became *as one* before Him. So we see that unity of a *composite* character was recognized by God Himself as existing within the world which He had created. . . .
>
> If the United States should be attacked by a foreign power, everyone would "rise as one" to the defense of the country. Yet no one would say that everyone had instantaneously become "one person." Rather, we would be one in a *composite unity*, one in purpose or will to work toward a common goal. . . . Why then should we not accept composite unity where the nature of God is concerned? Certainly the Scriptures do not prohibit such a view.[37]

Despite this admission in the segment omitted from the last paragraph quoted above, Dr. Martin denies that this concept can be applied to God.

Scripture, however, indicates that the doctrine of the trinity of God is far above the idea of mere agreement of will or goal; it is a unity of the basic Scriptural nature of substance, and Deity is that substance (John 4:24; Hebrews 1:3).[38]

Dr. Martin does not define "the basic Scriptural nature of substance," nor demonstrate that there is any real scriptural support for such a nature, and the passages he cites neither clarify nor define it. (E.g., Heb. 1:3, cited by Martin, says Christ "sat down on the right hand of the Majesty on high." He does not explain what this has to do with the "nature of substance.") Therefore, it is uncertain what he had in mind, but the bulk of his remarks, quoted above, support the Mormon concept of composite unity in the Godhead.

But the scriptures have not left the issue shrouded in mystery. In His great intercessory prayer for his disciples (John 17), Christ states the exact sense in which His unity with the Father should be taken. The entire

37. Martin, *Essential Christianity,* 29.
38. *Ibid.*

chapter gives deep insight into the oneness of the Father and the Son, but verse 22 (NASB, emphasis added) is particularly instructive:

> And the glory which Thou hast given Me I have given to them; that they may be one, *just* as We are one.

This verse teaches that the sense in which the Father and the Son are one is *exactly the same* as the sense in which Christ and His disciples may be one. That is clearly a figurative or composite form of unity. Nothing more mysterious or paradoxical was intended by Christ's prayer. The word *homo-ousios* is notably absent from John 17. From this we should conclude that Christ did not want His disciples to join Him in some incomprehensible, co-substantial "what." Likewise, He and His Father are not one in that sense.

Even more important, John 17:22 shows how the Father and the Son became one (and, correspondingly, how Men may become one with Them). The passage says that the *glory* which the Father gave the Son was, in turn, given by the Son to His disciples so that they too could become one. Mormons understand that the "glory" of God is "light and truth" (D&C 93:36), which may also be called wisdom and knowledge, or *intelligence* (a term also used to describe that from which spirits are organized).

The Bible records that Christ received wisdom from His Father before the beginning of the earth (Prov. 8:22-26), and was taught by Him (John 8:28). This wisdom or knowledge He, in turn, gave to His disciples through His teachings. It follows that shared knowledge and understanding are what make the Father and the Son one, though They are separate individuals. Furthermore, the same "glory" can make Men one with each other, and with God, as Christ prayed in John 17:22.

Though Mormons frequently use the phrase "one in purpose" to describe this state of unity, the oneness of the Father and the Son involves much more than a shared goal. They are one in authority, understanding, judgment, will, preference, thought, intent and character, and the epitome of perfect union between separate individuals.

Jesus forcefully communicated this concept to the Jews in John 10:30 when He said: "I and *my* Father are one." Thinking there is some support for the Nicene Creed in this statement, Evangelicals reason as follows:

---

39. Trivanovich, *Speaking the Truth in Love,* 23.

> Furthermore, Jesus Himself did claim to be the same God in essence, as His Father. In John 10:30 Jesus says, "I and my Father are one." The Greek word for "one" is neuter and demands the meaning of "one in essence." This does not mean one person, but two persons who constitute one God. The Greek text literally reads, "I and my Father, We are one (essence)."[39]

The Greek word *heis* (neuter) is commonly translated "one" in the New Testament, implying unity. "One essence" would be an unusual translation. But even if that translation were used, nothing in this Greek word contradicts the biblical teaching of the Godhead or supports the Nicene Creed. If the Lord meant to convey the *Nicene* concept of God, He would certainly have used the word *homo-ousios* here, but neither that word, nor any form of it, appears in John 10:30 (or anywhere else in the Bible). Thus, while Christ taught that He and the Father are one, He did not teach that He was *homo-ousios* (or co-substantial) with the Father.

Christ's expression of unity with the Father in John 10:30 was filled with metaphor, not paradox. The figure conveyed was a Hebrew concept that the Jews grasped immediately. When they heard Christ say He and His Father are "*heis*," they understood that He was implying equality with the Father. By using the word "one" in the neuter tense, Christ alluded to a degree of oneness characteristic of identical (but separate) neuter objects.

In English, this characteristic is called "fungibility," and is best illustrated with dollar bills. Each dollar bill is much more than physically identical to all other dollar bills. One dollar bill can be exchanged for any other with no loss of value. It does not matter to the holder which dollar bill he possesses because fungible objects are *legally* interchangeable. The Lord's use of the word *heis* communicated the understanding that He is not only like God, but has the right to stand in His Father's place. The Jews understood exactly what Christ meant, and prepared to stone Him, explaining: "You, being a man, make Yourself out *to be* God." (John 10:33 NASB.)

Evangelicals try to use passages like this, which teach of Christ's resemblance to the Father, to support the Nicene Creed. An example of their reasoning is the following analysis of Hebrews 1:3:

> This same verse calls Him the "express image" of His person. This word (*charakter*) was used in classical Greek of a

40. Trivanovich, *Speaking the Truth in Love,* 27.

> branding iron or stamp impressed into coins and seals, giving the exact reproduction of the original.[40]

But this analysis only shows how erroneous Nicene doctrine is. The Greek word *charakter* refers to an exact **reproduction**, *not* the original. Use of this word, like Christ's use of the word *heis* in John 10:30, conveys the understanding that Christ is exactly *like*, not the same person as, the Father. In fact, the use of a word commonly connected with the stamping of coins in Hebrews 1:3 supports the concept of fungibility used in John 10:30.

An understanding of these principles clarifies such passages as John 14:9, in which Christ told Philip, "he that hath seen me hath seen the Father." He did not mean that Philip actually saw the Father when he looked at the Son He meant that the Son's *appearance* is like the Father's. By observing the Son, an exact reproduction (*charakter*) of the Father, Philip knew what the Father was like in every detail, both physically and spiritually.

Thus, the Bible teaches that there exists between the Father and the Son a type of oneness not foreign to Man's understanding, but beyond any degree common to human experience. With the Holy Ghost, They form a singular unit, the Godhead, that reigns over Man in such perfect unity that the Three constitute a singular Administration spoken of as "one God."

Jesus Christ Is Jehovah

To more fully understand the oneness of the Godhead, one must know how it is organized. To do that requires a biblical understanding of the relationship between the Father and the Son. That understanding begins with an accurate identification of the Son as He was known before his mortal incarnation. Every individual who has ever lived on earth has had a physical body of flesh and bones plus his own unique spirit which occupies and operates that physical body.

The same is true of Christ. The spirit that occupied His body before it took on earthly flesh was none other than that great Spirit usually identified in the Old Testament as Jehovah. Jehovah, as a spirit, had the appearance of a man (Exod. 33:18-23) because, as noted in the last chapter, the spirit of a man looks like a man (Luke 24:36-39).

The belief that Jesus and Jehovah are the same person is shared by many Evangelicals. However, their belief is based on the position that

Jehovah is a name for the Trinity. Some groups, like the Jehovah's Witnesses, claim that Jehovah is the name of God the Father. Evangelicals, who strongly disagree with Jehovah's Witnesses on that point, have developed many proof texts to disprove this vielo however there are occasins when it appears God the Father uses the same title as the Son(e.g Moses 2:1).

To demonstrate that the person usually identified by the name Jehovah in the Old Testament is not God the Father, or the triune God of the Creeds, one need merely observe that Jehovah is repeatedly referred to in the Old Testament as the One who will judge Man (see, e.g., 1 Sam. 2:10; 1 Chron. 16:33; Ps. 9:7-8; 72:2; 96:11-13; and Isa. 33:22). John 5:22 states that the *Father* will judge no man, but has committed *all* judgment to the *Son*. Therefore, Jehovah normally designated the Son, not the Father, and certainly not a triune God. (This passage also contradicts Bloesch's notion that each person in the Trinity "participates in the activity of the other."[41])

The conclusion that Christ was Jehovah is confirmed in many other scriptural references. For example, Jehovah is referred to frequently in the Old Testament as the Rock (see, e.g., Deut. 32:3-4, 15, 18, 31; Ps. 62:1-2,;118:22; and Isa. 17:10). Paul's testimony about the identity of the Rock of Israel is direct and unequivocal. He said, "that Rock was Christ" (1 Cor. 10:1-4). Notably, he does not say, "that Rock was the Father," or "that Rock was the Father, Son, and Holy Ghost."

Finally, in John 8:56-59 Jesus boldly revealed to the Jews exactly who He was. In verse 56, He told them, "your father Abraham rejoiced to see my day: and he saw *it*, and was glad." The Jews chided him, noting he was not even fifty years old, and asked tauntingly if he had seen Abraham.

His response stunned them, for in it He identified Himself by the very name Jehovah had used to address Moses on Mount Sinai, "I AM" (Exod. 3:14). This announcement was an unmistakable assertion that *He* was the God of Moses and of Abraham. The Jew's desire to stone Him for this assertion indicates they understood that He had identified Himself as Jehovah.

---

41. Bloesch, *Essentials of Evangelical Theology,* 35.

The Father and the Son vs. the Nicene Creed

Biblical analysis of the relationship between the Father and the Son reveals that there is a definite hierarchy, or organization within the Godhead. Arius taught this principle, but erred in his interpretation of its implications. He assumed it meant the Father and the Son were not equal, an idea that is contradicted by the Bible (see John 5:18 and Phil. 2:6). He too was steeped in Greek thinking and failed to grasp that the existence of a hierarchy within an organization does not mean the members of the organization are unequal. A hierarchy may exist among equals because of the benefits that lie in an organized administration. God's organization of the family is an example of just such a hierarchy.

The Hierarchy of the Godhead. The roles of the Father and the Son in the Godhead are noted by Paul in 1 Corinthians 8:4 (some enphasis added):

> As concerning therefore the eating of those things that are offered in sacrifice unto idols, we know that an idol *is* nothing in the world, and that there is none other God but one.
>
> For though there be that are called gods, whether in heaven or in earth, (as there be gods many, and lords many,)
>
> But to us *there is but* one God, the Father, of whom *are* all things, and we in him; and one Lord Jesus Christ, by whom *are* all things, and we by him.

Verse 6 describes the functions of the Father and the Son in the Godhead. Paul's description of the Father's role is like that of a sole shareholder in a large corporation. He is the *source* of all power (KJV: "*of* whom *are* all things"; NASB: "*from* whom are all things"). The Son, whose function is like that of the Chief Executive Officer, is the one who carries out the Father's plan (KJV and NASB: "*by* whom are all things").

The Kenosis. In Philippians 2:5-11, Paul gives further information about the relationship between God and Christ in the Godhead. As noted above, many Evangelicals cite part of this passage to support their teaching that the Father and the Son separated when Christ was born on earth. That interpretation reflects a basic misunderstanding of the Godhead, as will be shown below,and an impossibility for the Nicene Trinity.

Philippians 2:5-8 (NASB, brackets added), which describes what Bible scholars call the "kenosis" of Christ, reads as follows:

> Have this attitude in yourselves which was also in Christ Jesus,
> who, although He existed in the form of God, did not regard equality with God a thing to be grasped [as a robber clutches his spoils—see the KJV],
> but emptied Himself [i.e., laid aside His privileges], taking the form of a bond-servant, and being made in the likeness of men.
> And being found in appearance as a man, He humbled Himself by becoming obedient to the point of death, even death on a cross.

Nothing in this passage suggests that Christ was the same person as the Father, only that He was *like* Him. The Greek word *morphē*, translated "form" here, conveys the same meaning as do the Greek words *heis* and *charakter* in the passages discussed above. *Morphē*, implies that the nature, appearance, and characteristics of the Son are identical to the Father, in whose image the Son was created.

Paul used the same root word in Galatians 4:19, which reads (NASB emphasis added): "My children, with whom I am again in labor until Christ is *formed* in you." Paul does not mean that the Galatians will become co-substantial with Christ through Paul's labors, but that they should emulate Christ's characteristics until they are, in all moral respects, *like* Him. Similarly, *morphē*, in Philippians 2:6 indicates that Christ had the same characteristics as the Father.

Christ laid aside His privileges and responsibilities in the Godhead ("emptied Himself"), and took on a physical body that could be subjected to death. Though Christ was the very Jehovah of the Old Testament, verse 7 explains that He willingly accepted His mortal ministry, making Himself "of no reputation" (KJV), or in other words, unknown as to His true identity. He became "in fashion as a man" (verse 8, KJV).

One may ask if this means that He was *not* in form like a man before His incarnation. The passage, however, explains the essence of this change. He submitted to physical death. It was in this sense that His form was unlike mortal Men prior to His incarnation.That is, until then His spirit was not joined with a physical body capable of death.

Mormon theology teaches that the principles by which Christ became a man are not physiologically different from those by which all Men enter mortal existence. He had a physical father and a physical mother.

42. See also McConkie, *Mormon Doctrine,* 2d ed., s.v. "Virgin Birth."

However, Christ's physical father was *not* Joseph, the betrothed of Mary, nor any other earthly male. His natural, *physiological* father was God the Father (Luke 1:31-35), making Him *literally* the Only *Begotten* of the Father (John 1:14, 18; 3:16; 1 John 4:9).

The Virgin Birth. Because of this biblical teaching, Mormons are accused of denying the virgin birth of Christ, but that is a mistaken notion. Mormons emphatically believe in the virgin birth (see , 1 Nephi 11:18-20; and Alma 7:10).[42] The fact that Christ was the literal, physical Son of God the Father, as reported in Luke 1:31-35, does not require that His conception occurred by other than immaculate means.

It certainly does *not* require that God the Father had sexual relations with Mary.[43] In this day, when artificial insemination has become a commonplace reality, Men cannot hold to the argument that God's only means of causing Mary's pregnancy was physical intercourse.

Isaiah, speaking of Christ's mortal birth, said "a *virgin* shall *conceive*" (Isa. 7:14, emphasis added). The language of this passage implies that Mary *did* conceive in normal human fashion, but that the conception of Christ was accomplished in a way that left Mary a *virgin*. 1 Nephi 11:18-20 , describes Mary as a virgin *after* the Christ Child was born to her (consistent with Matt. 1:25).

Luke reported the angel's promise to Mary that she would conceive *in her womb* (Luke 1:31). When she asked how this could be done, seeing she was a virgin, it is obvious her intent was to *remain* a virgin (Luke 1:34). The angel responded, "the *power* of the Highest [meaning the Father] shall *overshadow* thee" (Luke 1:35). The Greek word translated "overshadow" is *episkiazō*. This word was used in Luke 9:34-35 to describe the effect of the cloud, from which the Father spoke, unseen, to Peter, James and John at the Transfiguration. To Mary, it implied that her conception would involve the most gentle and nonintrusive contact imaginable learning her a virgin. With that explanation, Mary agreed to bear the child of God (Luke 1:38).

The immaculate impregnation of a virgin is an accomplishment that can be duplicated by scientists today. There can be no doubt, therefore, that the

---

43. An opposing view has been expressed by some LDS leaders while teaching the LDS belief that Jesus is the literal son of God. That view has never been adopted by the LDS Church, and contradicts Isaiah 7:14 and 1 Nephi 11:20.

Father was capable of accomplishing the same feat without the intimacy involved in any form of sexual contact.

Though the Holy Ghost was involved in Christ's conception, apparently as a facilitator in some unrevealed manner ("the Holy Ghost shall come upon thee, . . ." Luke 1:35) Mormons aver that Jesus is the literal Son of the Father, "the Highest" (NASB: "the Most High"), not the Holy Ghost (Luke 1:35).

The assertion by some Evangelicals that the Holy Ghost is the father of Jesus, rather than God the Father, is refuted by dozens of passages in the New Testament in which Jesus and God the Father refer to each other as "Son" and "Father." All Men are created in the image of God (Gen. 1:26), but Paul spoke *literally* of Christ when he said, "in him dwelleth all the fullness of the Godhead *bodily*" (Col. 2:9, emphasis added).

Christ's Pre-mortal Exaltation. In Philippians 2:9-11 (NASB, emphasis and brackets added), Paul explains that, at some point in the past, God "exalted" Christ to His present position over Men:

> Therefore also God highly exalted Him [Jesus Christ], and bestowed on Him *the* name which is above every name,
>
> that at the name of Jesus every knee should bow, of those who are in heaven, and on earth, and under the earth,
>
> and that every tongue should confess that Jesus Christ is Lord, to the glory of God the Father.

By thus exalting Christ, God gave Him a title of such significance it is described as "*the* name which is above every name." At this name every knee will bow (verse 10). The name or title thus described could be none other than that which Men associate with the ultimate authority of God.

This observation is consistent with the events described in John 1:1 and Isaiah 9:6 (NASB). The latter passage reads as follows:

> For a child will be born to us, a son will be given to us;
> And the government will rest on His shoulders;
> And His name will be called Wonderful Counselor,[44]
> Mighty God,
> Eternal Father, Prince of Peace.

44. In the original Hebrew there is no comma between the words "Wonderful" and "Counselor" in this passage.

This passage speaks from an eternal perspective, teaching that Christ was first recognized by the name (or title) "Wonderful Counselor." While this designation gives Men assurance that He is an able counselor to each person in need, it is far more meaningful in describing His relationship to the Father (see, e.g., John 1:2-3; and Heb. 1:2). It teaches that, in the beginning, Christ worked with the Father in the creation of the earth, and hence was called "Wonderful Counselor." This is not to imply that the Father received counsel in the form of wisdom from the Son, but that the Son assisted Him in all things (Col. 1:16). Christ still retains this title. Indeed, His every act in the work of Man's redemption is directed to helping the Father (see, e.g., John 1:3; 7:16; and 8:26-28).

Next, as Philippians 2:2-11 indicates, He became the "Mighty God." He is, and will be called "Eternal Father"[45] (Mosiah. 15:1-5), and by virtue of His example and message to Man, He is "the Prince of Peace."

These passages (John 1:1 and Isa. 9:6) are often cited by Evangelicals to support Nicene doctrine as if they taught that Christ was "*with* God" (as His "Wonderful Counselor") and "*was* God," (meaning God the Father) at the same time. That interpretation is not consistent with the Greek text, and does not comport with common sense. A non-sensical interpretation should not be adopted when the passage is susceptible of sensible interpretation.[46]

The exaltation of Christ is mentioned in other Bible passages. For example, Psalms 45:6-7 (some emphasis added) reads:

> Thy throne, O God, *is* for ever and ever: the sceptre of thy kingdom *is* a right sceptre.
>
> Thou lovest righteousness, and hatest wickedness: therefore God, thy God, hath anointed thee with the oil of gladness *above thy fellows*.

This passage teaches that Christ was anointed by His God to a position *above* His fellows. Christ did not exalt Himself to that position, nor did He give Himself the name which is above every name. This had to be the act of a separate, and at that time, higher authority. The Greek word trans-

45. Christ is the father of all who follow His precepts (see Rev. 21:7; John 1:12; and D&C 39:4). But this name/title suggests He will one day have spirit children of His own, over whom He will reign, not as God the Son, but as their "God the Father."
46. Not specifically listed as a rule of hermeneutics in Chapter 1, this principle is adopted from the rules of statutory construction used in the legal profession.

lated "exalted" in Philippians 2:9, means to "lift up above." If that word has any meaning at all, it is that Christ did *not* have the name which is above every name *before* He was thus exalted. He was thus raised from the position "Wonderful *Counselor*" to the position "Mighty *God*".

Having appointed the Son over all creation, the Father made the following acknowledgment of Christ's authority in Hebrews 1:8-9 (emphasis added):

> But *unto the Son he saith*, Thy throne, *O God*, *is* for ever and ever: a scepter of righteousness *is* the scepter of thy kingdom.
>
> Thou hast loved righteousness, and hated iniquity; therefore God, *even thy God*, hath anointed thee with the oil of gladness above thy fellows.

In verse 8, the Father calls the Son, "*O* God," but not "*My* God." In so doing, He acknowledges Christ's title and authority over Men, but not over Himself. The Father's paraphrase of Psalms 45:7 in verse 9 reiterates His act of exalting the Son, but affirms His own position as Christ's God. Clearly, Christ was *not* exalted above the Father.

In 1 Corinthians 15:23-26 (NASB) Paul expands on this understanding. He tells of the kingdom and mission given to Christ by the Father, and even designates its consummation. After explaining that all Men will be resurrected, Paul states:

> But each in his own order: Christ the first fruits, after that those who are Christ's at His coming,
>
> then *comes* the end, when He delivers up the kingdom to the God and Father, when He has abolished all rule and all authority and power.
>
> For he must reign until He has put all His enemies under His feet. The last enemy that will be abolished is death.

Death entered this world through the Fall of Adam.[47] Apparantly, when Adam and Eve fell, Christ was given the mission to redeem Men from death and return creation to its pre-fallen state. At the end of Christ's reign He will deliver up the "kingdom" to His Father, having subdued all

47. Since Christ's reign or mission is complete upon His conquest of death, it may be inferred that His reign began when death was introduced by the Fall of Adam. C.I. Scofield notes, "Jehovah is distinctly the redemption name of Deity" (*The New Scofield Study Bible,* 142 (footnote to Exod. 34:6).

enemies under His feet, the last enemy being death. This makes Christ the "Alpha and Omega" of the Bible (Rev. 1:8, 11; 21:6; 22:13), the beginning and end of Man's redemption.

Paul goes on in 1 Corinthians 15:27-28 (NASB, brackets added) to confirm the limitations of Christ's exaltation to the title of "Mighty God" as follows:

> For He [the Father] has put all things in subjection under His [the Son's] feet. But when He says, "All things are put in subjection," it is evident that He [the Father] is excepted who put all things in subjection to Him [the Son].
>
> And when all things are subjected to Him [the Son], then the Son Himself also will be subjected to the One [the Father] who subjected all things to Him [the Son], that God may be all in all.

The understanding that Paul conveys in this passage requires careful review of the wording. Paul says that, in subjecting "all things" to Christ, the Father did not subject Himself to Christ. *He* was an exception to the scope of Christ's dominion. Though "every knee should bow," the Father's knee is not, and will *never* be, included. The Son will *always* be in subjection to the Father.

Now, if Christ were the same Being as the Father, as Trinitarians claim, these passages would say that Christ is in subjection to Himself. That is not what these verses describe. That isn't even subjection in any conceivable sense of the word. If the Father and the Son were a singular Being, as taught in Nicene doctrine, there could be no separation of authority between them with One in subjection to the Other, as Paul taught in this passage.

Furthermore, if Christ were exalted, as indicated in Philippians 2:9-11, 1 Corinthians 15:23-26, and Psalms 45:6-7, He could not always (i.e., eternally) have been co-equal with the Father, for if He had been equal with the Father before His exaltation, the act of elevating Him would necessarily have put Him above the Father. Such an arrangement conflicts with Hebrews 1:8-9 and 1 Corinthians 15:27-28.

Most telling of all, the Greek word translated "fellows" in Hebrews 1:9 means "partners, holding with others." If Nicene doctrine were correct and God had no other spirit children at the time of Christ's exaltation, this term could only refer to the Holy Ghost and the Father, the word "fellows" being plural. According to Hebrews 1:9 and Psalms 45:7 Christ was anointed *above* his "fellows." That would mean He was exalted above the

Holy Ghost and the Father. But Christ was *not* exalted above God the Father. He never was, and never will be, in a position over His Father (1 Cor. 15:27-28). Hence, Nicene theology cannot be harmonized with the Bible under any satisfactory hermeneutic.

In the Godhead, the Father's position is chief. From Him, the chain of command extends to the Son. All things, even prayers to the Father, must be done "in the name of Christ" (Moses 1:17), for no one may approach the Father except by the Son, and no one can be saved except by His name (Acts 4:12; to the same effect, see also, 2 Nephi 25:20; 31:21; and Mosiah 3:17). Christ is the one and only mediator between God (the Father) and Man (1 Tim. 2:5).

A Vertical Line of Authority. These passages reveal a *vertical* line of authority in the Godhead, but Evangelicals imagine that Mormons believe in three separate Gods over the earth.[48] That implies a horizontal line of authority. This is emphatically not the case. Christ's statement that, "No man can serve two masters: for either he will hate the one, and love the other; or else he will hold to the one, and despise the other" (Matt. 6:24) demonstrates the folly of such an organization.

Evangelicals make this assumption because *they* view the Trinity horizontally—three persons of equal authority who are, conglomerated into one Being. If the Trinity were not co-substantial in Evangelical theology, Men would be confronted with three separate autonomies, three Gods, any one of whom they might elect to worship and obey. Such an arrangement would lead to universal chaos. This may be one reason for their resistance to the idea of three separate individuals in the Godhead.

The biblical view of Heaven from Man's perspective reveals a *singular* autonomy—not three separate autonomies. *One* Authority exercised by three Persons, acting in perfect unity and organized in a monolithic vertical administration—*one God!* This single authority in which the three act as one, is proclaimed by the Bible and taught in Mormon theology. It is the characteristic that makes Mormonism, of all Christian religions, most emphatically *monotheistic*.

Conclusion

There is no convincing argument that the Nicene Creed is either logical or biblical, and the claim that Men simply do not understand it because

48. Trivanovich, *Speaking the Truth in Love,* 20.

God's basic nature is beyond their comprehension is equally contrary to biblical authority. Acceptance of the Nicene formula constitutes a statement that, like the ancient Samaritans, "Ye worship ye know not what" (John 4:22). The Trinity makes of God a paradox, and places a conceptual barrier of insurmountable proportions between God and Man. This is contrary to the will of the Father who made Man in His image (Gen 1:26-27), and wants all Men to know Him (John 17:2-3). Most importantly, the Trinity contradicts or is inconsistent with numerous important Bible passages.

The singular authority over the heavens and the earth is "the Godhead," a term that may also be rendered "God" or "Deity" in a sense that refers to the *position* itself. The Father, the Son, and the Holy Ghost, three separate individuals, are members of the Godhead, each having the right to be designated by the title "God." These Three are not one *individual*, but are so united that they display the profoundest sense of composite unity, making them describable only as "*one God*."

4

God and Man

Among Evangelicals, Mormon doctrine about the relationship between God and Man is perhaps the most misunderstood of any subject in LDS theology. Typical of Evangelical opinion on this theme of biblical Mormonism is the following:

> Satan is deceiving the Latter-day Saints to believe in exaltation to godhood. . . .
>
> The doctrines of "exaltation" and "celestial glory" (people can evolve into gods and goddesses) are rooted in ancient witchcraft. Yet these doctrines, complete with the same terminology, are being perpetuated through the Mormon Church today.
>
> The Bible is clear, salvation cannot include godhood. God Himself proclaimed in the Bible that "before Me there was no God formed, neither shall there be after Me" (Isa. 43:10). As a matter of fact, throughout the Bible, God condemns in the strongest terms anyone practicing the belief of becoming like God. We are not saved to become a god.[1]

The idea that Men can become like God (known in theology as *deification*) is as old as Adam (see, Gen. 3:22). Any variation on this concept that may have been taught in ancient witchcraft was obviously perverted from the more ancient doctrine understood by Adam. Mormonism, as it is called today, is the same Gospel, the same theology and the same plan of salvation God taught in the Garden of Eden. *It* is the source from which apostate forms arose (such as the occult), not the other way around.

As for the biblical citations used to support Evangelical criticism of this doctrine, they remind one of the man caught stealing chickens, who

1. Trivanovich, *Speaking the Truth in Love,* 43.

justified his act by saying, "I can prove I was doing right by the Bible! It says, 'go therefore and steal . . .'"

"Why don't you finish the passage?" the judge asked.

"I've gone far enough to prove my point," the man replied.

Typical of such hermeneutics, Isaiah 43:10 is taken grossly out of context in the quotation above. In this passage Christ declares that, there is but one ultimate authority over Man. Men can not become separate Gods, then can become one with God (John 17:21-23). This does not contradict the numerous passages in which Christ teaches that His brothers and sisters can become like Him and their Father. Indeed, the Bible repeatedly teaches that all Men can become like their Father (or Mother) in Heaven.

Children of God

The Bible refers to God as the Father of *all* Men, not just of Christ (see, e.g., Mal. 2:10; Matt. 5:48; Luke 11:2; John 20:17; Eph. 4:6; Heb. 12:9).[2] It teaches that Men are the children of God, both physically—through Adam-and spiritually. The Evangelical argument that all these filial affirmations are to be taken figuratively would be more convincing if the scriptural message weren't so pervasive. By the sheer number of His repetitions, one would think His children might eventually take Him at His Word, and acknowledge God as their literal *Father* in Heaven.

The first inkling of this truth appears in the account of Man's creation when they were made in the image and likeness of God (Gen. 1:26-27; 1 Cor. 11:7). As noted in Chapter 2, the words "image" and "likeness" imply a genetic link between a father and his son, and a connection that results in similarities of a spiritual dimension.

After His resurrection, Christ emphasized the relationship between God and Man in His instructions to Mary (John 20:17, NASB):

> Jesus said to her, "Stop clinging to Me, for I have not yet ascended to the Father; but go to My brethren, and say to them, 'I ascend to My Father and your Father, and My God and your God'."

2. Some Evangelical scholars claim God is only referred to in the scriptures as the Father of Christ and of believers. That conclusion can only be reached using a very strained interpretation, of these verses.

In this passage, Christ intentionally defined the link between Himself and Man and declared our mutual relationship to God. He indicates that Men have the same Father and the same God as He, and that He and other Men are "brethren."

Paul preached extensively on this subject. In his speech to the Athenians on Mars Hill, he concluded with these words (Acts 17:28-29):

> For in him we live, and move, and have our being; as certain also of your own poets have said, For we are also his offspring.
>
> Forasmuch then as we are the offspring of God, we ought not to think that the Godhead is like unto gold, or silver, or stone, graven by art and man's device.

In this passage, the word "offspring" is translated from the Greek word *genos*, meaning "race." This word forms the basis for such English words as "genetics" and 'genes." It indicates that Men are the same *species* as God. The word is used in Revelation 22:16 to describe Christ as the "root and *offspring* of David." That reference clearly recognizes the literal *genetic* link between Christ and David (through His mother, Mary, who like her husband Joseph, was also a descendent of David). The same genetic link between God and Man is conveyed by the word *genos* in Acts 17.

Paul taught the Hebrew understanding of the nature of God, declaring that, if Men are the race or offspring of God, they ought not to think that the Godhead is like gold or silver or stone. What then should Men think about the nature of the Godhead? If Men are as different from God as Evangelicals claim, Paul asked the Greeks to think of God as an incomprehensible triune being. But Paul said "we are also his offspring." It follows that he wanted them to realize that God is a Man.

Paul taught the Romans the same principle in even more detail. In Romans 8:14-17, he states:

> For as many as are led by the Spirit of God, they are the sons of God.
>
> For ye have not received the spirit of bondage again to fear; but ye have received the Spirit of adoption, whereby we cry, Abba, Father.
>
> The Spirit itself beareth witness with our spirit, that we are the children of God:

> And if children, then heirs; heirs of God, and joint-heirs with Christ; if so be that we suffer with *him*, that we may be also glorified together.

The word "sons" in verse 14 is from the Greek *huios*, meaning "mature children," or "heirs." As Men allow themselves to be led by the Spirit of God, they become, in a figurative sense, mature children, obedient to their parents and ready to be made heirs. But the word translated "children" in verses 16 and 17 is the Greek word *teknon*, meaning "one born," i.e., literally related by birth. This word communicates the truth that Men are the literal children of God.

The distinction between "mature children" and "offspring" was drawn by Christ in John 8:37-44. He spoke to the Pharisees, who claimed salvation because they were the "seed" (descendants) of Abraham. Christ acknowledged their *physical* lineage in verse 37 (NASB emphasis added), saying, "I know that you are Abraham's *offspring*," but He accused them in verse 39 (NASB emphasis added) as follows: "If you are Abraham's *children*, do the deeds of Abraham." Thus, Christ distinguished between the literal *genetic* relationship of the Jews to Abraham, and their moral kinship with that righteous patriarch. Men may be the literal offspring of God, but they do not become *children* of God in the fullest sense unless they learn to *act* like their Father.

The phrase "joint-heirs with Christ" in Romans 8:17 confirms that Men have a fraternal relationship to Christ. Christ and Man are *brothers* (John 20:17). This does not mean that all Men are related to Christ through the same physical parents. There is a deeper meaning in this profession of Christ's brotherhood. The Bible teaches that God is the father of the *spirits* of all Men (Num. 16:22; Mal. 2:10; Eph. 4: 6), just as He is the Father of Christ's spirit. Thus, Christ is a literal brother to all Men—we are all spirit children of the same Father.

The lineage of Man's spirit is compared with his physical parentage in Hebrews 12:9:

> Furthermore we have had fathers of our flesh which corrected us, and we gave *them* reverence: shall we not much rather be in subjection unto the Father of spirits, and live?

This verse acknowledges that, although God is the ultimate physical ancestor of Man in that He created Adam and Eve in His image, He is not the natural parent of each man or woman's physical body. Men have a literal parent-child relationship with a fleshly father, who corrects them here on earth. But "the Father of spirits" is none other than God the Eternal Father, to whom it is more important that Men submit.

Each person has a spirit that inhabits and operates his or her physical body. This is clear from numerous Bible teachings (see, e.g., Job 32:8; 1 Cor. 6:20). Man's spirit was created by being born of God as a literal spirit child (Zech. 12:1). He does not call Himself "the Father" because He spoke Man into existence out of nothing. Men were not told to address Him as "Our Father" (Matt. 6:9) because He wanted to use a metaphor to teach us proper behavior toward other members of our species. He is called our "Father" because He *is*! Men must learn to treat each other as literal brothers and sisters, for all Men are truly part of the same *family*, both in heaven and on earth (Eph. 3:14-15).

The Pre-Mortal Existence of Spirits

That the birth of all Men as spirit children of God occurred long before their birth in the flesh is apparent from many Bible passages. God spoke intimately of His relationship with Jeremiah in Jeremiah 1:5, implying that their acquaintance extended long before Jeremiah's birth: "Before I formed thee in the belly I knew thee; and before thou camest forth out of the womb I sanctified thee, *and* I ordained thee a prophet unto the nations." In this reference to God knowing Jeremiah, sanctifying him, and ordaining him a before he came out of the womb, the word "knew" implies a personal acquaintance more extensive than the period of gestation.

It also speaks of an act requiring an interpersonal relationship—He ordained Jeremiah a prophet. Ordination to such a calling is accomplished by the laying on of hands (Num. 27:22-23). There is no reason in sound hermeneutics that Jeremiah 1:5 should be interpreted figuratively. Rather, it is consistent with the understanding gained above. Jeremiah, like all Men, lived with his Father as a spirit child for an unknown duration before being born on this earth.

Angels. The realization that Men live with God as His spirit children before their sojourn on earth explains many otherwise mysterious Bible teachings. First, it solves a great mystery about the origin and nature of the spiritual hosts referred to in scripture as *angels*. These servants and messengers of God are none other than the spirits of Men, God's spirit children. The early saints understood this truth and for they referred to the spirit of Peter as "his angel" (Acts 12:15).

The term "angel" is often used in the Bible to refer to messengers and ministering spirits (e.g., Heb. 1:13-14). As spirit children of God, the spirits of Men often act in this capacity to do His bidding. (Some act in a similar capacity for Satan—see Rev. 12:7-9). Angels are usually spirits, but the term can be used to designate physical messengers of God, such as the three who visited Abraham on their way to oversee the destruction of Sodom and Gomorrah (Gen. 18:1-8).[3]

Job 38:7 (NASB) speaks of Earth's cornerstone being laid, "When the morning stars sang together, And all the sons of God shouted for joy" The word translated "sons" in this verse is the Hebrew word "*ben*," which literally means "offspring." Use of this word confirms that "the sons of God" (Heb: *beni elohim*) refered to here were Men, described by Paul as the "offspring" of God in Acts 17:28-29. The term "sons of God" is a reference to the spirits of Men in pre-mortality, and this verse tells of their joy at the prospect of earth's creation (Job 38:4-7).

Hebrews 2:7 (quoting Ps. 8:5) says of Man, "Thou madest him a little lower than the angels." The word "madest" is not in the Greek text, but is part of the word translated "lower." It does not imply creation, but movement. Thus, the phrase, "madest him a little lower than the angels" implies that Men were *transported* to a, place lower than where the angels reside.

The context of Hebrews 2:7-8 recalls the act of God placing Adam in the Garden of Eden and giving him dominion over the earth. Thus, when the spirits of Men were sent from their heavenly abode to earth, to inhabit fleshly bodies, they were conveyed to a location that is lower than the place where they lived with the other angels, their spirit brothers and sisters.

Another implication of this passage is significant. Men could not have been transported *from* the home of the angels if they did at some time occupy that heavenly realm.

Finally, the NASB indicates that the phrase "a little" in "a little lower than the angels" (KJV) has *temporal* significance. The translation is "Thou hast made him *for a little while* lower than the angels" (Heb. 2:7, NASB

3. One of these may have been the Father, Himself. According to Justin Martyr in his *Dialogue With Trypho*, Genesis 19:24 refers to two "LORDS," one on the earth directing down the fire and brimstone, and the other in heaven unleashing it.

emphasis added). Thus, Man's departure from the home of his Heavenly Father, Mother, brothers, and sisters, was viewed in God's perspective as one of brief duration.

This further clarifies Christ's kenosis. He too "was made a little lower than the angels," i.e., His spirit was sent down to this earth to put on flesh, for the express purpose of "suffering death" so He could fulfill His mission and be crowned with glory and honor (Heb. 2:9-11).

From Adam until the meridian of time,[4] Christ was known to Men on Earth as Jehovah, the God of Abraham, Isaac, and Jacob, and He acted in that capacity. Thus, His descent from the circumstances He enjoyed in pre-mortality to life on earth involved a monumental condescension (as described in Phil. 2:5-8).

An understanding of pre-mortality also gives crystal clarity to Ecclesiastes 12:7 (emphasis added), which states: "Then shall the dust return to the earth as it was: and the spirit shall *return* unto God who gave it." Certainly that is the intent of all spirits who leave their Heavenly Home "for a little while" to be in a place "lower than the angels." They want to return to their Father, and, if their hope is realized, their end will be greater than their "first estate," their occupancy in that Heavenly realm (see Jude 6). This explains the joy expressed when the foundations of the earth were laid (Job 38:7).

Evil Brothers. Unfortunately, not all the sons of God "kept their first estate" (Jude 6). Job 38:7 refers to "the morning stars" singing together. The mention of "stars" in this passage is not a reference to distant suns, as astronomers use the term. It refers to a special group of spirits among the "sons of God." In Numbers 24:17 (NASB), Christ is called "a star" which "shall come forth from Jacob," and in Revelation 22:16, Jesus states that He is "the bright and morning star" (NASB: "the bright morning star"). Surely "the morning stars" mentioned in Job included Christ, "the bright morning star," in His pre-mortal state.

But Job 38:7 speaks of "morning stars" in the plural. Christ is uniquely designated "the *bright* morning star," but there must have been others in that group. Surprisingly, Isaiah 14:12 (NASB) refers to *Satan* as "a star of the morning." That evil one was once among the select group spoken of by Job.

4. Theoretically the meridian of time would be 0 A D, but the Georgian calendar, upon which all modern calendars are based, doesn't have a zero point to mark the birth year of Christ.

Indeed, the name by which he was first known, Lucifer, means "the shining one."

That Satan was a "son of God" is clear from Job 1:6 (NASB): "Now there was a day when the sons of God came to present themselves before the LORD, and Satan also came among them." Since it is the same author and the same wording, the term "sons of God" used in this verse must be taken in the same sense as in Job chapter 38. The phrase "Satan also came among them" indicates that Satan was also a son of God. It is incongruous to suppose that he crashed this meeting, especially in light of the extensive and parental conversation God has with him on seeing his arrival (Job 1:7-12).

Thus, the Bible teaches that Lucifer, one of the sons of God, was a spirit brother of Christ (and of all Men), and one of that elite group designated as "the morning stars." Distasteful as that relationship may be to Evangelicals, it is biblical doctrine.

Of course, the relationship between Christ and Lucifer ends with their common parentage. Satan, like all Men, was free to make evil choices in his first estate (Jude 6), and he did so in a big way (Rev. 12:7-9[5]). So basic and far-reaching were his evil choices, that now, though they are sons of the same Father, there is certainly no other form of kinship between Christ and Satan.

To charge Mormons accusingly with the belief that "Christ is the spirit brother of Lucifer," is an attempt to shock Evangelicals who don't know what the Bible teaches on this subject. It is a verbal form of "yellow journalism," where a truth is intentionally and repeatedly phrased so that recipients will reject it rather than investigate and learn of its truth. Evangelicals who use this phrase do not explain the Latter-day Saint teaching, nor examine its scriptural basis—they only assert that Mormons believe in a

5. Evangelicals believe the "war in heaven" is yet to occur. But Lucifer was a "star [or "son"] of the morning" at the time the foundations of the Earth were laid (Isa. 14:12; Job 38:7). That is a positive designation, one he shared with Christ. But he later appeared to Eve in the Garden of Eden as the great deceiver (Gen. 3:1-5). Further, his followers, called "evil spirits," "demons," or "devils," are referred to in both the New Testament (e.g., Matt. 8:28) and the Old (e.g., 1 Sam. 16:23). In Job, the oldest book in the Bible, Satan's appearance at a meeting of the "sons of God" (1:6, et seq.) suggests he had fallen by then. All this indicates his rebellion and the "war in heaven," the war with Michael in which he and his followers were cast out of heaven, occurred between the time the foundations of the Earth were laid (Job 38:6-7) and the time when Eve entered the Garden of Eden (Gen. 2:21-25).

"different Jesus" because the Mormon Jesus is the "spirit brother of Lucifer." By so stating a half truth, they imply something different than the reality that Christ is the brother of *all* God's spirit children (John 20:17).

Satan's parentage is a fact taught in the Bible. It is an important biblical truth that should be neither ignored nor demeaned, a sobering reminder of how far Men can fall (Isa. 14:12).

Fellows. Psalms 45:7 says of Christ, "Thou lovest righteousness, and hatest wickedness: therefore God, thy God, hath anointed thee with the oil of gladness above thy fellows." (That this passage is addressed to Christ is evident from Hebrews 1:8-9.) From this verse it is clear that, as spirits, Men were capable of making choices and were given free agency to choose evil, as Satan did, or good, as Christ did, and that rewards followed (for Satan's reward, see Rev. 12:9; also, Jude 6; 2 Pet. 2:4).

The word "fellows" was examined in the previous chapter where it was noted that the term couldn't have included God the Father. Only a knowledge of Man's pre-mortal existence makes this reference comprehensible. Christ's "fellows" were His brothers and sisters, the other spirit children of God the Father. As noted in the last chapter, "fellows" means "partners, holding with others," so it may also have had specific reference to "the morning stars" mentioned in Job 38:7.

Foreknowledge. The knowledge that Men existed as spirit children of God before coming to Earth explains one of the most perplexing teachings found in the Bible—the doctrine of predestination. During Man's pre-mortal existence, God was able to observe each individual and their choices. He became completely and perfectly acquainted with every personality, and "foreknew" the choices they would make during their lives on earth (Rom. 11:2). Many were chosen, or elected, knowing they would accept the gospel message and accomplish specific callings in His service (1 Pet. 1:2). Truly, He has "chosen us in him from before the foundation of the world" (Eph. 1:4).

The doctrine of predestination can only be appreciated through a knowledge of Man's pre-mortal existence. "For whom he did foreknow, he also did predestinate *to be* conformed to the image of his Son, that he might be the firstborn among many brethren" (Rom. 8:29). Foreordination was a pre-earthly consecration (a predestination) to an earthly calling in Christ's service. By responding to that pre-earthly call and making the right choices on earth, this verse anticipates that many of Christ's brethren will be able to return to the abode of God with Him.

Only with this understanding is it clear that God is not guilty of arbitrary or capricious acts of favoritism in consecrating or ordaining (Jer. 1:5) Men to various callings in this life. Man's free agency remains intact, and his choices are determinative of his rewards. Election is a calling based on God's pre-mortal knowledge of each person's capabilities. Because the memory of that calling, and of the pre-mortal existence itself, is veiled (1 Cor. 13:12; 2 Cor. 5:7) it remains for each individual, as a free agent, to live up to the calling, election, *predestination*, or *foreordination* he or she received in pre-mortality.

Memories. The veil over Man's memory of his pre-mortality has many purposes. The first is physical. If spirits could remember their pre-earth life, they would experience overwhelming difficulty coping with the slow and demanding process of physical growth a baby must endure. Like evil spirits occupying the bodies of men or beasts, they would quickly destroy their developing physical tabernacles (Matt. 8:31-32).

The veil also makes this existence a kind of closed-book test where Men are placed on their own, separated from God, to show their true mettle. Of course, the proof is not for God's benefit, but for Man's. All Men must bow their knee to Him and confess that His judgments are just (Rom. 14:11; Mosiah 16:1).

In Job 38:4 (NASB) God asks, "Where were you when I laid the foundation of the earth? Tell *Me*, if you have understanding." Here God asks Job if he has a knowledge of where he was when God laid the foundation of the earth. This questioning acknowledges that Job was *somewhere*. Of course, God knew that Job did not recall his pre-mortality. The question wasn't meant as an insult, but as a reminder that Job's perspective was limited.

Job, like all Men in this life, underwent a test. This reminder of Job's limited perspective teachs that God's administration of that test should not be questioned by Man. Without their memory of the pre-mortal existence, Men are incapable of seeing things from God's point of view. This is a necessary aspect of the test. If Men could recall their pre-mortal existence, this life wouldn't provide the opportunity for self-realization and development God intended.

Intelligences. As indicated in Chapter 2, Mormons believe that *nothing* is created out of nothing. Even the spirits of Men were organized out of something. In Mormon theology that something consists of *intelligences* (Abraham 3:22-23). The nature and character of intelligences has not been revealed to Man, and is not within his scope of understanding at this time, but it is believed by most Mormons that they are self-conscious and differ in personality one from another.

From other LDS scripture, it appears that, like God, each individual intelligence has always existed as a fundamental building block of life that cannot be created (D&C 93:29), that is,it is "uncreate." This eternal element within each man and woman is critical to their ultimate destiny—deification.

Men have progressed from intelligences, to spirit children of God, to physical embodiments in a mortal world. Their ultimate goal is to be resurrected to a glory and eternal life like that enjoyed by Christ, and return to live forever with their Father in Heaven. What this means in terms of Man's potential is regarded by Evangelicals as one of the most controversial subjects in Mormonism, and will be discussed next.

Becoming Like God

Each day Men grow older they take on an appearance closer to that of their earthly fathers and mothers. Since Men are the children of God, it should surprise no one that, as they mature, they can become more like Him. Evangelicals have a very odd reaction to this doctrine. While they teach it themselves (more or less), using such passages as 1 John 3:2 to show that Men will be resurrected and become like God in some vague, figurative sense, they condemn Mormons, along with many of their own cohorts, for teaching the biblical truth that Men can become like God in a literal sense.

Understanding this doctrine is difficult for many. One famous televangelist, Kenneth Copeland, teaches that Men are "little gods," but he sounds more like a charismatic New-Ager than a Mormon. In reacting to the error he mixes with truth, it is not surprising that mainline Evangelicals have misconstrued and rejected Mormon teachings on this subject.

A typical misunderstanding is reflected in the statement of Craig Hawkins, a former co-host of "The Bible Answerman." He thinks Mormons believe they can become part of the Trinity.[6] But Mormons do not even accept the trinitarian concept of co-substantiality, however, this notion is not from Mormon doctrine.

Mr. Hawkins' comments however, reflect an important distinction that must be drawn in order to understand what the Bible (and the Mormon Church) teaches on this subject. There is literally a *generation* of difference between teaching that "Men can become *like* God," and saying "Men can become God." No one in the current generation of God's spirit children, except Christ, will become God over this earth.[7]

This distinction was also communicated by Christ, as Jehovah, in Isaiah 43:10: "before me there was no God formed, neither shall there be after me." To the extent, if any, these words apply to Men rather than idols, they may be applied to those who have delusions of grandeur extending beyond the plane of this existence. Mormons do not claim that any member of the current generation of God's spirit children, save Christ alone, is or will be God over their fellow Men.

Christ alone was "anointed . . . with the oil of gladness" *above* His "fellows" (Ps. 45:6-7; Heb. 1:8-9). He became "the Mighty God" over all Men (Isa. 9:6; see, also, John 1:1). Mormons certainly do not believe that the progress of Men toward God-like-ness will ever allow them to assert authority over God the Father or Christ. The extent to which they may assist Christ in exercising authority over their brothers and sisters on this earth is unknown. But **no other God than Christ** will be appointed, "formed," or "constituted" to rule and reign over this generation of spirits. Though a man may one day become as God is now, He will remain subject to the Father, and will always honor, worship and obey God through Jesus Christ.

This truth is typified in the relationship that should exist between parents and children on earth. The fifth commandment does not say "Honor thy father and thy mother, until you become adults like them" (see Exod. 20:12). Becoming like his father is each man's genetic destiny. Some day most men and women will have families of their own. When that day comes, their children will owe them honor. But each parent will still owe honor to his or her own father and mother.

Likewise, each Man, no matter what his destiny, must honor, worship and obey his Heavenly Father, despite the fact that he may someday become like Him, even to the extent of having spirit children of his own.

The Bible condemns the idea of Men exalting themselves over God. It was this egomaniacal desire that led Satan to his just condemnation. When he did not receive the glory given to Christ, his brother (Phil. 2:9-11), he sought to usurp all honor and authority from the Father. These events are

6. "The Bible Answerman," syndicated by the Christian Research Institute, Irvine, California, c. 1989.

7. It is possible, however, for them to join Christ on the throne of His Father at some point in the distant future (Rev. 3:21).

described in Isaiah 14:12-17, a passage frequently misunderstood by Evangelicals. The passage reads in the NASB as follows:

> "How you have fallen from heaven,
> O star of the morning, son of the dawn!
> You have been cut down to the earth,
> You who have weakened the nations!
> "But you said in your heart,
> 'I will ascend to heaven;
> I will raise my throne above the stars of God,
> And I will sit on the mount of assembly
> In the recesses of the north.
> 'I will ascend above the heights of the clouds;
> I will make myself like the Most High.'
> "Nevertheless you will be thrust down to Sheol,
> To the recesses of the pit.
> "Those who see you will gaze at you,
> They will ponder over you, *saying*,
> 'Is this the man who made the earth tremble,
> Who shook kingdoms,
> Who made the world like a wilderness
> And overthrew its cities,
> Who did not allow his prisoners to *go* home?'"

As in Job 38, the term "stars" is a reference to the spirits of Men. Thus, verse 13 ("I will raise my throne above the stars of God") explains that Satan jealously sought to exalt himself over his fellow spirit brothers and sisters.

In verse 14 ("I will make myself like the Most High"), Satan assumes an ability he does not have. The humility of Christ's submission to the Father in all things (John 5:19-20; 6:37-38; 7:16-18, 28-29; 8:49-50, 54-55; Heb. 5:5-6), stands in stark contrast to the attitude of insurrection expressed here by Satan.

The remaining verses indicate that Satan never actually sought to be *like* the Father. His actions and motives were evil. He shook kingdoms, made the world a wilderness and overthrew cities. Verse 17 says he "opened not the house of his prisoners" (KJV). In contrast, Christ was able to "bring out the prisoners from the prison" (Isa. 42:7; cf., 1 Pet. 3:18-19). This is a reference to His atoning sacrifice and work of salvation for the dead that makes it possible for God's spirit children "to go home." Though Satan aspired to the authority of Christ, he refused to emulate His works—for his path was in the opposite direction.

Mormon doctrine teaches that Men are just as unable to "make [themselves] like the Most High" as was Satan. Men, being imperfect, can only become like God through the atonement of Jesus Christ and by His gift of eternal life. It is God alone who bestows this gift on Men. But Men will not be invested with so exalted a state if their behavior, like that of Satan described above, is inconsistent with the character of God. Thus, an understanding of Man's potential is an understanding of his need for salvation. The only way Men can attain the goal of becoming like the Father is through His plan of salvation.

Satan was not condemned for seeking to be like God, for he never made that effort. He was condemned for seeking to usurp God's authority in wickedness. Christ commanded all Men to make it their *goal* to become like God (Matt. 5:48). In so doing, Men must subject themselves to Christ, as He subjected Himself to the Father (1 Cor. 15:27-28). If they do that, the Bible clearly teaches that Men may become as much like the Son as He is like the Father (John 17:18-23).

Many passages say that Men will be changed into the image of God. "But we all, with open face beholding as in a glass the glory of the Lord, are changed into the same image from glory to glory, *even as* by the Spirit of the Lord" (2 Cor. 3:18); "And as we have borne the image of the earthy, we shall also bear the image of the heavenly" (1 Cor. 15:49; see, also, Col. 3:10). The clearest declaration of this principle is found in 1 John 3:2-3, where the Apostle taught:

> Beloved, now are we the sons of God, and it doth not yet appear what we shall be: but we know that, when he shall appear, we shall be like him; for we shall see him as he is.
>
> And every man that hath this hope in him purifieth himself, even as he is pure.

What an incredible promise! "We shall be like him." This glorious assurance is made to all who can number themselves with John as "the sons of God." This is a literal promise that Men may be endowed with the same *infinite* characteristics God displays.

That John meant this promise to be taken literally is evident from his closing phrase in verse 2: "for [Greek: *hoti*, meaning "because"] we shall see him as he is." God is an infinite being whose characteristics are incomprehensible to mortal Men. It would be impossible for beings restricted to finite vision, as Men currently are, to see God, an infinite being, *as He is*. But John asserts that those who are transformed into God's image *will* be able to see Him *as He is*, requiring that they have the same infinite vision God enjoys. Only *because* they have that ability, will Men know they have become truly like Him.

Paul describes this transformation in 1 Corinthians 15:52. "For the trumpet shall sound, and the dead shall be raised incorruptible, and we shall be changed." The raising of "the dead" incorruptible (1 Cor.15:53-54) speaks of the resurrection of all Men. The reference to being "changed," however, is restricted by the personal pronoun "we." Since that pronoun is inclusive of the author (Paul), it must refer to those, like Paul, who can look forward to the transformation John promised. This is an exciting prospect for all who, like Paul and John, "purifieth [themselves], even as He is pure" (1 John 3:3).

Christ's Testimony of Man's Potential

A powerful testimony of these truths was given by Christ in John 10:30-36. In John 10:30, Christ stated His equality and oneness with the Father, as noted previously. The idea that a man could become as God was as difficult for the Pharisees to accept then as it is for Evangelicals to believe now. Thus, the Pharisees said, "You, being a man, make Yourself out *to be* God" (John 10:33, NASB). A similar criticism is leveled by Evangelicals at Mormons today. Of course, in Christ's day it was more than a theological criticism—it was a charge of blasphemy under the Law of Moses, the punishment for which was death by stoning.

Christ's response to that charge is enlightening. It was as follows (John 10:34-36, NASB):

> Jesus answered them, "Has it not been written in your Law, 'I said, you are gods'?
>
> "If he called them gods, to whom the word of God came (and the Scripture cannot be broken),
>
> do you say of Him, whom the Father sanctified and sent into the world, 'You are blaspheming,' because I said, 'I am the Son of God'?"

The quotation in verse 34 is from Psalm 82: 6. Evangelical commentators claim this Psalm has nothing to do with *Men* being "gods." They say it was directed at the *judges* in Israel, who were derogatorily called "gods" in this passage because of the way they wielded the power of life and death over their people.[8] There is no valid hermeneutic to support this strained interpretation. In fact, it undermines Christ's use of the passage in John 10:34, directly contradicting the interpretation Christ gave it when He quoted it to the Pharisees.

Psalms 82 reads, in full, as follows:

> God standeth in the congregation of the mighty; he judgeth among the gods.
>
> How long will ye judge unjustly, and accept the persons of the wicked? Selah.
>
> Defend the poor and fatherless: do justice to the afflicted and needy.
>
> Deliver the poor and needy: rid *them* out of the hand of the wicked.
>
> They know not, neither will they understand; they walk on in darkness: all the foundations of the earth are out of course.
>
> I have said, Ye *are* gods; and all of you *are* children of the most High.
>
> But ye shall die like men, and fall like one of the princes.
>
> Arise, O God, judge the earth: for thou shalt inherit all nations.

This Psalm encourages *all* Men to judge righteously and to be merciful to the poor and orphaned. When Christ reiterated this admonition in His Sermon on the Mount, He did not restrict it to the judges in Israel (Matt. 7:1-5). *All* Men should do what they can to see that the poor and needy are delivered out of the hands of the wicked. It is verse 6 that reveals the audience to whom the Psalm was directed. It says, "all of you *are* children of the most High." Clearly, "you" refers to all "children of the most High," not just to the judges of Israel.

Christ said that Psalms 82:6 was directed to those "to whom the word of God came" (John 10:35, NASB). The word translated "came" in John 10:35 is not *erchomai*, the usual word in Greek that means "to come" in the sense of arriving at a destination. It is *ginomai*, which is discussed in

8. Martin, *The Maze of Mormonism,* 77.

Chapter 2. The phrase could be rendered, "in whom the word of God, comes alive."

Did Christ miss something in this Psalm? According to the Evangelical interpretation, He should have said that Psalm 82 was directed "unto the wicked judges of Israel." But He didn't. Instead, He said it refers to those in whom the word of God comes alive. These are they who purify themselves as John directed in 1 John 3:3, so that they become "sons of God" (1 John 3:2). As the phrase "children of the most High" in Psalm 82:6 implies, these are "children" (or "sons") who have learned to behave in a way that reflects their lineage (see Rom. 8:14).

Christ cited Psalm 82 as a defense against the charge of blasphemy. By using it, He countered a threat from the legalistic Pharisees who thought they had finally found evidence that would justify putting Him to death. He deftly parried their charge using Psalms 82:6, which He noted "could not be broken." His purpose would have failed if Psalm 82 was nothing more than a derogatory reference to wicked judges in Israel, intended to be taken in a figurative sense, as Evangelicals assert.

If the Evangelical interpretation were correct, it would also mean the Pharisees misunderstood Christ's statement in John 10:30. He did *not* make Himself out to be God, as the Pharisees surmised, but used the term "god" in a derogatory and figurative sense. This interpretation suggests Christ merely corrected their misapprehension of His claims. There is no justification for that conclusion even in Evangelical teaching. Not only does it insult Christ's ability to communicate, it presents a woefully inadequate response to the Pharisaical charge of blasphemy.

The Pharisees knew exactly what Christ said. His claim must not be taken in some derogatory and figurative sense. He told them He was God. They understood that claim and regarded it as blasphemy, a capital offense under the Law of Moses. To counter that claim, Christ proved that it was not blasphemy because scripture refers to all Men ("unto whom the word of God came") as Gods (potentially). He did that with Psalm 82:6.

It is fortunate the Pharisees did not misunderstand this passage the way Evangelicals do today. Otherwise, they would have been justified in putting Him to death before His earthly mission was completed.

Of course, in the next verse, the Psalmist, in humbling tone, points out that, although "children of the most High" are "gods," they are all subject to death, and will be struck down in due time. This places Man's lofty origins in the proper perspective. It is an appropriate reminder of Man's current state of vulnerability, lest he forget and be overcome with the egotistical mania that prompted Satan's rebellion.

Men have not yet attained anything like their potential, but if they purify themselves as Christ is pure, so they are true children in whom the word of God has come alive, they will one day realize the blessing of these promises. Though lowly and finite in their present state, Men may yet be changed so they can actually see God as He truly is, being like Him in His glorified, infinite, and perfect nature.

Eternal Families

That Men are the spirit children of God implies that God is capable of having children. The idea of having children in Heaven is totally foreign to Evangelicals. They categorically reject such a prospect. That position is based on a single passage in the Bible that has been woefully misinterpreted.

Other critics of the Mormon belief in eternal procreation, say that it makes no sense for resurrected beings, with bodies of flesh and bone, to have spirit children. With their vast knowledge about the syngamy of resurrected beings, they contend that resurrected men and women should reproduce only resurrected (or at least, physical) children.[9] An appropriate response to these detractors is given in Job 38:2 (NASB): "Who is this that darkens counsel by words without knowledge?" There is absolutely no reason to assume that a resurrected human being cannot reproduce a spirit version of itself.

Mormons believe in both eternal marriage and eternal families, and these beliefs imply the procreation of children in the same way God created Men as His spirit children. This concept follows logically from the Bible's teachings about the resurrection. Human bodies, as formed by God, are fully capable of reproduction. The perfect restoration of the body suggests these capabilities will remain intact after the resurrection (Ezek. 37:1-14).

Job used very emphatic language to declare that his resurrected body would be in the same form as his mortal body (Job 19:26-27):

> And *though* after my skin *worms* destroy this *body*, yet in my *flesh* shall I see God:

9. E.g., J. Edmund Decker on "The Bible Answerman," c. January 13, 1992.

> Whom I shall see for myself, and mine eyes shall behold, and not another; *though* my reins be consumed within me.

Christ appeared to His apostles in the exact form He had during His mortal life (Luke 24:36-39). If Men are thus raised in the exact bodily form they enjoyed during this life, why should theologians expect resurrected beings to be sterile?

The only Bible passage that raises the possibility of resurrected being having their reproductive organs removed is found in Matthew 22:23-30 (and Mark 12:18-25) where Christ is misunderstood by Evangelicals to have said that *all* Men "neither marry, nor are given in marriage" in the resurrection. A careful analysis of this passage reveals that its message was limited to the individuals specified in the example. That passage, along with several other Bible verses, must be grossly misinterpreted to arrive at any other conclusion. Matthew 22:23-30 (NASB) reads as follows:

> On that day *some* Sadducees (who say there is no resurrection) came to Him and questioned Him,
>
> saying, "Teacher, Moses said, 'If a man dies, having no children, his brother as next of kin shall marry his wife, and raise up an offspring to his brother.'
>
> "Now there were seven brothers with us; and the first married and died, and having no offspring left his wife to his brother; "so also the second, and the third, down to the seventh.
>
> "And last of all, the woman died.
>
> "In the resurrection therefore whose wife of the seven shall she be? For they all had her."
>
> But Jesus answered and said to them, "You are mistaken, not understanding the Scriptures, or the power of God.
>
> "For in the resurrection they neither marry, nor are given in marriage, but are like angels in heaven."

This passage describes a confrontation between Christ and a group of Sadducees—members of a sect who did not believe in the literal resurrection of the body. The Sadducees did not come to Christ to seek understanding. They came to confront Him with a situation they thought would demonstrate the foolishness of His teachings and vindicate their own belief that there is no resurrection. They concocted a clever trap by carefully drafting a hypothetical question based on what they knew to be a teaching of Christ.

The question they chose would not have served their purpose if Christ had not been teaching eternal marriage. They assumed Christ would say that each marriage in their story continued after the resurrection. If His answer had been consistent with their meager understanding of eternal marriage, it would have proved that Christ's teachings result in a state of intolerable confusion. God is not the author of confusion but of order (see, e.g., 1 Chron. 15:12-14; 2 Chron. 29:35). They hoped Christ would be caught in this trap.

If Christ had not been teaching eternal marriage, their question would not have fitted into their plot. It would simply have allowed Christ to bear further testimony of the resurrection. From the parenthetical reference to the Sadducees' disbelief in the resurrection (Matt. 22:23), it is obvious they would not have wanted that. Hence, it is clear that Christ taught eternal marriage, and the Sadducees knew He did.

In fact, just three chapters earlier Matthew recorded Christ's teachings on eternal marriage. There He addressed the Pharisees in response to their question about divorce. In Matthew 19:3-6 (NASB, see also Mark 10:2-9) it reads:

> And *some* Pharisees came to Him, testing Him, and saying, "Is it lawful *for a man* to divorce his wife for any cause at all?"
>
> And He answered and said, "Have you not read, that He who created *them* from the beginning made them male and female,
>
> "and said, 'For this cause a man shall leave his father and mother, and shall cleave to his wife; and the two shall become one flesh'?
>
> "Consequently they are no longer two, but one flesh. What therefore God has joined together, let no man separate."

God joined Adam and Eve when they were immortal (Gen. 2:18-25), and He commanded no man to part them. Would that same God later separate them himself? Certainly not! That was the point of Christ's instruction (especially verse 6). What God does remains forever (Eccl. 3:14). Christ's message was that the joining of husband and wife was ordained of God, and was meant to be *eternal.*

The Pharisees, who believed they could divorce their wives on the flimsiest of grounds, were rebuked by this teaching, and obviously reported Christ's teachings to the Sadducees, with whom they disagreed as to the resurrection. The Sadducees saw in this an opportunity to discredit Christ on both doctrines (resurrection and eternal marriage). This explains why the Pharisees came together on this occasion with the Sadducees.

What then does Christ's response to the Sadducees' mean? Christ contradicted the Sadducees' assumptions in verses 29 and 30, but the implications of His contradiction are not as broad as Evangelicals assume. He did not deny eternal marriage. He said that the *specific* marriages identified in this question were not eternal (verse 30: "For in the resurrection *they* neither marry, nor are given in marriage," emphasis added). This is particularly clear from the book of Tobit, still in Catholic Bibles, which contains a story describing the very circumstances posed by the Sadducees. So what was it about the marriages in this example that differed from the marriage of Adam and Eve cited by Christ in Matthew 19?

The basis for the Sadducee's error was that they did not understand (1) "*the Scriptures*," or (2) "*the power of God*" (Matt. 22:29). Lack of scriptural knowledge is evidenced by their failure to note that Adam and Eve's marriage had been performed *by God*, and would therefore "be forever" (Eccl. 3:14). They also failed to note that the purpose of marriage to the brother of a deceased spouse was only to raise up a mortal posterity for the deceased spouse (Deut. 25:5-6). One would not expect, therefore, that any of the subsequent marriages would last after the first brother and his wife were restored to each other in the resurrection. This is evident from the version of this example that appears in the Book of Tobit, with which they should have been familiar. Finally, they failed to note that God's laws are spiritual (Rom. 7:14), and no *spiritual* purpose would be served by a marriage performed by God if it could not continue after the resurrection.

In Matthew 16:19, just a few chapters before Christ taught the Pharisees about eternal marriage, He explained that the *power of God* includes the power to bind on earth and have it bound in heaven. Such authority (or "power") is needed to ensure that an earthly marriage is contractually binding in the eternal realm. As Christ noted, the Sadducees knew nothing of this power, and their question failed to mention its use in connection with *any* of the marriages. Hence, *none of them* would be binding in Heaven.

Christ did not contradict Himself, nor change His mind between Matthew 19 and Matthew 22. What His answer to the Sadducees demonstrates is that, through "the power of God," marital relationships are maintained in an orderly manner in heaven. This answer completely frustrated the Sadducees' trap.

The most important aspect of the message of Matthew 22:23-30, however, was not the way in which Christ foiled the Sadducees, but the implications of His answer to them. Marriages performed under Man's authority alone, as in the Sadducees' example, will not remain in effect after the resurrection. The power of God must be used to bind men and women in order for their marriages to last forever. Those who are not married by such authority, like the men and woman in the Sadducees' example, remain as the angels in heaven—messengers only, separate and single forever.

This interpretation of Matthew 22 is consistent with Paul's teachings on the subject (1 Cor. 11:11, emphasis added): "Nevertheless, neither is the man without the woman, neither the woman without the man, *in the Lord*." The phrase "in the Lord" refers to Man's ultimate state of rest in the Kingdom of Heaven. Paul says that in that realm, the relationship of men and women is the same as that of Adam and Eve, who, in their immortal state, were joined by God as one flesh. As in Eden, the creation of such a relationship requires the power of God, specifically the power given by Christ to Peter in Matthew 16:19. For those who are bound by that power, unlike those in the Sadducees' example, Heaven will include the promise of continued marital bliss, and with it, parenthood.

Gods Many and Lords Many

It is now possible to put in context some of the statements of early Mormon leaders that are commonly misinterpreted by Evangelical critics. The Bible teaches that Men may become like God. Like God, Men may also have spirit children of their own, with the concomitant duty to care for them and see to their development just as Men have been nurtured and developed by their Father in Heaven.

This suggests to the mind an eternal pattern, one that not only continues in the future, but may have been repeated innumerable times in the past. Man's Heavenly Father may have had His own Father in Heaven, and may have passed through an existence, like that of Christ, on an earth populated by His own brothers and sisters. Support for this conjecture can be found in the Bible, most notably in John 5:19 (NASB), which reads as follows:

> Jesus therefore answered and was saying to them, "Truly, truly, I say to you, the Son can do nothing of Himself, unless *it is* some-

> thing He sees the Father doing; for whatever *the Father* does, these things the Son also does in like manner."

The implications of this verse are profound. The language suggests that the Father, at some unknown time in the eternal past, did the same thing on the world to which He was sent as Jesus Christ did here. The Son was able to review His Father's actions, and prepare for His own mission on this earth. This is consistent with Matthew 5:48 in the original Greek which implies that, as Men must become spiritually, nature ("perfect"). So God the Father became spirirually nature.

These passages are short on details, but some early Mormon leaders have exposited on the concepts they imply, consistent with the doctrines considered in this chapter. Their statements must be taken in that context. They are the thoughts and opinions of inspired men about a profound subject on which the Lord has revealed little.

Likewise, statements of LDS leaders about many gods are consistent with the comments of Paul in 1 Corinthians 8:4-6, in which Paul, speaking of food offered to idols, made a very meaningful comment:

> As concerning therefore the eating of those things that are offered in sacrifice unto idols, we know that an idol is nothing in the world, and that *there is* none other God but one.
>
> For though there be that are called gods, whether in heaven or in earth, (as there be gods many, and lords many,)
>
> But to us *there is but* one God, the Father, of whom *are* all things, and we in him; and one Lord Jesus Christ, by whom *are* all things, and we by him.

Since Paul was speaking of idols, Evangelicals assume that verse 5 refers to false gods, the creations of Men. That assumption is inadequate to explain the language of that verse. Paul may have been referring to idols when he said, "there be that are called gods, . . . in *earth*," though more likely he had in mind such instances as Moses being called a "god" to Pharaoh (Exod. 7:1). Heaven has also called them "gods, to whom the word of God came" (see John 10:34-35 and Ps. 82:6). But it is entirely unlikely that idols have ever been "called gods . . . in *heaven*."

The most startling aspect of Paul's language in verse 5 is his parenthetical statement that "*there* **be** *gods many, and lords many*." This is a positive indication of the actual existence of many gods and many lords that cannot be ignored the way Evangelicals do. Paul did not say "there be *false* gods many and *false* lords many." He said there actually *are* many "gods" and many "lords."

If this were not the clear meaning of his remarks, it would have been entirely unnecessary for him to state at the beginning of the next verse, "But *to us* there is but one God." He would certainly have left the italicized words out if he had not just verified the actual existence of many gods and lords in the universe. Paul's attitude toward idols is clearly indicated in verse 4—they are "nothing." If Paul were talking about idols in verse 5, there would have been no need to personalize the statement in verse 6 with the words "*to us*." He could have ended his comments with the simple affirmation that "there is but one God! " Instead, having digressed into a deep subject, giving Men a short but profound look at the universe, it was necessary to restore proper perspective with the phrase "*to us* there is but one God," thus confirming the composite unity with all who are thus designated.

The same view is offered briefly in the first verse of Psalm 82. The NASB notes that the literal translation of that verse is: "God takes His stand in the congregation of God; He judges in the midst of the gods."

What exists in the universe concerning the many gods and lords referred to by Paul and in Psalm 82 is not revealed in scripture, but Man's powers of reason have lead some to deep speculation. The speculative statements of early LDS leaders on this subject should not alarm Evangelicals. Like any non-canonical exposition on John 5:19, 1 Corinthians 8:5, Psalm 82:1 and others, these statements should be viewed with some latitude for opinion.

Above all, Mormons, like Paul, believe that, *to Man*, there is but one God—the Father—and one Lord—His Son, Jesus Christ. Mormons do *not* teach that any Man, save Christ, will occupy that position over those who are his fellow brothers and sisters (Isa. 43:10).[10] Nor will Men establish eternal families in the near future (speaking cosmologically). There is too much left to be done in the work of redeeming their brothers and sisters.

10. Though referred to as God in the Bible, the Holy Ghost has a communicative, rather than administrative, function in the Godhead (see, e.g., Neh. 9:30; Isa. 11:1-3, Matt. 12:18; Mark 13:11). Though he may be one among the current generation of God's spirit children who was elevated to Godhood, he too is subject to Christ.

Conclusion

This chapter presents insights on the teachings of the Mormon Church regarding Man and his relationship to God and the potential inherent in that relationship. They are the teachings of the Bible. They tell much about where Men came from, why they are here, and where they may be going in their eternal future. Having learned of his potential, Man's earnest desire should be to understand the means by which he may achieve the goal of becoming like his Father. That goal can only be attained through salvation, which is available only in and through the Gospel of Jesus Christ.

Part II

MORMON SOTERIOLOGY

5

Who's Preaching Another Gospel?

The second reason Evangelicals label Mormonism a cult is that they differ with LDS teachings about the Gospel of Jesus Christ. Viewing themselves as the modern heirs of historic Christianity, Evangelicals believe they are the ones who teach the original Gospel of Jesus Christ. They condemn Mormons for preaching a different Gospel from the one they teach, as if that was the same as teaching a different Gospel from the one taught by the early Apostles.

In fact, it is Evangelicals who teach a different gospel, one that became popular during the Protestant Reformation, a gospel that is indistinguishable from *antinomianism* (the heresy that behavior is unrelated to faith).[1] On many crucial points, in fact, the Evangelical gospel is still being debated among their own theologians today.

Paul warned the early Galatians (Gal. 1:6-9):

> I marvel that ye are so soon removed from him that called you into the grace of Christ unto another gospel:
>
> Which is not another; but there be some that trouble you, and would pervert the gospel of Christ.
>
> But though we, or an angel from heaven, preach any other gospel unto you than that which we have preached unto you, let him be accursed.

1. Antinomianism teaches that Christians are not bound by any moral law, and was condemned early in the Protestant Reformation by Martin Luther. (Martin Luther, "Table Talk" in *Luther's Works,* ed. Helmut T. Lehman, trans. Theodore G. Tappert, 55 vols. (Philadelphia: Fortress, 1967), 54:248). However, it inevitably insinuates its way into any system of theology that denies the necessity of obedience to God as a basis for obtaining salvation.

> As we said before, so say I now again, If any *man* preach any other gospel unto you than that ye have received, let him be accursed.

The revealed nature of Mormonism is often criticized by Evangelicals because of this passage, but Galatians 1:8 does not condemn receipt of the Gospel from angels, the means by which it was taught to Joseph Smith. The language of that verse is meant to emphasize Paul's point. Like Joseph Smith, Paul personally received the Gospel from heaven, not from his fellow mortals (Gal. 1:12). It is inconceivable that Paul believed an angel from heaven would actually preach a gospel different from the one he had received from that very source.

What this passage requires is that teachers of the Gospel determine with certainty that they are teaching the same Gospel Paul taught. The teachings of the Apostles set the standard, not the teachings of the Protestant Reformation nor of modern theologians. This chapter will explore the basic difference between the Evangelical and the LDS Gospel, and demonstrate that it is The Church of Jesus Christ of Latter-day Saints that embraces the Gospel taught in the Bible.

What Is the Gospel?

Evangelicals teach that the Gospel consists entirely of the good news that Christ died, was buried, and has been resurrected.[2] The passage they cite in support of this position is 1 Corinthians 15:1-5 (NASB):

> Now I make known to you, brethren, the gospel which I preached to you, which also you received, in which also you stand,
> by which also you are saved, if you hold fast the word which I preached to you, unless you believed in vain.
> For I delivered to you as of first importance what I also received, that Christ died for our sins according to the Scriptures,
> and that He was buried, and that He was raised on the third day according to the Scriptures,
> and that He appeared to Cephas, then to the twelve.

Verse 1 of this passage indicates that Paul had previously preached the Gospel to his Corinthian audience. They had received it, and were "stand[ing]" in it at the time this epistle was written. Verse 2, suggests that

2. Trivanovich, *Speaking the Truth in Love,* 31-33.

the good news Paul previously preached was the *means* by which the Corinthians were saved (if they remembered what he taught, and had not believed "in vain."[3])

In verse 3, Paul says that what he delivered to them was "of first importance," and what follows in verses 3 through 5 is certainly the first and most important aspect of the Gospel of Jesus Christ. These verses express two essential truths about Christ's atonement: first, Christ died for Man's sins, and second, He rose from the dead on the third day. Christ's death for sins made possible salvation from spiritual death, while His resurrection provided salvation from physical death. (The mention of Christ's burial and His appearances after the resurrection confirms the certainty of His death and gives percipient evidence that He arose.)

Mormons also teach that Christ's death and resurrection are the core of the Gospel. Joseph Smith said:

> The fundamental principles of our religion are the testimony of the Apostles and Prophets, concerning Jesus Christ, that He died, was buried, and rose again the third day, and ascended into heaven: and all other things which pertain to our religion are only appendages to it.[4]

However, if the death and resurrection of Christ are the good news of *first* importance, there must also be good news of *second* importance. All of the gospel that Paul taught was necessary for salvation, otherwise he would not have told the Corinthians to "keep in memory what I preached unto you" (1 Cor. 15:2). It is not enough simply to comprehend the core of the Gospel. One must know how Men can be saved as a result of Christ's death and resurrection. Otherwise, it does little good to know that those momentous events occurred.

That the death and resurrection of Christ does not constitute the entirety of the Gospel is confirmed by Christ's own preaching in Mark 1:14-15 (NASB, emphasis added). Before He ever taught that He would die or rise from the dead, His message was recorded as follows:

> And after John had been taken into custody, Jesus came into Galilee, preaching the *gospel of God*,

3. Paul's use of this phrase implies either that belief alone is not salutary, or that the degree of salvation Men can experience in this life is not intrinsically permanent, or both.

4. Smith, *Teachings of the Prophet Joseph Smith,* 121.

> and saying, "The time is fulfilled, and the kingdom of God is at hand; repent and believe in the *gospel*."

The metaphor given by Christ in Matthew 12:40 appears to be the first time He referred to His pending death, burial, and resurrection. The events described in Mark 1 occurred well before those described in Matthew 12. What then was "the gospel of God" Christ asked the people to believe?

The answer is in verse 15 ("The time is fulfilled, and the kingdom of God is at hand"). It was the news that Messiah had come in fulfillment of the law and the prophets. This too was part of the momentous news from God that comprises the entire Gospel message to Man.

Laws or Ordinances in the Evangelical Gospel

The entirety of the Gospel message is curtailed in Evangelical theology by their belief that the Gospel contains no laws and ordinances requiring human obedience. One expression of the Evangelical position is the following:

> The Third Article of Faith [of the LDS Church] states:
>
> "We believe that through the Atonement of Christ, all mankind may be saved, by obedience to the laws and ordinances of the Gospel."
>
> There are, however, no laws and ordinances in the true gospel. Christ's death for our sins, His burial and resurrection have nothing to do with man's obedience.[5]

Evangelicals cite a number of passages in support of this position, but none actually sustain their premise. For example, they point to Ephesians 3:1-6, which says that the Gentiles participate in "his promise in Christ by the gospel." They also cite Galatians 5:1-6, in which Paul instructed the Galatians to "stand fast . . . in the liberty wherewith Christ hath made us free" rather than practice circumcision for salvation. Romans 1:16 is often cited. This is Paul's declaration that the gospel is "the power of God unto salvation." None of these passages gives any suggestion that the Gospel is without laws and ordinances.

Nevertheless, Evangelicals teach that "if we add law again after being justified by Christ, then we are transgressing against God."[6] This claim is

5. Trivanovich, *Speaking the Truth in Love,* 34.
6. Trivanovich, *Speaking the Truth in Love,* 45.

a corollary to their basic premise stated above. Both misunderstandings stem from a failure to distinguish between law, in general, and *the Law*, meaning the Law of Moses, which was fulfilled and abrogated by Christ's atonement (Heb. 7:18-19; Acts 15:5-29).

Consider Paul's warning in 2 Thessalonians 1:7-8 (emphasis added):

> And to you who are troubled rest with us, when the Lord Jesus shall be revealed from heaven with his mighty angels,
>
> In flaming fire taking vengeance on them that know not God, and that *obey not the gospel of our Lord Jesus Christ:*

If "the gospel of our Lord Jesus Christ" had no laws and ordinances, there would be nothing to "*obey*," as required by Peter in this passage. Clearly, there are laws and ordinances in the Gospel, or there would be no reason to identify the punishment that awaits those who "*obey* not the gospel"[7] (emphasis added).

The writer of Hebrews explains that a new and greater *covenant* was intended to replace the Law of Moses. The term *covenant* is an ancient legal concept, "an agreement or promise to do or not to do a particular thing."[8] To covenant means "to enter into a formal agreement; to bind oneself in contract."[9] The nature of a covenant is such that the promises of one party are conditioned upon performance by the other party of the obligations they accept.[10] The use of this term in the Old and New Testaments confirms that God's promise of salvation is conditioned upon Man's obedience to the Gospel.

The new covenant that the Lord promised in the Old Testament is the Gospel of the New Testament (Heb. 9:11-15). Referring to that new covenant, Hebrews 8:10 (quoting Jer. 31:33, some emphasis added) promises:

---

7. Some Evangelicals (e.g., G. Michael Cocoris) claim 2 Thess. 1:7-8 establishes two conditions, both of which must be satisfied in order to reap God's vengeance. That is, they believe they will not be objects of God's wrath unless (1) they do not know God, *and* (2) they do not obey the gospel. If they "know . . . God," but do not obey His Gospel, they will yet avoid His vengeance. Unfortunately, those who do not obey God do not know Him (1 John 2:3-4).

8. Steven H. Gifis, *Law Dictionary* (Woodbury: Barron's Educational Series, Inc., 1975), s.v. "covenant."

9. *Ibid.* Emphasis in original.

10. *Ibid.*

> For this *is* the covenant that I will make with the house of Israel after those days, saith the Lord; I will put my *laws* into their mind, and write them in their hearts; and I will be to them a God, and they shall be to me a people:

This passage speaks specifically of "laws." If there were no laws in the Gospel of Jesus Christ, there would be nothing to write into the minds and hearts of God's people. In truth, there are *mutual* promises stated in this passage. Men must have God's laws in their minds (an *intellectual* understanding of His Gospel) and in their hearts (a *love* for, and devotion to, Him and His gospel), if they expect to be His people and receive the benefits of having Him as their God.

The fact that salvation is by grace (Eph. 2:8-9) does not negate the existence of laws and ordinances in the Gospel. Paul notes the relationship between the gift of God's grace and the efficacy of law in Romans 3:31 (NASB): "Do we then nullify the Law [or, *law*] through faith? May it never be! On the contrary, we establish the Law." It is certain that the Apostles never established the Law of Moses, so what Law does Paul refer to in this verse, if not the Law of the Gospel?

If there were no laws in the Gospel, there would be no sin (Rom. 5:13). Sin is defined as the transgression of law (1 John 3:4). If there were no sin, there would be no necessity to warn Men against it. Christ and His Apostles wouldn't have bothered to preach against sin, since there would be no such thing, and Satan's temptations would be superfluous. It would be a waste of time to tempt believers into committing acts that are not sin (because they violate no laws).

But this is not biblical reality. That the greatest call of the Bible is to repent proves unequivocally that the Gospel contains laws.[11]

The Fulfillment and Abrogation of the Law of Moses

Many passages cited by Evangelicals in their attempt to prove that there are no laws in the Gospel actually relate to the changes in God's

11. Some Evangelicals (e.g., Bob George, syndicated radio evangelist from Dallas) teach that the only law of the Gospel is faith, and that repentance only means to turn from unbelief. But John stated exactly what "His commandment" is: "And this is His commandment, that we believe in the name of His Son Jesus Christ, and love one another, just as He *commanded* us" (1 John 3:23, NASB, emphasis added). These two commandments include all the law and the prophets (Matt. 22:36-40).

law that occurred when the Law of Moses was fulfilled by Christ's great and last sacrifice. The Law of Moses was filled with symbolism intended to lead Israel to Christ, whose sacrifice would provide the means for their justification. When Christ came, the preparatory law, the Law of Moses, was replaced with the higher law of Faith (see Gal. 3:23-25).

For many Jews, this was not an easy transition. Paul preached in Galatia against false teachings about the continued efficacy of the Law of Moses, specifically its requirement of circumcision (Gal. 2:1-14). The Galatians were then being confronted by false teachers who claimed that, to be saved, the Gentiles had to obey certain Mosaic requirements, especially circumcision (see Gal. 5:1-3).

Paul taught against this misconception, explaining that salvation does not come by the "works of the law [of Moses]" (Gal. 2:16, brackets added); otherwise, God would have had Men obtain salvation through obedience to some law (e.g., the Law of Moses) instead of requiring the sacrifice of His Only Begotten Son (Gal. 2:21; 3:21). But Men are unable to abide by law without making some mistakes. They have all sinned, and hence require a Savior (Gal. 3:22).

Paul also explained that Abraham received the promise of salvation through faith in Christ (Gal. 3:7-9). He quoted Habakkuk 2:4 ("the just shall live by his faith") to prove that faith was the basis for salvation even in the Old Testament (Gal. 3:11), then noted that the Law of Moses was given 430 years after Abraham and was not intended to change the promise of salvation given to that great patriarch (Gal. 3:16-18). Instead, the Law of Moses was given "because of transgressions" (Gal. 3:19). It established a strict standard and was intended to school Men in obedience so they would be better prepared to live the law of faith in Christ (Gal. 3:24-26).

Nothing in Paul's teachings supports the Evangelical doctrine of salvation without obedience to law. The fact that no law is sufficient by itself to redeem Men does not mean they will be saved without law. The fact that the Law of Moses was fulfilled and abrogated does not mean that the Gospel has no laws. As stated in Romans 3:31, Paul *established* law. He explained to the Galatians exactly what law he established in Galatians 5:19-25. That passage reiterates all the teachings of Christ, both sins of commission (Gal. 5:19-21), and sins of omission (Gal. 5:22-25). Clearly, when the schoolmaster (the Law of Moses) was done away

(Gal. 3:24-25), God intended that Men should *school themselves*, not play hooky for the rest of eternity.

No inspired writer has ever suggested that fulfillment of the Law of Moses left no laws in the Gospel. Though Christ fulfilled the Law of Moses and freed Men from its burdensome requirements, He taught that true liberty is exercised *through* law, not without it (John 8:31-32). Likewise, though America is considered a free country, its freedom comes through law, not by its absence.

Living under the Law of the Gospel, rather than the Law of Moses, may be compared to matriculation at a university. Early schooling (comparable to the Law of Moses) subjects the student to strict and often burdensome rules, the purpose of which is to instill good work habits. Upon reaching the university level (comparable to the law of faith), the student is freed from these petty requirements. However, he is *not* freed from the necessity of passing tests and meeting the requirements for graduation. If Men do not impose good work habits on themselves (by putting them "into their mind, and [writing] them in their hearts"), they will fail the test of life, and miss the goal of salvation because they misunderstood and misused their liberty.

Differentiating Mormonism from the Evangelical Gospel

To pinpoint where LDS teachings about the Gospel diverge from Evangelical soteriology (the branch of theology that deals with doctrines of salvation) is a difficult task. To clarify the issue, Evangelical and Mormon answers to a series of questions about salvation are given below.

> **Question 1:** "Did Christ die for the sins of all Men?"
> **Evangelical Answer:** "Yes."
> **Mormon Answer:** "Yes."

It is without contest that Christ, through His atoning sacrifice, paid the penalty for all the sins of all Men who have or ever will live upon this earth (John 1:29; Rom. 5:18; 1 Tim. 2:6; Heb. 2:9; 1 John 2:2). Most Evangelicals do not understand that Mormons agree with them on this point. Some have claimed that "[t]he LDS Church teaches that Christ died for Adam's transgression, not for ours."[12] Such statements evidence

12. Trivanovich, *Speaking the Truth in Love,* 33.

a significant misunderstanding of the Mormon faith. While Mormons do believe that Christ died for Adam's transgression, they unequivocally assert that He also died for all the sins of humanity (see Alma 34:8-14).

Question 2: "Then, are all Men saved?"
Evangelical Answer: "No."
Mormon Answer: "No."

Although Christ died for the sins of all Men, it is clear that *not all* will be saved (Heb. 9:28; Rom. 5:15). Salvation is *conditional* (see, e.g., 1 John 1:7 (emphasis added): "But *if* we walk in the light, as he is in the light, . . . the blood of Jesus Christ his Son cleanseth us from all sin").[13] Mormons and Evangelicals may not agree on what those conditions are, but both acknowledge that a response by Man to Christ is necessary (even pure Calvinists, who believe that the response is prompted solely by Christ).

Question 3: "What must Men do to be saved?"
Evangelical Answer: "Have faith in Christ."
Mormon Answer: "Have faith in Christ."

Many Evangelicals are surprised to learn that their understanding of the Bible's answer to this question is the same as Mormon doctrine. Some argue that Mormons do not really teach this truth, but the fact is that Mormon theology is in agreement with Evangelical teaching up to this point. The New Testament makes it clear that Men are saved "through faith" (Eph. 2:8). However, that is not the end of the inquiry.

Question 4: "What is faith?"

Evangelical Answer: "The essence of faith consists in believing and receiving what God has revealed, and may be defined as that trust in the God of the Scriptures and in Jesus Christ whom He has sent, which receives Him as Lord and Savior and impels to loving obedience and good works."[14]

---

13. On this point even Walter Martin agrees. Apparently unaware that his position expresses Mormon doctrine with considerable accuracy, he states: "Paul never taught that the reconciliation provided by God the Father would eventually be accepted by all men. [Contrary to Dr. Martin's misinformation about Mormonism, Mormons have never taught this either] He taught that the grace of God provided redemption, so that potentially all men might be saved if they repented and accepted the gospel." *Maze of Mormonism,* 254, (emphasis in original).

> **Mormon Answer:** "Faith is the assurance which men have of the existence of things which they have not seen, and the principal of action in all intelligent beings. If men were duly to consider themselves, and turn their thoughts and reflections to the operations of their own minds, they would readily discover that it is faith, and faith only, which is the moving cause of all action in them; . . ."[15]

These two answers have at least one similarity. Each recognizes that faith plays a significant role in human behavior. But the real distinction between Mormonism and the Evangelical gospel is revealed by the last question in this series:

> **Question 5:** "To be saved, do Men have to obey the commandments of that God in whom they have faith?"
> **Evangelical Answer:** "No!"
> **Mormon Answer:** "Yes!"

Mormons teach that salvation comes when Man's faith results in his obedience to God (Heb. 5:9: "And being made perfect, he became the author of eternal salvation unto all them that obey him"). Evangelicals teach that *permanent* salvation comes *before* Man's faith is demonstrated by any form of obedience.[16] In the Evangelical economy, Man is eternally saved *first*, after which obedience will (or may) follow.

While the intent—obeying God—may be the same, the practical differences between these two positions are enormous. The Evangelical answer amounts to putting the cart before the horse in a spiritually disastrous misinterpretation of the Gospel message. Mormons reject the Evangelical position as unbiblical, and believe instead that Men must learn to live *like* God before they will be privileged to live *with* Him.

Mormon doctrine on this point should not be misconstrued, however. The difference between Mormonism and the Evangelical gospel is more subtle than many imagine.

---

14. *The New Scofield Study Bible,* 1731 (footnote to Heb. 11:39). While many different definitions of faith are given by Evangelical scholars, this one expresses the most universally accepted elements of the Evangelical concept.
15. Joseph Smith, Jr, "Lecture First" in *A Compilation Containing the Lectures on Faith,* comp. N.B. Lundwald (Salt Lake City: Bookcraft, Inc., n.d.), 7.
16. John F. MacArthur, Jr., *Faith Works: The Gospel According to the Apostles* (Dallas: Word Publishing, 1993), 24 (citing Eph. 2:10).

Mormons do not teach that Men must obey a difficult and complex set of rules for a defined period of time in order to merit salvation. Instead they teach that, to be saved, a person who believes in Christ must *confess openly* that they are *willing* to obey His commandments (Rom. 10:9). This is done through ordinances that God has established as symbols of commitment to Him, declaratory acts that are performed in front of witnesses.

God has made salvation surprisingly easy to obtain. All that is required to step into the light of His Spirit and taste the joy of communion with Him through the Holy Ghost is a degree of faith in Him manifested by a willingness to obey Him and confirmed through an open commitment to do so. From then on, Men remain saved . . . as long as they *continue* to obey God. If they falter from that course, they must recommit themselves to a life of obedience in order to reestablish the relationship with God that constitutes their salvation (1 John 2:1).

Though they require self-discipline, God's laws are fundamentally simple and easy to obey. Of course, it takes many years to learn perfect obedience, but God extends to each person the time he needs to repent (e.g., Rev. 2:20-23). Thus, a man can and must strive always not to "live the rest of *his* time in the flesh to the lusts of men, but to the will of God" (1 Pet. 4:1-2). If they do that, Men can be assured that God's grace is sufficient to save them, though their sins have been as scarlet (Isa. 1:18).

The Lordship Salvation Controversy

In the American Evangelical movement a major controversy has flared that relates directly to the issue of obedience and *who* may be the beneficiaries of permanent salvation. Those who espouse what has reluctantly been dubbed *Lordship Salvation* rebel at the apparent insincerity of many who claim salvation by grace without obedience. They assert that real faith *inevitably* produces a changed life.[17] According to this school of thought, genuine believers may stumble and fall, but they are dedicated to following Christ and *will* persevere in that effort.[18] Hence, they conclude that those who later turn away from Christ, or show no change in their lifestyle as a result of their confession of faith, were *never* actually saved.[19]

17. MacArthur, *Faith Works,* 24 (citing 2 Cor. 5:17).
18. MacArthur, *Faith Works,* 25 (citing 1 Cor. 1:8).

In its practical application, though close to the Mormon (and biblical) view, this position can be extremely confusing. If it can be proven later that a convert was never really saved when, at the moment of his conversion, he truly thought he believed in Christ enough to receive the permanent salvation promised by Evangelicals, the issues of salvation are thrown into a state of chaos. If one does not have saving faith without demonstrating obedience, and saving faith is necessary for permanent salvation, it follows that a demonstration of obedience is also necessary for salvation. But that is the very result Evangelicals wish to aviod.

Those who reject Lordship Salvation (the *No-lordship* camp), note that pistis (translated "faith" in the New Testament) means "to trust." They claim that trusting Christ means to accept and rely on what He did for Men. Thus, they teach that, to be saved, Men need merely trust that Christ has done all their obedience for them. At the moment they adopt this view (an act the No-lordship camp regards as so epiphenomenal that it couldn't possibly be classified as a meritorious work), they are instantly and permanently saved.

An example of this teaching comes from former radio evangelist and pastor of the Church of the Open Door, Dr. G. Michael Cocoris. He explains that to be saved Men need only believe (that is, "trust") in Christ, and nothing else. "[Trust] in Christ, plus nothing else, for salvation," is his message.[20] "Depend on Him for the forgiveness of sin. Rely on Him, plus nothing else, to get you to heaven."[21]

In the face of such a call to Christ, one cannot help but feel he has been invited to a feast without directions to its location. If a man is not saved and wants to be, and he is told that he must do *nothing* except "depend" and "rely" on Christ, he will naturally think: "If I do absolutely nothing, how will my condition change? I wasn't saved the last time I did nothing. How do I depend and rely on Christ without doing *anything*?"

Dr. Cocoris gives no clear answer to these questions. He only explains what a new believer should do *after* he is saved.[22] How one depends and relies on Christ in order to obtain salvation is not explained by him, nor by any other No-lordship advocate.[23] Indeed, the idea itself is anathema to those who call on Men to do *nothing* in order to be saved.

---

19. MacArthur, *Faith Works,* 25 (citing 1 John 2:19).
20. G. Michael Cocoris, *Lordship Salvation: Is it Biblical?* (Dallas: Redención Viva, 1983), 18.
21. *Ibid.*
22. *Ibid.*

The noted Evangelical scholar C. I. Scofield tried to shed some light on this issue in a footnote to Romans 3:31, as follows:

> The sinner upholds the law in its right use and honor by confessing his guilt and just condemnation. Christ, on the sinner's behalf, upholds the law by obediently keeping its precepts [citations], and by enduring its penalty, death.[24]

Does this mean Men need merely confess that they are sinners and worthy of condemnation in order to be saved? What of commitment? What of obedience? Can a complete abandonment of self-control be equated with depending and relying on Christ? Can Men really leave the helm of their Soul to the winds of fate and expect it to arrive at the port of Salvation?

Unfortunately, some who espouse No-lordship teachings do so precisely *because* it justifies continuing in sin.[25] The benefits of a plan of salvation that does not require the obedience of its recipients as a condition to permanently conferring on them its greatest blessing, are immediately obvious to those who love sin more than God. No-lordship advocates may not intend such a system, but the gospel they preach invites what some Evangelicals have labeled *easy believism*—condoning, or at least countenancing (though not advocating), lasciviousness in the name of grace. For biblical condemnation of that approach, none is more to the point than Jude 4, which warns of "ungodly men, turning the grace of our God into lasciviousness."[26]

Both Lordship and No-lordship Evangelicals try to distinguish their gospel from such unadulterated license, but the more they require evidence of true faith in the form of obedience, the closer they come to the truth they adamantly reject. There is a glaring and unresolved inconsistency between their position that Men need not obey God in order to be saved and their effort to encourage obedience among believers. Witness, for example, the following attempt to explain Evangelical soteriology:

> The Bible does not teach "believe in God, do what you want, and you're saved." Having faith in Christ does not mean having an intellectual belief in the facts. Even the demons believe and they

23. MacArthur, *Faith Works,* 49.
24. *The New Scofield Study Bible,* 1591 (footnote to Romans 3:31).
25. MacArthur, *Faith Works,* 123-24.
26. See, also, David Hocking, *Grace and God Works: A Study of Titus* 2:11-15 (*La Mirada: Biola Hour Ministries,* 1989), 3-6, 9.

> tremble (James 2:19)! The Bible urges us to "believe" in Christ for salvation. The Greek word for "believe" (*pisteuo*) means to "place trust in."
>
> True faith is trusting in Jesus Christ alone for our salvation. The response to true faith will be a desire to obey Him—*commit* yourself to a lifetime relationship of obedience to Christ (Eph. 2:10, Rom. 6:17-18). It is important to understand that it is not this commitment that earns you eternal life. Our good works cannot earn acceptance before God because we are imperfect and therefore do not live up to His standard of perfection (Isa. 64:6). True faith is simply the hand that receives God's free gift of eternal life.
>
> Nevertheless, salvation is far from "easy believism"![27]

There is not the slightest indication in this rhetoric of whether or not Men must actually change their behavior (in response to their desire to obey God) in order to receive the benefits of salvation. Nor is there any hint of what would happen if they made no change as a result of their professed belief, or if they ceased to obey once they entered upon a course of obedience. Isn't this the very "easy believism" decried in the last sentence quoted above?

The truth is that placing trust in Christ means relying on *what He has told Men to do*. In other words, relying and depending on Christ means trusting Him enough to obey Him.

Some No-lordship teachers accept their gospel as a form of easy believism, and claim that God will eventually bring the saved sinner around to obedience.[28] This view is at least consistent with the general Evangelical position that obedience is not necessary for salvation. However, the expectations of these teachers are certain to be frustrated. Their hopes will always be shortcircuited because any failure to recognize that Men *must* obey God in order to be saved will undercut the attempt. The only exception is when a No-lordship believer finally awakens to the realization that a continuing life of sin is *not* going to result in his salvation and decides to change his behavior.

To make matters worse, many Lordship as well as No-lordship teachers claim that Men, being imperfect, *cannot* live up to God's standard of

27. Trivanovich, *Speaking the Truth in Love,* 37-38.

28. This appears to be the view of Dr. Cocoris, in *Lordship Salvation,* and of Dr. Charles Stanley, "In Touch Ministries," Atlanta, Georgia.

perfection.[29] The necessity of learning obedience, which Mormons espouse, is viewed as "Mission Impossible" by these teachers.[30]

This position is clearly contrary to the Bible (1 Cor. 10:13), and provides yet another disincentive to obedience. If Men are told they do not have to obey Christ in order to be saved, most will lack the motivation to bring their behavior in line with His. It is even easier to be overcome by evil if Men are told that obedience to God is *impossible*. Why should anyone try to live the commandments, if to do so is both unnecessary *and* impossible?!

The result of this theology is best exemplified by the alleged salvation of Larry Flint, who continued to publish *Hustler* magazine while claiming to be born again. Obviously, the gospel Larry Flint accepted is one taught by No-lordship advocates.

This form of the gospel was condemned by the Lord as far back as the prophet Jeremiah, who said of certain false prophets, "they say unto every one that walketh after the imagination of his own heart, No evil shall come upon you" (Jer. 23:16-22[31] see, also, Psalms 119:155).

The Book of Mormon prophesied against radical No-lordship teachers in the latter days (2 Nephi 28:8):

> And there shall also be many which shall say: Eat, drink, and be merry; nevertheless, fear God—he will justify in committing a little sin; yea, lie a little, take the advantage of one because of his words, dig a pit for thy neighbor; there is no harm in this; and do all these things, for tomorrow we die; and if it so be that we are guilty, God will beat us with a few stripes, and at last we shall be saved in the kingdom of God.

While those in the No-lordship camp would not admit to speaking these exact words, Nephi's description is an honest summary of their teachings, and agrees with Dr MacArthur's indictment of the No-lordship gospel.[32] In the early Church, such false teaching arose as a form of liberty in Christ. It was soundly condemned by the Apostles (see 2 Peter 2, especially verses 18-19; Gal. 6:7-8; James 2:14-26; 1 John 3:7-10; and Jude 4).

---

29. John F. MacArthur, Jr, *The Gospel According to Jesus* (Panorama City: Word of Grace, 1988), 177.

30. Trivanovich, *Speaking the Truth in Love,* 48.

31. This passage was directed to believers. In fact, it was God's word against the "prophets" of Jeremiah's time (Jer. 23:13-14, NASB).

Paul prophesied that teachers having "a form of godliness" but who practiced sin and denied "the power" of godliness, would reappear in the last days (2 Tim. 3:1-7). The term *godliness* literally means "God-likeness," that is, being or behaving like God. The power of godliness is denied by No-lordship teachers who claim that obedience to the laws of God is unnecessary for salvation. What they are saying is that being or behaving like God (Godlike-ness) has *no power* to save Men.

In the No-lordship system the concept of trust in Jesus Christ has been transformed into the passive acceptance of that glorious gift which unrepentant Men suppose they can snatch from the bleeding hands of the Savior. The faith of those who have such expectations is indistinguishable from the belief of demons. "You believe that God is one. You do well; the demons also believe, and shudder" (James 2:19, NASB). Why doesn't the demons' belief in God give *them* "the hand that receives God's free gift of eternal life?"[33] What is the difference between the belief that saves and the sincere belief expressed by demons (Matt. 8:29)?

The answer is obvious (see Matt. 7:21; Prov. 20:11; Rom. 2:13; and James 1:22). It is *deeds* that make the difference (Ps. 28:4; Isa. 59:18; Jer. 25:14; Luke 23:41; Rom. 2:5-8). The reason demons are not saved as a result of their belief in Christ is they do not obey His commandments! Men can expect no different treatment if they merely acknowledge God without obeying Him.

Those who believe in Lordship Salvation, on the other hand, have an excellent understanding of what faith really is,[34] but they make the same mistake all Evangelicals do. They believe in salvation *without* obedience. If it is not necessary to obey God's commandments, why is *any* obedience necessary? If obedience is necessary to some extent, how will a little obedience meet the demands of a just and perfect God (see, e.g., James 2:10-11).

There are only two tenable positions in the debate over obedience as a requirement for salvation. Either Men *must* obey God in order to be saved, or they may be saved without obeying Him *at all*. No middle ground exists. If God will countenance *any* sin, He must countenance all sin. If He will countenance no sin, *any* sin will keep a man out of His Kingdom.

32. MacArthur, *Faith Works,* 28-29.

33. Trivanovich, *Speaking the Truth in Love,* 38.

34. MacArthur, "Without Faith it is Impossible to Please Him," Chap. 3 in *Faith Works,* 37-54.

Those who espouse Lordship Salvation recognize the evil in saying that God will countenance all sin, but they refuse to accept the Bible's affirmation that He won't countenance any sin (Deut. 23:14; Gal. 5:19-21; Eph. 5:5; Matt. 5:48).

Permanent Salvation

The real flaw that leads Evangelicals into the Lordship debate is the idea that salvation is *permanent* once it is obtained. That notion is based on the idea that Christ's blood cleanses believers of all the sins they *have* committed, all they *are* committing, and all they *will yet* commit, at the moment faith is first generated in them. What follows inevitably from this assumption is that believers are free from then on to commit any sin they choose. Lordship teachers accept that premise, but deny its inevitable conclusion. Thus, they are drawn into a theological dilemma.

David Hocking, in *Grace and Good Works: A Study of Titus 2:11-15* (La Mirada: Biola Hour Ministries, 1989), 5-6, identifies this dilemma in the following words:

> If one is yielded to Christ, there should be evidence—dare we say "good works"? Some Bible teachers believe that if there is no evidence of such yieldedness in an individual's life, that person is not truly a Christian.
>
> On the other hand, most evangelical scholars would also agree that an individual fully yielded to the Lordship of Christ would show virtually perfect behavior. Is there a Christian dead or alive who has ever demonstrated such perfection?
>
> The controversy over this issue, then, often centers on what is good works and how much good works "proves" an individual to be a Christian. The inevitable result of such an argument is a return to the old "formula" approach to pleasing God: If I just do this or that, then I am pleasing God. Frankly, I don't think theologians will ever resolve this problem.

Those who espouse Lordship Salvation also recognize this quandary, but offer no solution to it. In *Faith Works: The Gospel According to the Apostles* (Dallas: Word Publishing, 1993), 31, John F. MacArthur, Jr., the principle advocate of Lordship Salvation, states:

> Of course Christians sin. They disobey. They fail. We *all* fall far short of perfection in this life (Phil. 3:12-5 [sic]). "We all stumble

> in many ways" (James 3:2). Even the most mature and godly Christians "see in a mirror dimly" (1 Cor. 13:12). Our minds need constant renewing (Rom. 12:2). But that doesn't invalidate the truth that salvation in some real sense makes us practically righteous. The same epistle that describes the Christian's hatred of and battle with sin (Rom. 7:8-24) first says that believers are free from sin and slaves of righteousness (6:18). The same apostle who wrote, "If we say that we have no sin, we are deceiving ourselves" (1 John 1:8) later wrote, "No one who abides in Him sins" (3:6). In one place he says, "If we say that we have not sinned, we make Him a liar, and His word is not in us" (1:10), and in another, "No one who is born of God practices sin, because His seed abides in Him" (3:9).
>
> There's a true paradox—not an inconsistency—in those truths. . . .

Thus, Evangelicals are led once more by Greek notions of theology. Instead of rejecting false doctrine because it has led to an unresolvable inconsistency, they wrap it in mystery and label it a "paradox." The truth is that there are no paradoxes in the Bible or in the universe God created. Those who refuse to let go of a false doctrine in the face of its inconsistencies resort to Hellenistic rationalization rather than change their personal theology.

Of course Christians sin. But the belief that they will *remain* saved when they do so lies at the heart of Evangelical misunderstanding about the Gospel. The idea that believers can sin and still be considered righteous in God's eyes because they have received the benefits of a once-and-for-all justification, is tantamount to the heresy of *antinomianism* (the belief that behavior is unrelated to faith). It is theologically impossible to reject *antinomianism*, as Lordship believers profess to do,[35] and still teach that Men are saved by grace *without* the necessity of obedience to God.

Rather than admit that believers can only be saved as they stand in obedience, Lordship teachers look for some special quality in the nature of a "true" believer's faith ("saving faith").[36] Unfortunately, the Bible doesn't teach that there is a magical intensity of faith that, if experienced at a single moment in time, will result in permanent salvation apart from obeying

35. MacArthur, *Faith Works,* 91-94.

God. There is nothing about the faith of one convert that results in permanent salvation, despite his disobedience, while another, who experiences the same conviction, must be told that he was *never* saved because his disobedience is more significant or enduring.

If *anyone* obeys God, he can obtain salvation. If *anyone* disobeys Him, he cannot, unless he repents and learns to obey Him. That is justice, and God is always just, as well as being "the justifier of him which believeth in Jesus" (Rom. 3:26).

John expressed this truth as follows: (2 John 9, NASB emphasis added):

> Anyone who goes too far and does not *abide* in the teaching of Christ, does not have God; the one who abides in the teaching, he has both the Father and the Son[37].
>
> Christ gave the same message in the Parable of the Sower (Matt. 13:3-23; Mark 4:3-20; Luke 8:4-15). According to that Parable, believers who fall away are allowing Satan, the cares of the world or their own weakness in the face of tribulation, to destroy the faith they once had. The difference is not found in any quality intrinsic to the seed of faith scattered by the Sower. It is found in the behavioral response of the soil in which the seed is planted (see, e.g., Matt. 13:5-8).

Another Gospel?

Neither Lordship nor No-lordship teaching successfully deals with the basic flaw in the Evangelical gospel, the failure to acknowledge that Men must obey God in order to be saved. The Gospel of Jesus Christ is the power of God unto salvation (Rom. 1:16), and it operates on the lives of Men through laws Men must obey in order to avoid God's vengeance or just punishment (2 Thess. 1:7-8). The notion that the Gospel demands nothing more of unrepentant sinners than the acceptance of a free gift may sound good to Evangelicals, but it is not supported by the Bible, and will *not* result in their salvation.

---

36. MacArthur, *Faith Works,* 166-172.

37. To "abide" in the teaching of Christ means to maintain obedience to His commandments on a daily basis, to live the Gospel or walk in the light (1 John 1:7). See, *MacArthur, Faith Works,* 167.

The Mormon gospel teaches that Men must strive to obey God's commandments in order to be and to remain saved. No one wants to hear that they must overcome their carnal nature and obey the commandments of God in order to obtain salvation. Even with John's reassurance that His commandments are not grievous (1 John 5:3), and Christ's promise that His yoke is easy and His burden is light (Matt. 11:30), it is difficult for Men to take up their cross, and follow Him (Matt. 10:38).

The Evangelical gospel teaches that permanent salvation occurs before any obedience on the part of the believer, and is independent of such obedience. True faith, they say, *will*, or *may* (depending on whether one adopts the Lordship or the No-lordship gospel), impel the new believer to obedience, but Men do not have to obey God in order to be saved. In fact, they are usually told it is impossible to do so (though Lordship teachers at least say they should persist in the effort).

The difference between these two messages is vital. It has been summarized from the Evangelical viewpoint, with a kind of ironic accuracy, as follows: "The Mormon gospel is centered on man trying to obtain salvation through obedience. The [Evangelical] gospel is centered on what Jesus Christ has done for our salvation."[38] Unfortunately, this couplet misses the point. "What Jesus Christ has done for our salvation" is to make it available through obedience to Him.

In what direction is the Evangelical gospel taking Men? Which of the great forces that influence Men has always taught that they do not need to obey God in order to get what they want? Satan told Eve in the Garden of Eden that there would be no consequences of her disobedience, she would not die if she partook of the forbidden fruit (Gen. 3:1-6), but Adam and Eve experienced an inescapable death by following Satan's advice instead of obeying God (Gen. 5:5). The same advice will condemn all who seek salvation through a gospel that requires no obedience to the One who issued the first command to Adam and Eve.

John admonished the early church (1 John 3:7-8, emphasis added):

> Little children, let no man deceive you: he that *doeth* righteousness is righteous, even as he is righteous. He that committeth sin is of the devil; for the devil sinneth from the beginning.

---

38. Trivanovich, *Speaking the Truth in Love,* p. 34.

Conclusion

It has always been and will ever be Satan who is the promoter of any plan of salvation that offers the fruits of salvation while disclaiming the necessity of obeying God. Satan preached that gospel to Eve in the Garden (Gen. 3:1-7), it was condemned by Paul in Galatians 1:8-9, and it must be rejected by Evangelicals today if they are to find salvation, and stop preaching "another gospel."

6

The Gospel of Faith

After an exposition on obedience as a requirement for salvation, Evangelicals could feel vindicated in their claim that Mormon soteriology is a system of *works righteousness* like the Pharisees had in Christ's day. But that would be a grave misconception. Sadly, a great deal of Evangelical criticism directed at Mormon theology is the result of just such misinformation and misunderstanding.[1]

Peter taught concerning Jesus Christ: "Neither is there salvation in any other: for there is none other name under heaven given among men, whereby we must be saved" (Acts 4:12). Most Evangelicals do not realize that Mormons emphatically teach the same doctrine (see, e.g., Mosiah 3:17; 5:8). These passages negate any possibility that Men can get to Heaven on their own.

This chapter will attempt to dispel some of the misunderstandings that lie at the heart of Evangelical criticism of Mormon soteriology. In so doing, it will provide an explanation of the Gospel of Jesus Christ that places obedience in its appropriate biblical perspective as an element of the Law of Faith by which Men are saved. Before examining the Gospel of Jesus Christ, however, it is helpful to identify its goal. If the goal is not in view, passages that relate to its attainment can be misinterpreted.

From and for What Are Men Saved?

In the Bible, to be *saved* means to be spared from the ultimate consequences of spiritual mistakes. "And she will bear a Son; and you shall call His name Jesus, for it is He who will *save* His people *from their sins*"

1. See, e.g., the complete jumble of misinterpretation and the lack of correlation between quotations that appears in Walter Martin, "Salvation, Blood Atonement and Eternal Judgment," Chapter 9 in *The Maze of Mormonism,* 237, et seq.

(Matt. 1:21, NASB, emphasis added; see, also, Eph. 1:7; Col. 1:13-14; and 1 Thess. 1:10). Since the "wages of sin *is* death" (Rom. 6:23), the ultimate goal of the Gospel is to save Men from *death*.

Death is simply a form of separation (Isa. 59:2), and two forms are identified in scripture. Each is a consequence of sin. *Physical Death* is the separation of Man's spirit from his physical body (James 2:26). It resulted from Adam's transgression, which caused the Fall. *Spiritual Death* is the separation of Man from God (Isa. 59:2; Ps. 51:10-12; Rom. 8:5-10), also a consequence of the Fall, but one that is directly connected to Man's own transgressions. The "good news" of the Gospel is that God has provided a way for Men to be saved from these two forms of death or separation.

Salvation from Physical Death. 1 Corinthians 15 focuses on Christ's triumph over Physical Death through His resurrection, and makes the following promise to all Men (1 Cor. 15:20-22, NASB):

> But now Christ has been raised from the dead, the first fruits of those who are asleep.
>
> For since by a man *came* death, by a man also *came* the resurrection of the dead.
>
> For as in Adam all die, so also in Christ all shall be made alive.

No Man can escape the result of Adam's transgression, so there is nothing Men can do to overcome Physical Death. One aspect of the good news from God is that Christ rose from the dead and brought to pass a physical resurrection whereby the bodies of all Men will be made "alive" (that is, physically immortal), thus defeating the bonds of Physical Death.

Physical Death was not part of God's original creation. God made Men physically immortal in the Garden of Eden. Physical Death entered the world because of a sin committed by Adam and Eve. Christ's atonement overcame Physical Death making it possible for all to return to the original condition of their creation—immortality. All Men, even unbelievers, will receive Christ's free gift of salvation from Physical Death (Acts 24:15), for Christ is "the Savior of *all* men, especially of believers" (1 Tim. 4:10, NASB, emphasis added).

Salvation from Spiritual Death. While salvation from Physical Death is a "free gift" (Rom. 5:12-15), salvation from Spiritual Death, though a gift, is not free in the sense of being unconditional. Unlike Physical Death, Man's *own* transgressions cause Spiritual Death. Justice demands, and the Bible clearly teaches, that there are conditions Men must meet in order to overcome the separation from God caused by their own sins (Rom. 6:23).

Indeed, if salvation from Spiritual Death were not conditional, it would be impossible to distinguish Heaven from Hell.

Eternal Life. Salvation from Spiritual Death is frequently referred to in the Bible as eternal or everlasting *life* (see, e.g., Matt. 19:16; 25:46; Mark 10:17, 30; Luke 18:18; John 3:15; 4:36; 5:39; 6:54, 68; 12:25; 17:2-3; Rom. 2:7; 5:21; 6:23; 1 Tim. 6:12, 19; Titus 1:2; 3:7; Jude 21). "Everlasting life" and "eternal life" are identical. The Greek word in each instance is *aionios*, literally translated "age-lasting." When the Bible uses the word "life" (with or without the modifying adjective), it is usually speaking of salvation from Spiritual Death (see, e.g., Ezek. 33:11-19; 1 John 1:2; 5:11).

There are a variety of rewards that await those who do good (Matt. 10:42; John 14:2; Rev. 22:12), but the greatest of the gifts of God is eternal life (Mark 10:29-30). Eternal life is **to know God** (John 17:3), and ultimately to live with Him (Rev. 21:1 to 22:6). To know God, the separation between God and Man known as Spiritual Death must be overcome. This is possible to a limited degree in this life when Men know God (1 John 4:7) and have His Spirit with them (1 John 3:24), but eternal life in the sense of living with God in heaven represents Man's *ultimate* salvation, and will not be experienced until after the resurrection.

The scriptures also describe salvation from Spiritual Death as "inheriting the kingdom of God" and similar promises of residence in the realm where God dwells. Some Evangelicals teach that there is a difference between "inheriting the kingdom of God" and "inheriting eternal life," but Matthew 25:31-46 (NASB) dispels that misconception.

It indicates that the Lord will judge all nations, including the righteous and the wicked, "Then the King will say to those on His right [the righteous], 'Come, you who are blessed of My Father, *inherit the kingdom* prepared for you from the foundation of the world.'" (verse 34, emphasis added). Verse 46 (emphasis added) contrasts the fate of the righteous and the wicked, saying: "these [the wicked] will go away into eternal punishment, but the righteous into *eternal life*."

Thus, the reward of the righteous is described in one verse as going "into eternal life," and in the other as inheriting "the kingdom." Clearly, these two rewards are equivalent (see, also, Col. 3:23-24). The essence of Spiritual Death is separation from God, and Men are not separated from God when they are living with Him in His kingdom.

Evangelicals speak of the "tenses of salvation," claiming they *have been saved* from the guilt and penalty of sin, *are being saved* from the habit or pollution of sin, and *will be saved* from the result or presence of sin.[2] This theological rhetoric, however nicely phrased, can be misleading. Men always feel guilty when they commit sin, unless their conscience has been completely desensitized ("seared" 1 Tim. 4:2). Guilt is God's Early Warning System to help Men repent and live righteously (Rom. 2:14-15). One should not ignore its presence on the claim that they were saved at some time in the past. When guilt is present, sin is usually the cause, and there is no salvation *in* sin.

Sin has serious earthly consequences as well—physical, emotional, and legal. God wants Men to be happy, and the reason He has forbidden sin is that it has the opposite effect—here and hereafter. Guilt and earthly penalties for sin may seem harsh, but they are intended to benefit Man. They encourage repentance and allow Men to exercise and develop their moral agency.

Salvation involves something much more serious than earthly penalties for sin. It involves relief from God's *ultimate* punishment for sin (Matt. 1:21; Rom. 6:22-23). The big stakes are not the earthly concerns, but Man's ability to live the rest of eternity with God. To achieve that end, Men must be clean, for no unclean thing can enter God's presence (Deut. 23:14; Gal. 5:19-21; Eph. 5:5), and nothing that would defile His Kingdom or detract from its perfection will be allowed to enter (Rev. 21:27). Therefore, Men must learn to live in sinless perfection (Matt. 5:48), and they must be cleansed from the mistakes they make before and during the learning process (Job 25:4).

A definitive statement of the plan God has provided to accomplish that end ("the Plan of Salvation") is contained in Ephesians 2:8-9, a popular passage among Evangelicals:

> For by grace are ye saved through faith; and that not of yourselves: *it is* the gift of God: Not of works, lest any man should boast.

Mormons believe this statement as strongly as do Evangelicals. However, they disagree with the interpretation of it offered by Evangelicals. Because these verses contain a summary of God's all-important plan for the salvation of Men, it is essential to have an accurate exposition of their meaning.

---

2. See, e.g., *The New Scofield Study Bible,* 1586 (footnote to Rom. 1:16).

"By Grace Are Ye Saved . . . and That Not of Yourselves"

The atoning sacrifice of Jesus Christ is frequently referred to in the Bible as the "grace" (Ps. 84:11; Prov. 3:34; Acts 15:11; Rom. 3:24) or "gift" (Rom. 5:17-19; 2 Cor. 9:15; Heb. 6:4; 1 Pet. 4:10) of God. Mormons believe Christ, the Son of God, infinite and eternal (Alma 34:9-14), suffered the penalty of sin for all Men, to make His grace available as an unmerited gift offered to all.

That Mormons believe in salvation by grace will come as a shock to those who know no more about Mormonism than Dr. Walter Martin revealed in his grossly slanted critique, *The Maze of Mormonism* (Ventura: Regal Books, 1978). The real differences between Mormonism and Evangelical teachings are far more subtle than they appear in that misguided tome. The place to start is with an accurate knowledge of the Gospel taught by The Church of Jesus Christ of Latter-day Saints.

Past, Present, and Future Sin. To understand how the Gospel provides salvation for all, it is necessary to view sinful behavior as a function of time. As Men travel through time, they experience a cyclical chronology of sin. They contemplate committing sin in the *future*, and they commit it in the *present*. It then becomes part of their *past*, a growing store of previous sins that affect future behavior.

Left to their own devices, Men quickly become enslaved by sinful habits through this pattern (John 8:34; Rom. 6:16; 2 Pet. 2:19). The Gospel was intended to break the chain, and free Men from the bondage of sin (Rom. 6:18-19; 1 John 1:7).

Men can improve their present behavior if they will turn from sin. This can only be done through *repentance* (Acts 26:20; 1 John 1:9; Luke 3:7-9; Rev. 2:5). Men can refrain from contemplating sin in the *future*. This is part of what the scriptures call *enduring to the end*, a determined perseverance by which a believer strives throughout life to overcome sin (Mark 13:13; Heb. 12:1; and 1 Pet. 4:2). It means looking forward with a sense of commitment to a sin-free life, spiritually at home with God.

If this were all that is necessary for Men to enter God's presence and enjoy eternal life, everyone could be saved by the program Evangelicals condemn—a system of righteous works, attaining salvation through obedience to the laws of God. But the biggest problem in the enslaving cycle of sin is unaffected by Man's best efforts to do good and turn from evil. All Men have committed at least some sin in their *past* (Rom. 3:23,

1 John 1:10). As guilty sinners, they have *already* earned condemnation to an eternity of separation from God (Rom. 5:12).

Men can do nothing about the sins of their *past* (i.e., the sins Men have committed up to the present moment of their existence). They are as powerless to affect their past actions as they are to raise themselves from the dead (Job 24:22; cf., John 10:18). Thus, Men *cannot* save themselves from Spiritual Death any more than they can save themselves from Physical Death.

Men would like to think their past sins will be forgotten if they repent, or their good deeds will erase their bad ones. But this is not how orderly and civilized societies function. Perfect justice requires that all violators of law receive the same punishment for the same acts or omissions under the same circumstances. Discrimination is not a trait of God (Acts 10:34), nor is disorder.

A law that provides no punishment for its disobedience may be broken with impunity by all. Thus, God cannot maintain law and, at the same time, overlook *any of* Man's past indiscretions (Rom. 3:25-26). In His perfect system of justice, *all* who "have sinned, and come short of the glory of God" (Rom. 3:23) have earned the wages of sin (Rom. 6:23)—death!

No present or future action by Man can change this result. Time travel is *not* a reality in anyone's future, and repentance is legally ineffectual. If reality were otherwise, one might expect that a man who has jumped off a high building could prevent his destruction on the sidewalk below by merely promising (on the way down) that he will never jump off the building again. Without some *external* assistance, Man's cries of repentance must go unheeded by a God who carries out perfect justice in the same way He maintains the law of gravity.

Sadly, the realization of this, Man's just condemnation for the sins of his past, robs Him of the motivation to break the bonds of sin. Why cease from sin, if, having made one mistake, Man is condemned to an eternity of separation from a perfect God? The sense of hopelessness that inevitably arises from contemplation of past imperfections only encourages continued sin. *Past* sins, therefore, are the most crucial links in the chain of sin.

To overcome that damning link, Men need an Intercessor who can do for them what they cannot do for themselves. That Intercessor must be One who is *entitled* to Salvation, and thus possesses the safety net needed to stop Man's spiritual plummet into the depths of Hell. He must also be the One entitled to mete out the punishment for spiritual sins. Otherwise, He would be just another victim of wrath.

With such an Intercessor, Men can lift their heads, knowing that their efforts to overcome sin and learn obedience to God will not be frustrated by condemnation for the errors they inevitably make during the learning process.

Justification. The precept which operates to save Men from their past sins is called *justification*. Paul revealed the principles of justification in great detail in his epistle to the Romans, beginning with Romans 3:21-26, which reads in the NASB as follows (some emphasis and brackets added):

> But now apart from the Law [of Moses] *the* righteousness of God has been manifested, being witnessed by the Law [of Moses] and the Prophets,
>
> even *the* righteousness of God through faith in Jesus Christ for all those who believe; for there is no distinction [between Jew and Gentile];
>
> for all have sinned and fall short of the glory of God, being *justified as a gift by His grace* through the redemption which is in Christ Jesus; whom God displayed publicly as a propitiation in [or by] His blood through faith. *This was* to demonstrate His righteousness, because in the forbearance of God He passed over the sins *previously committed;*
>
> for the demonstration, *I say*, of His righteousness at the present time, that He might be just and the justifier of the one who has faith in Jesus.

The Pharisees, a Jewish sect to which Paul once belonged, believed that salvation came through obedience to the Law of Moses. To contradict that misunderstanding, Paul explains in verse 21 that the righteousness of God exists apart from the Law of Moses, but is demonstrated in that Law and the teachings of the prophets. In verse 22, he tells the gentile Romans that the righteousness of God is attained through faith in Christ, and that both Jew and Gentile have the same access to it. Verse 23 explains why Man needs a Savior to attain the righteousness of God. Though all have sinned and thus fallen short of His righteousness, they can be "justified" as a gift which can be given because of the *grace* of Christ (verse 24).

Verse 25 says that redemption comes through Christ because His suffering and death constituted a publicly visible payment or "propitiation" for the sins that Men "*previously committed*" (KJV: "sins that are past").[3] Thus, it is *past* sins, from which Men are powerless to save themselves, to which the atonement applies.

As Men deal with the present necessity of learning obedience to God, the distinction between their past sins and the sins they now commit, or will commit in the future, is strategic. Present and future sins can and must be dealt with by Men, who cannot be allowed to think they are given a free ride into Heaven by God's grace. Hence, Paul's specific indication that the atonement applies only to past sins.

In verse 26 Paul explains that, without the atonement, it would be unjust favoritism, and a violation of God's holy and perfect character to forebear from punishing some, while others must receive full punishment. Were it not that Christ voluntarily undertook to suffer the punishment earned by those who have faith in Him, justice would not allow God to *pass over* any of Man's transgressions. Through the atonement, God can be *both* "just and the justifier" of those who have faith in Christ.[4]

Men cannot justify themselves (Job 9:20; Luke 10:29, 16:15). Justification is a judicial act performed by the Judge of all the earth. It literally means "to declare right or righteous." C. I. Scofield correctly explains the nature of justification in these words (emphasis in original):

> Justification . . . may be defined as the *judicial act of God whereby He justly declares and treats as righteous the one who believes in Jesus Christ.* The justified believer has been declared by the Judge Himself (Rom. 3:31) to have nothing laid to his charge (Rom. 8:1, 31 34).[5]

Paul rejoiced in this great boon as he continued his exposition in Romans 3 (verses 27-28):

> Where *is* boasting then? It is excluded. By what law? of works? Nay: but by the law of faith.

3. This is not a reference to sins committed by Men before the time of Christ's sacrifice. God is able to pass over "the sins previously committed" by all Men, whether they lived before or after Christ (see Romans 4:1-5).

4. See Alma 34:8-16 in the Book of Mormon for an insightful reiteration of these principles. Since the people living in the western hemisphere had no contact with Paul, the Lord revealed the same truths to their prophets.

5. *New Scofield Study Bible,* 1591 (footnote 18 to Romans 3:28).

> Therefore we conclude that a man is justified by faith without the deeds of the law [of Moses].

This passage confirms the reality that Men are not justified by the rituals of the Law of Moses or anything else they can do. No matter what the Lord asks of them, no matter how perfect their obedience throughout the *rest* of eternity, all Men would *have* to be condemned for their *past* sins if Christ had not paid the price for them. If there had been no atonement, all Men would have to serve the eternal sentence they deserve for the crimes they previously committed.

Justification is the decree of God that a Man's past sins are forgiven (Acts 13:38-39; Rom. 3:23-26; 4:7-8). In the Bible, the word "justify" or "justification" is often used in lieu of "forgiveness of sins" (see, e.g., Luke 18:14; Acts 13:39; Rom. 3:20; 1 Cor. 6:11; Gal. 2:17). This great boon, according to Paul, may be obtained only "by the law of faith" (Rom 3:27; see, also, Isa. 53:11; Acts 5:31; Eph. 1:7; Col. 1:14).

Sanctification. When a Man has been justified, all his *past* sins are blotted out (Acts 3:19). As long as he doesn't commit any *new* sins, he is clean in the eyes of God and entitled to receive His Spirit—he is *saved,* he is ready to commune with God, to know Him, and have His Spirit with him. The challenge, however, is to maintain that state.

Evangelicals assume, without biblical support of any kind, that justification occurs but once in a person's lifetime.[6] But justification occurs before death, while Men are still subject to temptation. After justification has cleansed a new believer of his or her past sins, most will commit additional sin. This new sin (which, by its commision, becomes a *past* sin) adversely affects the individuals relationship with the Lord. They no longer stand spotless or blameless before Him, and hence, are no longer in a state that will allow them to know God (1 John 2:3-4). It is always a man's *present* status that is the focus of God's examination (2 Cor. 13:5, Ps. 26:2). This question must always be asked: "Is there any sin in the believer *now?*"

God is patient with repentant believers who are sincerely striving to obey His commandments (Rom. 2:4, 9:22; 2 Pet. 3:9; 1 John 2:1), but, like any other past sin, new sins must be forsaken and remitted, that is, justified. Thus, although Christ's act of atonement was accomplished once for

6. MacArthur, *Faith Works,* 90 and 109.

all Men (Heb. 9:25-28; 1 Pet. 3:18), each Man's *need* for the atonement recurs throughout earthly life (see, e.g., 1 John 1:9). The process of repeated justification for new sins repented of (until Men learn perfect obedience to God) is called *sanctification*, meaning to consecrate or make holy—to dedicate to the Lord (see, e.g., Gen. 2:3; Exod. 13:2; Lev. 20:26; 27:14-15).

While the Bible speaks of sanctification being by the Lord (Jer. 1:5; Ezek. 20:12, 37:28; John 10:36; 1 Thess. 5:23; Jude 1), it also indicates that Men have a part in it as they exercise their will and moral agency in an effort to maintain a state of holiness (Exod. 19:10; Lev. 19:2; Deut. 32:51; and Isa. 29:23). Although the Lord provides the means for sanctification, He expects all Men to sanctify themselves to Him (Exod. 19:10; Lev. 11:44; Num. 20:12; Deut. 32:51; Ezek. 20:41; 36:23; 1 Pet 1:16).

Paul explained the elements and process of sanctification in Titus 2:11-14 as follows:

> For the grace of God that bringeth salvation hath appeared to all men,
>
> Teaching us that, denying ungodliness and worldly lusts, we should live soberly, righteously, and godly, in this present world;
>
> Looking for that blessed hope, and the glorious appearing of the great God and our Saviour Jesus Christ;
>
> Who gave himself for us, that he might redeem us from all iniquity, and purify unto himself a peculiar people, zealous of good works.

The grace of God brings salvation to Men through justification for their past sins. This principle teaches Men that they must live righteously, repenting and receiving justification anew each time they fall and commit new sin. Men should look forward to salvation as God purifies and redeems them "from *all* iniquity," until they become "a peculiar people, zealous of good works."

The dual role of God and Man in the sanctification process is illustrated in 1 Thessalonians 4:3-8 (NASB) as follows:

> For this is the will of God, your sanctification; *that is*, that you abstain from sexual immorality;
>
> that each of you know how to possess his own vessel in sanctification and honor,
>
> not in lustful passion, like the Gentiles who do not know God;

> *and* that no man transgress and defraud his brother in the matter because the Lord is *the* avenger in all these things, just as we also told you before and solemnly warned *you*.
>
> For God has not called us for the purpose of impurity, but in sanctification.
>
> Consequently, he who rejects *this* is not rejecting man but the God who gives His Holy Spirit to you.

This passage places upon Men the responsibility of maintaining the state of moral holiness that comes through justification. That is why Men are commanded throughout the Bible to repent and endure to the end, even *after* they have been justified. They are saved while in obedience to God, a state of holiness which they will learn to maintain for longer and longer periods at a time, until they are ready for *eternal* obedience in the Kingdom of God.

Paul illustrates the relationship between salvation and the sanctification process in 2 Thessalonians 2:13 as follows:

> But we are bound to give thanks alway to God for you, brethren beloved of the Lord, because God hath from the beginning chosen you to salvation through sanctification of the Spirit and belief of the truth:

Ultimate salvation is obtained only through the process of sanctification. By this process Men are prepared to live eternally with God in His Kingdom. The scriptures teach this principle: "Pursue peace with all men, and the sanctification without which no one will see the Lord" (Heb. 12:14, NASB). The expression "see the Lord" refers to the time when Men will be ready to enter the actual presence of God.

Paul taught the same truths to King Agrippa in Acts 26:18. There he announced that Christ had sent him to the Gentiles:

> To open their eyes, *and* to turn *them* from darkness to light, and *from* the power of Satan unto God, that they may receive forgiveness of sins, and inheritance among them which are sanctified by faith that is in me.

Peter teaches the same principle in 1 Peter 1:2. There, addressing believers throughout the world, he describes them as:

> Elect according to the foreknowledge of God the Father, through sanctification of the Spirit, unto obedience and sprinkling

> of the blood of Jesus Christ: Grace unto you, and peace, be multiplied.

This means that Men are saved by faith in Christ and numbered among the "elect" (a term that relates to salvation) through sanctification.

These passages also demonstrate that the purpose of sanctification is to learn obedience. To be *fully* sanctified is to arrive at a state of consistent obedience that, in conjunction with justification for past sins, will allow Men to live in perfection with God. Men who have achieved this goal during their life on earth were referred to as "perfect" (Gen. 6:9; 1 Kings 15:14; 2 Chron. 15:17; 2 Kings 20:3; Job 1:1; 2:3; Ps. 37:37; 1 Cor. 2:6; Phil. 3:15; 2 Tim. 3:17). Even though they were not perfect from birth, as Christ was, they learned obedience through the process of sanctification and were justified with respect to their past sins through the grace of Christ.

The scriptures say that Men are sanctified by God's truth (John 17:17), through Christ (1 Cor. 1:2; Heb. 10:10; 13:12), by the Spirit of God (1 Cor. 6:11), through the influence of others (1 Cor. 7:14), by obedience to the ordinances of the Gospel, notably baptism (Eph. 5:25-26), and by the word of God and prayer (1 Tim. 4:5). It is clear, therefore, that a *mutual* effort is necessary to bring Men into a state of holiness that will allow them to enter God's presence.

The Power of the Gospel. The Law of Faith is the means by which Men are cleansed from *all* their sins. They are cleansed from their *past* sins through *justification*, from their *present* sins through *repentance*, and from their *future* sins through *endurance to the end.* This Law of Faith, also referred to as the Gospel, gives Men the power to obtain real and everlasting salvation (Rom. 1:16).

Of course, Man's cooperation in the sanctification process does not *merit* his salvation. The grace of God is essential to the process and is "not of yourselves" (Eph. 2:9). The scriptures are clear that Men must repent *before* they can be prepared through justification and sanctification to enter His Kingdom. (Matt. 3:2; 4:17; Mark 1:15; Luke 13:3, 5; Acts 2:38; 3:19; 8:22—note that the command to repent *precedes* the promise in each of these passages). God will not justify the wicked (Exod. 23:7), but only the righteous (Deut. 25:1), that is, those who, through repentance, have turned to God and are willing and ready to become righteous.

God is just and holy, and those who come to Him must do so in holiness (1 Pet. 1:14-16; Lev. 19:2). God understands that Men encounter great difficulty in attaining holiness, so He is "longsuffering to us-ward, not willing that any should perish, but that all should come to repentance" (2 Pet. 3:9). But God's longsuffering is waiting for Men to *repent*, not just to believe in Him. If Men do not "come to repentance," they cannot take advantage of God's patience, and the grace of Christ will *not* save them.

"You Have Been Saved"

Some Evangelical misconceptions about the Gospel are due to their misunderstanding of the statement in Ephesians 2:8 that seems to address the timing of salvation. The phrase is "ye are saved," or, as it is more accurately translated from the Greek, "you have been saved" (Eph. 2:8, NASB). Unfortunately, this assurance is immediately appropriated by Evangelicals as a promise to them personally, without consideration of the context, or how they compare to the ancient Ephesians to whom Paul spoke these words.

Evangelicals believe that salvation occurs at the moment true faith is experienced by the new convert.[7] That moment is often called "the moment of faith,"[8] and supposedly occurs independent of any effort or intent to be obedient to God's commandments.[9] It happens before any trial of the new convert's faith, and is not in any way a work.[10] While some speak of submitting their will to Christ as a result of their faith in Him, all Evangelicals claim that personal obedience has nothing to do with salvation. At most, they believe that obedience is a *characteristic* of the redeemed. It is never considered a *condition* for redemption.[11]

The distinction between this teaching and the truths taught in the Bible (and Mormonism) is subtle, but very important. It is found in the Evangelical belief that the saved state of a believer persists irrespective of his or her continuing obedience. The words, "you have been saved," do not invite that conclusion, and a thorough review of relevant biblical passages make that clear.

By far the majority of references to salvation in the New Testament are

7. Zane Hodges, *Absolutely Free!* (Grand Rapids: Zondervan, 1989), 107.
8. G. Michael Cocoris, then head pastor of the Church of the Open Door, letter to the author, November 3, 1989.
9. MacArthur, *Faith Works,* 24 (citing Eph. 2:10).
10. MacArthur, *Faith Works,* 24 (citing Eph. 2:1-5, 8).
11. MacArthur, *The Gospel According to Jesus,* 188.

in the *future* tense. Many say that Men *shall* be saved (e.g., John 10:9, Acts 2:21; 16:31; Rom. 5:9-10; and 10:8-9, 13). Others have a contingent wording, promising that Men *may* be saved (John 6:40; 1 Cor. 5:5). Some speak of the *hope* of salvation (e.g., Rom. 5:1-2; 10:1; Heb. 6:11-12; 1 Thess. 5:8; and Titus 1:1-2), while others treat salvation as a process or "way," saying that Men are "being saved" (e.g., Acts 16:17; Rom. 1:16; 13:11; 2 Cor. 3:18; and Acts 2:46-47; 1 Cor. 1:18; and 2 Cor. 2:15, in the NASB).

In fact, there is only one instance in the Bible where a specific individual is said to "have been saved" at a specific moment in time (Luke 7:36-50, esp. 48-50). In that case, a devoted and abjectly penitent woman was forgiven of her sins by Christ when she anointed His feet with oil. After He forgave her, Christ said, "Thy faith hath saved thee; go in peace."

This is consistent with the exposition above. The woman's sins having been forgiven by God Himself, she was, at that moment, in a state of perfect holiness before Him and thus "saved." But the Bible does not say she remained in that state.

Besides Ephesians 2:8, there are a few other passages in the writings of John that use the present perfect tense to describe the enjoyment of eternal life by those who believe (e.g., John 3:15, 36; 6:47; and 1 John 5:13). These passages require an understanding of what John meant when he used the term "believe," and will be discussed later in this chapter. *No* biblical reference speaks of personal salvation in the past tense alone (e.g., "I was saved in Jerusalem at the Feast of Pentecost").

Therefore, before assuming that all Men remain permanently saved because Ephesians 2:8 says "you have been saved," as Evangelicals do, it would be well to exegete Ephesians 2:8 further. Ephesians 2:1-7 places Ephesians 2:8 in context, and reads in the NASB as follows (some emphasis added):

> And you *were* dead in your trespasses and sins,
>
> in which you *formerly walked* according to the course of this world, according to the prince of the power of the air, of the spirit that is now working in the sons of disobedience.
>
> Among them we too all *formerly lived* in the lusts of our flesh, indulging the desires of the flesh and of the mind, and were by nature children of wrath, even as the rest.
>
> But God, being rich in mercy, because of His great love with which He loved us,

> even when we *were* dead in our transgressions, made us alive together with Christ (by grace you have been saved),
>
> and raised us up with Him, and seated us with Him in the heavenly *places*, in Christ Jesus,
>
> in order that in the ages to come He might show the surpassing riches of His grace in the kindness toward us in Christ Jesus.

This passage indicates that the Ephesians had learned not to walk in sin by the time Paul said they were saved. They had turned from their evil ways, and lived in obedience to God's commandments. At least that is the assumption on which Paul's comment about their salvation is based. There is no promise in the passage that any of the Ephesians so addressed would *remain* saved should they turn back to evil.

In fact, the Book of Revelation, written some 30-50 years after the Epistle to the Ephesians, compliments the Ephesians on many points, but calls them to repentance, and threatens to "remove thy candlestick out of his place, except thou repent" (Rev. 2:1-6). Thus, even though Paul told the Ephesians "you have been saved" in 60 A.D., their ultimate salvation was by no means assured when the Book of Revelation was written decades later.

There is another sense in which the phrase "you have been saved" was used by Paul. In Ephesians 2:6, Paul speaks of events that are clearly in the future as though they were in the past. This is a writing technique Paul uses to make promised future blessings sound more immediate and vital. Paul's statement, "you have been saved" in Ephesians 2:8, is a similar literary technique, referring to the future blessing of ultimate salvation as though it were a present reality.

The statement, "you have been saved," cannot be taken as a generalized assurance of permanent salvation. Christ has already made His atoning sacrifice, and hence, in one sense *all* Men "have been saved." This does not mean any single individual is guaranteed of that condition irrespective of his or her state of current repentance.

"Through Faith"

Paul's statement in Romans 3:27-28 that Men are justified by "the law of faith" is the same principle he expressed in the phrase "through faith" in Ephesians 2:8. If salvation were automatic in any sense, Paul would have left that phrase out of his formula. But Men must choose salvation "through" faith in the Lord Jesus Christ. Because of its importance as Paul's summary of the means by which Men receive the benefits of the atonement, it is critical to understand exactly what he meant by "faith."

If obedience is the means to salvation, as Mormons teach, why did Paul use the word *pistis* (Gr., "faithfulness" or "steadfastness") instead of *hupakoē* (Gr., "obedience") in his formula? One answer is that *Pistis* is more inclusive. It not only conveys the necessity of obedience, it designates He in whom the believer should trust as the source of those precepts to be obeyed. It also implies the attitude believers should have toward their Exemplar. Trust is more than mere obedience. It includes loyalty and confidence in the person whose advice is followed.

Faith is the foundation of all action.[12] Thus, only to the extent Men obey Christ and emulate His example can it be said that they have faith in Him. If there is faith, there is obedience to that in which the believer has placed his faith. If there is no obedience, it is because there is insufficient faith in the principle which the believer does not obey. Only those who obey Christ completely have complete faith in Him (see e.g., John 8:31; 13:35; 15:8; Matt. 19:25-29; Rev. 2:23).

However, most believers' faith in Christ is not black or white—there is some obedience, demonstrating some faith, and some disobedience, demonstrating a need for faith to grow. The greater the faith, the greater the obedience, and the greater the obedience, the closer Men come to perfect obedience and their ultimate salvation (Rom. 13:11).

Paul's emphasis on faith rather than obedience alone, also shows that a call to faith is easier to accept than a command to obey. Paul was always concerned to express himself in a way that would persuade to his audience (1 Cor. 9:20-22). Faith involves *following* righteous leadership, and it is always easier to follow than to be pushed.

A good attorney will ask his client to trust him, as opposed to saying, "Obey me." Of course, the attorney wants the client to follow his instructions, otherwise, the client will not prevail, but the client must have confidence, or trust, in the attorney. During a course of business, the client cannot do whatever he wants and expect to avoid legal problems. That is not possible in any system that involves justice. His legal salvation, so to speak, depends on whether or not he trusts his attorney enough to follow

12. Joseph Smith, Jr, "Lecture First" in *A Compilation Containing the Lectures on Faith,* 7.

his advice. Spiritual salvation is much the same. Men must have enough confidence in their Advocate with the Father (1 John 2:1) to follow His advice.

Paul's choice of the word "through" is significant as well. If a man were told that he could obtain a position of great importance "through education," would it be reasonable for him to think that stepping into a classroom for an instant would qualify him for the promised station? Certainly not! Most people understand that the phrase "through education" implies years of effort and training. Only if a person persists in learning will the promises of a good education be his.

"Through faith" communicates the same concept. The phrase was meant to summarize the process of sanctification, by which Men grow and learn to obey the commandments of God, exercising their faith in Him and following the advice and instructions of He in whom they place their trust. Thus, obedience is so intrinsic to the principle of faith, a call to trust in Christ *is* a call to obey Him.

God's Standard

In requiring obedience for salvation, the Bible sets a single standard. Christ commanded: "Be ye therefore perfect, even as your Father which is in heaven is perfect" (Matt. 5:48). That is God's standard, and it has never been changed or repealed (Gen. 17:1; Deut. 18:13; 1 Kings 8:61; 1 Chron. 28:9; 2 Cor. 13:11; Col. 1:28; 4:12; Heb. 12:23; 13:21; James 1:4). Evangelicals try to soften this commandment by pointing out that the word "perfect" in the New Testament is translated from the Greek *teleioo* or *teleios,* "having attained the end or purpose" (sometimes rendered "fully developed in a moral sense").[13] They contend that perfection, God's goal for Man, is not an attainable reality.[14]

Such rationalization is completely without scriptural support. *Teleioo* is a word that accurately describes the sanctification process, the goal, "end,"

---

13. Walter Bauer, *A Greek-English Lexicon of the New Testament and Other Early Christian Literature,* 4th Ed., trans. William F. Arndt and F. Wilbur Gingrich (Chicago: University of Chicago Press, 1957), s.v. "teleios."

14. Frank E. Gaebelein, ed., *The Expositor's Bible Commentary,* 12 vols. (Grand Rapids: Zondervan, 1984), 8:161 ("this must not encourage us to conclude that Jesus teaches that unqualified perfection is already possible for his disciples"); George A. Buttrick, ed., *The Interpreter's Dictionary of the Bible: An Illustrated Encyclopedia,* 4 vols. (New York: Abingdon Press, 1962) s.v. "perfection."

or "purpose" of which is present tense perfection. "Perfect" is the ideal translation, and was retained in Matthew 5:48 by the translators of the NASB. Indeed, the same word (*teleioo*) is used in that verse to describe "your Father which is in heaven." There can be no argument that *He* is anything but perfect in every sense of the word.

In this verse, Christ commanded Men to become like God (see, also, Luke 6:36). As difficult as that may seem, it has been achieved in this life by certain individuals named in the Bible. It is an eternal goal, one the fulfillment of which will take most Men much longer than their earthly life to achieve. But it is not an impossible goal. All Men can achieve that goal if they patiently strive to learn obedience until they can regularly adhere to the spirit and letter of God's laws. This is true because God's commandments are not "grievous" (1 John 5:3), and He has promised to help (cf., Phil. 2:13).

"Not of Works"

Because Mormons accept God's standard and strive (with typical human frailty) to reach the goal He set, the Evangelical cry against them is that "Satan is deceiving [them] to believe that works must be added to God's grace" in order to obtain salvation.[15] Such rhetoric has no basis in reason or reality. Mormons add nothing to the Bible's requirements for salvation. They acknowledge what God has commanded them to do. They look with gratitude to the grace of Christ for the crucial remission of their past sins, while recognizing their need to repent and endure to the end.

Still, Evangelicals warn: "Consider carefully what we're implying if we believe we must add works to God's grace. We're implying that Christ's work on the cross was not adequate and that we must help Him out."[16] If that logic is correct, Evangelicals must be equally guilty of trying to "help Him out." They believe Men must *trust* in Christ to be saved. That too implies "Christ's work on the cross was not adequate and that we must help Him out" by trusting Him.

But Mormons do not add works to God's grace any more than Evangelicals add their version of trust to His grace. Their criticism seems valid only to those who do not understand what Christ sought to accomplish on the cross.

15. Trivanovich, *Speaking the Truth in Love,* 44.
16. Trivanovich, *Speaking the Truth in Love,* 45.

Mormons do not deny the necessity of God's grace for their salvation; they do not teach that the works of the Law of Moses are necessary for Men to be saved; and they do not teach that Men can obtain salvation by present or future compliance with any law or ritual. Mormons teach that obedience to the laws and ordinances of the Gospel has no efficacy whatever apart from the atoning sacrifice of Jesus Christ (2 Nephi 2:6-8; 11:6; Mosiah 13:28; 15:18-19; Alma 34:9-14)

Such protestations, however, are generally made to no avail in discussions with Evangelical theologians, who have gone to Pharisaical extremes in their interpretation of the phrase, "not of works." They cannot accept the fact that Men, of necessity, have *something* to do with their own salvation, for fear it will detract in some way from the work of Christ.[17] So extreme is this view that *any* form of obedience to God's commandments is seen as a meritorious work that cannot save.[18] This notion fails to recognize that justification is not needed for obedience, only for past sins.

Paul was trained as a Pharisee to believe in the importance of an outward show of obedience to the letter of the Law of Moses. Yet, though he preached against Pharisaical thinking, there is no passage in his writings that suggests obedience to God's commandments should be considered a "meritorious work." In fact, the latter phrase appears nowhere in the Bible.

Generally, when Paul used the word *works*, he referred to the works or "deeds" of the Law of Moses (Rom. 3:20, 28, KJV; also note that C.I. Scofield footnotes every use of the word "law" in Galatians 2 with the indication that it refers to "the Law of Moses"[19]). This is apparent from Paul's statement to the Galatians in Galatians 2:16 (emphasis added):

> Knowing that a man is not justified by the *works of the law*, but by the faith of Jesus Christ, even we have believed in Jesus Christ, that we might be justified by the *faith of Christ*, and not by the *works of the law*: for by the *works of the law* shall no flesh be justified.

The apostle James, however, used the word "works" differently. He didn't limit that term by the use of any prepositional phrase, as Paul did in Romans 3:28 (NASB), "*works of the Law*." James used the word "only" to modify the word "faith" (James 2:24). This distinction indicates that

17. *Ibid.*
18. Cf., MacArthur, *The Gospel According to Jesus,* 33.
19. *The New Scofield Study Bible,* 1656 (footnote 9).

James' use of the words "works" and "faith," unlike Paul's usage of those words, was intended to separate the concept of intellectual assent from the behavioral response of Men to their beliefs. To James, the word "faith" refers only to thought processes, the intellectual acceptance of facts, ideas and opinions, while the word "works" identifies Man's behavior based on those thought processes.'

Paul never used words of limitation, like "only," in connection with the word *faith*. His approach is from a different perspective. To Paul, faith is much more than mere Pharisaical adherence to the outward requirements of the Law. He sees "faith" and "belief" as *inclusive* of obedience. Faith is a state of the heart that includes *both* mental assent and a devotion reflected by heart-felt obedience. Paul's use of the term *faith* is closer to the meaning of the Greek word *pistis*, which encompasses three aspects, identified by theologians as *noticia* (a knowledge of truth), *assensus* (intellectual acceptance of truth), and *fiducia* (trust and confidence manifested by obedience to truth).[20]

This understanding resolves an otherwise glaring contradiction between Paul's statement in Romans 3:28 ("For we maintain that a man is justified by faith apart from works of the Law," NASB; cf., Eph. 2:9), and the statement of James in James 2:24 ("Ye see then how that by works a man is justified, and not by faith only"). The latter passage either contradicts Paul, or as suggested above, is based on different terminology. If it is understood that Paul used the word "works" here to refer to the dead works of the Law of Moses and assumed that faith includes obedience, and if James used the word "faith" to mean mental assent without obedience, then the method by which Men are saved, according to each author, is the same.

Some who reject this conclusion dismiss the writings of James altogether, claiming they are not an inspired addition to the canon of the Bible.[21] Fortunately, most Evangelical scholars reject that position, but, in accepting James' writings, they must confront a significant doctrinal contradiction. Surprisingly, they resolve that conflict in much the same way Mormons do.[22]

James says that mere intellectual assent to facts, ideas, and opinions (*noticia* and *assensus*), without obedience (*fiducia*), does not constitute

---

20. Compare this analysis to that of John MacArthur in *Faith Works,* 139-155.

21. This argument lacks any scholarly basis. See, *The Expositor's Bible Commentary,* 12:163.

22. See, e.g., MacArthur, *Faith Works,* 139-155.

the faith Paul said would save Men. To illustrate, Romans 4:1-5 reads as follows:

> What shall we say then that Abraham our father, as pertaining to the flesh, hath found?
>
> For if Abraham were justified by works, he hath *whereof* to glory; but not before God.
>
> For what saith the scripture? Abraham believed God, and it was counted unto him for righteousness.
>
> Now to him that worketh is the reward not reckoned of grace, but of debt.
>
> But to him that worketh not, but believeth on him that justifieth the ungodly, his faith is counted for righteousness.[23]

By way of contrast, James notes Abraham's famous act of obedience, and says (James 2:21-23, emphasis added):

> Was not Abraham our father *justified by works*, when he had offered Isaac his son upon the altar?
>
> Seest thou how faith wrought with his works, and by works was faith made perfect?
>
> And the scripture was fulfilled which saith, Abraham believed God, and it was imputed unto him for righteousness[24] and he was called the Friend of God.

In Romans 4:1-2 Paul asks what Abraham, the father of the Jews, understood about salvation, and notes that, if Abraham were justified by "works," he would have had reason to boast, but such boasting would not have been "before God" (verse two). That is, God would not have been the source of Abraham's salvation if he had been obedient to the Law of Moses all his life, as Christ was. In that case, Abraham would have earned salvation as a debt owed to him, the same as Christ did.

Does this contradict James teaching that, in fact, Abraham was justified by works? Certainly not! Paul says Abraham was not justified by perfect obedience to the Law of Moses. In fact, the Law of Moses had not been given when Abraham lived (though animal sacrifice, looking

23. To be "counted for righteousness" means that Abraham was justified. That is how justification operates to effect the forgiveness of sins.

24. The phrase "imputed unto him for righteousness" indicates that Abraham was justified. Again, that is the way justification functions to allow forgiveness of sins.

forward to the last and great sacrifice of Jesus Christ, was required in his day—Gen. 22:1-14). Abraham was saved through the Gospel of Jesus Christ, the same Gospel Paul asked the Gentiles to receive (cf., Eph. 2:11-17; Gal. 3:26-29), and that Gospel requires obedience, as demonstrated earlier.

In Romans 4:5 Paul notes that the principle of justification is available to all that "worketh not." What did he mean by that? Does the word "worketh" in this phrase refer to obedience? Was Paul contradicting James, saying that justification is available to those who *do not* obey the commandments of God? If so, righteous Abraham was a poor example. He obeyed God, and, according to James, was justified by his works.

To James, the word, "works," included Abraham's obedience in general. To Paul the word, "worketh" meant only to perform the works of the Law of Moses. While they both used the same word, each had a different meaning in mind. To best understand Paul's statement, "him that worketh not," it must be contrasted with the phrase "him that worketh" in Romans 4:4. That verse promises to "him that worketh" the "reward" as an obligation of the Father earned by perfect obedience to the Law of Moses. The only person who ever earned salvation in this manner is Jesus Christ. Thus, He is the only person referred to in verse 4.

By contrast, the rest of humanity is referred to in verse 5 as "him that worketh not." The contrast Paul draws is between the perfect obedience of Christ and the imperfect obedience of the rest of mankind. It is not between obedience and no obedience. Even those who have tried to do the works of the Law are included in verse 5 because, unlike Christ, they failed to live the Law perfectly. Thus, "him that worketh not," refers to all Men, who, being unable to live God's laws perfectly from their birth, need the Savior's atonement to justify their past sins.

Abraham *learned* obedience. Thus, he needed the Savior's atonement as much as the Gentiles do to justify the sins that all Men commit in the learning process. James notes that Abraham *succeeded* in learning to obey God, and hence was saved through the atonement of Jesus Christ for his past sins. The comparison of Paul and James demonstrates the point that *both* the atonement of Christ *and* the obedience Men are necessary for salvation.

Faith, a Work? A serious theological problem arises from the overbroad interpretation of the term *works* adopted by Evangelicals. It is the question of whether or not faith itself is a work. Evangelicals admit that faith in Christ is necessary for salvation, yet it is a commandment of God to have faith in Christ (Matt. 23:23; Mark 11:22; 1 Tim. 1:5; 6:11-12). Hence, if Men believe in Christ, they are obeying a commandment of God.

Given Evangelical theology on this point, such obedience would have to be classified as a meritorious work, which cannot save. That conclusion, overturns the entire Law of Faith.

To avoid this result, Evangelicals like John MacArthur claim that "faith is a gift of God, not a work of man."[25] For this proposition Pastor MacArthur cites Ephesians 2:1-5 and 8. However, those verses contain nothing that supports his thesis. Ephesians 2:1-5 doesn't even address the issue. Verse 8 ("For by grace you have been saved through faith; and that not of yourselves, *it is* the gift of God" NASB) does *not* say that "the gift of God" is "faith," as Pastor MacArthur assumes. The better interpretation of the Greek is that "the gift of God" referred to in that verse is "grace." Grace, after all, is the subject of Paul's sentence.

The Bible is clear that faith in Jesus Christ as the Son of God comes to Men through revelation from the Father (Matt. 16:15-17). However, it is equally clear that a man must exercise his free will to accept that revelation.[26] As Paul, himself, explained in Romans 10:17, "So then faith *cometh* by hearing, and hearing by the word of God." Men must *hear* the "word" given to them by God before they can have faith. Hearing, used in this sense, is an act of will that involves *acceptance* of God's message. It cannot be theologically distinguished from any other act of human obedience.

Faith *must* be voluntary, for God desires all Men to accept Him of their own free will and choice. "But without faith *it is* impossible to please *him:* for he that cometh to God must believe that he is, . . ." (Heb. 11:6). If faith was bestowed on Men without an act of will from them, its absence would be God's fault, and hence the forgoing verse would be a sham. God calls all Men to Him (John 12:32), and only because of that call do Men come to Him (John 6:44, 65), but they must come of their own free will and choice. God is not responsible for Man's positive response to His call. Otherwise, God would be responsible for Man's evil choices as well as his good. If God were solely responsible for Man's faith in Him, it would be

25. MacArthur, *Faith Works,* 24.

26. The alternative is pure Calvinism. If Men cannot be saved by or because of anything they do, the only means for salvation is the inscrutable whim of God. Such a position completely destroys the free agency of Man.

injust for God to condemn Men because of their faithlessness (John 5:24). Thus, faith is clearly a "work" of Man, at least in part.

Paul did not intend the term "work" to be used as broadly as Evangelicals do (see Phil. 2:12). Their definition is more consistent with James' use of that term. Note, however, that when James uses that term in the same broad sense, he declares that Men are justified by their "works." Thus, James recognized, as Evangelicals should, that the efforts of Men are not only efficacious, but essential to their salvation.

In so saying, it is important not to lose sight of the point made by each of these great apostles. Men cannot redeem themselves from their past sins by any human effort. James does not say Men can work their way to heaven. He says that their works, *with* their faith, are necessary for their salvation.

The "Faith" of Other Inspired Writers

Other inspired writers also used the word "faith" in a way that suggests they intended it to be taken as inclusive of devoted obedience to God's laws. In chapter 11 of the book of Hebrews, the author of that volume defines faith in a way that includes specific reference to the *behavior* of each person whose faith is used as an example. James reviews Hebrews 11 in James 2, making specific note of the behavioral element in each example. A comparison of these two approaches demonstrates the truth about works noted above.

To illustrate, Hebrews 11:31 (emphasis added) says of Rahab the harlot: "*By faith* the harlot Rahab perished not with them that believed not, *when she had received the spies* with peace." James 2:25 (some emphasis added) reads: "Likewise also was not Rahab the harlot justified *by works, when she had received the messengers*, and had sent *them* out another way?" Hebrews 11:31 says Rahab was saved "by faith" when she received Israel's spies, while James 2:25 says Rahab was saved "by works," for that act.

There is but one way by which Men are saved. Hence, the reference to justification "by works" in James 2:25, must be equivalent to the statement in Hebrews 11:31 that Rahab's justification was "by faith." The writer of Hebrews must have intended the word "faith" to include the behavior James identified as "works." Thus, when the Book of Hebrews says Men are saved by "faith," it means they are saved by their acceptance of Christ's atonement, *and* their obedience based on that acceptance.

An analysis of the apostle John's writings leads to the same conclusion. He used the word "believe," translated from the same root word as *faith*, to include obedience. For example, John 6:47 (some emphasis added) states, "Verily, verily, I say unto you, He that *believeth* on me hath *everlasting life*," while 1 John 2:17 reads (emphasis added), "And the world passeth away, and the lust thereof: but he that *doeth* the will of God *abideth for ever*." The terms "everlasting life" in John 6:47 and "abideth for ever" in 1 John 2:17 are essentially identical in the Greek. The only difference between these verses is the *means* by which John says eternal life is obtained. In the first passage he says *belief* is the way, while in the second he says "he that *doeth* the will of God" will attain the goal. John is not contradicting himself. Rather, he intended the word "believeth" in John 6:47 to mean the same as *doing* the will of God (1 John 2:17). Thus, John, like Paul, used the word, "believeth," to include *fiducia* based on *noticia*, and *assensus*.

A similar example is found in John 17:3, where John taught that it is "life eternal" to "*know*" God. In 1 John 2:3-4, he makes it clear that, if Men do not keep God's commandments, they do not know God. Thus, John teaches that Men can only "know" God, (i.e., have "life eternal"), if they keep God's commandments.

John uses other phrases involving obedience to Christ's teachings as though they were equivalent to a belief in Him. In 1 John 4:16, he says (emphasis added): "And we have known and believed the love that God hath to us. God is love;[27] and he that *dwelleth in love dwelleth in God*, and God in him." The phrase, "dwelleth in God," refers to salvation, eternal life with God. Thus, he who dwells in love is saved, according to John. But what does it mean to dwell in love?

John quotes the Savior in John 15:10 as saying: "If ye keep my commandments, ye shall abide [i.e., *dwell*] in my love; even as I have kept my Father's commandments, and abide in his love." Thus, Christ taught that the way to "abide in love" is to keep God's commandments. Indeed, all the commandments of the Lord can be summarized in the single word, *Love* (Matt. 22:37-40; Luke 10:25-28). If he who dwells in love is saved (1 John 4:16), and dwelling in love means keeping God's commandments (John 15:10), it follows that Men must obey God's commandments in

27. This phrase does not mean God is an emotion. It is an idiom, like "Elvis Presley is Rock 'n' Roll!" It means that God perfectly epitomizes that emotion.

order to be saved and dwell with Him.

John even *defined* "the love of God" as obeying God's commandments. "For this is the love of God, that we keep his commandments" (1 John 5:3). For other examples of this point see 1 John 2:5-6, 17, 29; 3:6, 9; and 5:18.

John 15:10 is also helpful in correcting the most significant misunderstanding in the Evangelical gospel. In that passage, the promise clearly *follows* the condition. Christ said, "*if* ye keep my commandments, ye *shall* abide in my love," not the other way around. The Evangelical gospel would render this passage "*when* ye abide in my love, ye *shall* keep my commandments." That is not the gospel Jesus (or John) taught.

John's terminology must be kept in mind when reading his announcement of the Gospel in John 3:15-16, a favorite passage of Evangelicals:

> That whosoever believeth in him should not perish, but have eternal life.
>
> For God so loved the world, that he gave his only begotten Son, that whosoever believeth in him should not perish, but have everlasting life.

From the exegesis above it is clear that John used the phrase "whosoever believeth" to refer to those who keep God's commandments. To "believe" is to obey, as far as John is concerned. Those who do not obey, do not believe. Hence, John is saying "whosoever [obeys God's commandments] should not perish, but have everlasting life."

Christ Himself equated belief with works, not the works of the Law of Moses, but His own works. In John 14:12, He said:

> Verily, verily, I say unto you, He that believeth on me, the works that I do shall he do also; and greater *works* than these shall he do; because I go unto my Father.

At the conclusion of His Sermon on the Mount, Christ warned (Matt. 7:21, emphasis added)

> Not every one that saith unto me, Lord, Lord, shall enter into the kingdom of heaven; but he that *doeth* the will of my Father which is in heaven.[28]

---

28. As noted in Chapter 1, Dispensationalism holds that the Sermon on the Mount has "no application to the Christian, but only to those who are under the Law, and

The latter passage makes it clear that only those who *do* the will of God (i.e., Christ's works—John 14:12) will ultimately be saved. The requirement for entry into the kingdom of heaven is *doing*, not *saying* (and certainly not just *thinking*). While good works do follow the inception of true belief, *salvation* is only possible when Men stand in obedience to God's word and thus engage in good works.

Some Evangelicals are confused by the fact that John, who said "No one who abides in Him sins" (1 John 3:6, NASB), also said "If we say that we have no sin, we are deceiving ourselves" (1 John 1:8, NASB).[29] But there is no conflict in these passages at all.

While John acknowledges that all believers *have* sinned (Rom. 3:23), he unequivocally declares what Mormons have always preached, that no one can *be* saved if they are not currently abiding in a sinless state before God ("no one who abides in Him sins"). There is some sin in the past of every Man. That sin was atoned for by Christ. But, if Men wish to abide in Him, they must learn to sin no more.[30]

Christ confronted the Jews on a similar belief they maintained in His day—that they would be saved simply because they were the sons of Abraham (cf., Luke 3:8). That belief, like the Evangelical gospel, includes no requirement of obedience. Christ said that the Jews would *not* be saved, because their *works* were not the works of Abraham (see John 8:37-44). Evangelicals may expect no less if their works are not the works of Christ.

Thus, no matter how the writer expresses it, the message is always the same. The New Testament teaches that Men must obey God in order to be saved. Paul's phrase, "not of works," means that obedience, though *necessary*, is not *sufficient* to save Men. However insufficient, obedience remains necessary for salvation (Phil. 2:12).

"Lest Any Man Should Boast"

Though works are necessary (but not sufficient) to save Men, the strength Men need to do God's will comes from Him (Phil. 2:13). Thus,

---

therefore must apply to another Dispensation than this." Clarence Larkin, Dispensational Truth (Philadelphia: Larkin, 1918), 87. Mormons, as well as most Evangelicals, flatly reject this rationalization.

29. MacArthur, *Faith Works,* 31.

30. Compare this analysis with the paradox MacArthur sees in these two verses in *Faith Works,* 31.

no right-thinking believer could ever imagine that obedience is something in which he or she should boast. Men can just as easily boast of their faith in Christ, and not a few are guilty of that sin.

Contrary to Evangelical criticism, the Mormon belief that Men must obey Christ and do His works in order to be saved does not imply that Men can work their way to heaven, and no believer should hold that thought. Meeting the conditions set by Christ to receive His grace is not the same as doing works that merit salvation. Salvation remains a totally unmerited gift from God that comes by the atonement of Jesus Christ, not by any act ever performed or that ever will be performed by other Men.

When Paul says, "work out your own salvation with fear and trembling" (Phil. 2:12), he expresses the Gospel message taught above without suggesting that Men can, by their works, obtain salvation. He reminds Men that they must do their part, and seek the righteousness that comes "through the faith of Christ" (Phil. 3:9). Such faith grows in the believer (2 Cor. 10:15; Rom. 13:11), and as it does, Men close the gap between themselves and God until they attain that state of perfection to which Christ called them (Matt. 5:48; Phil. 3:8-17). But this is never done in a vacuum. It is only the gifts and grace of God that make it possible.

These truths were expressed in the Book of Mormon by the prophet-king Benjamin, who understood the efficacy of good works in the Plan of Salvation. Inspired writing contains no more eloquent explanation of the attitude Men should have toward the value of their works than the following scripture from the Book of Mormon, the words of King Benjamin, found in Mosiah 2:20-24:

> I say unto you, my brethren, that if you should render all the thanks and praise which your whole soul has power to possess, to that God who has created you, and has kept and preserved you, and has caused that ye should rejoice, and has granted that ye should live in peace one with another—
>
> I say unto you that if ye should serve him who has created you from the beginning, and is preserving you from day to day, by lending you breath, that ye may live and move and do according to your own will, and even supporting you from one moment to another—I say, if ye should serve him with all your whole souls yet ye would be unprofitable servants.
>
> And behold, all that he requires of you is to keep his commandments; and he has promised you that if ye would keep his

> commandments ye should prosper in the land; and he never doth vary from that which he hath said; therefore, if ye do keep his commandments he doth bless you and prosper you.
>
> And now, in the first place, he hath created you, and granted unto you your lives, for which ye are indebted unto him.
>
> And secondly, he doth require that ye should do as he hath commanded you; for which if ye do, he doth immediately bless you; and therefore he hath paid you. And ye are still indebted unto him, and are, and will be, forever and ever; therefore, of what have ye to boast?

The answer of Paul, with King Benjamin, to the last question above, is an unequivocal "Nothing!" That should always be the answer of even the most righteous believer.

Conclusion

Through faith, and because of the atonement of Jesus Christ, His suffering, death, and resurrection, all Mankind can be saved by obedience to the Gospel of Jesus Christ, the Law of Faith. The basic precept of that Law is faith in the Lord Jesus Christ. Faith in Christ is confidence and trust in Him reflected by obedience to His commandments. Men are merely giving lip service to Christ if they claim faith, but do not obey Him (Matt. 7:21; 15:8). Therefore, with faith comes repentance and an open commitment to Him through obedience to the ordinances of the Gospel which will be discussed next.

The fulfillment of the saving process is receipt of the Holy Ghost by the laying on of hands, which reestablishes the relationship between God and Man, a relationship that is perfected through the sanctification process that follows in Man's inevitable struggle to gain control of his flesh.

This is the original Gospel of Jesus Christ as delivered to the ancient saints by the Apostles of old. All who abide in it will be saved in the Kingdom of God. Those who reject it, will be the recipients of His just condemnation. Those who criticize it, preach another gospel.

7

The Necessity of Gospel Ordinances

The auditorium was hot with emotion and the breath and sweat of six thousand devotees who had shouted and sung and praised through the night at every call from the temporary pulpit on stage. The evangelist had reached the climax of his final exultation from the Word. In tones the more electric for their hushed energy, he calls for all who will accept Christ to come forward. Those who respond are assisted by aides who lead them in a short written prayer. They are given information on how they can grow in Christ and a list of local churches where they can be discipled. Those who say the prayer are assured they have received Christ and been saved. The joy of the moment is one the penitent will cherish for years to come.

Though never identified as such, the paragraph above describes a *ritual* or *ordinance*. A *ritual* is a "prescribed form or order of conducting a religious or solemn ceremony."[1] The word *ordinance* has the same meaning but comes from the Latin*ōrdināre*, meaning to put in order. The New Testament uses three different Greek words for "ordinance": *paradosis* (1 Cor. 11:2), which may also be translated "tradition"; *dogma* (Eph. 2:15), which is sometimes rendered "decree"; and *dikaióma* (Heb. 9), a "righteous ceremony," which is used in discussing the rituals of the new, as well as the old law.

Although Christ kept the Law of Moses perfectly, His death was the fulfillment of that Law. Its ordinances are no longer required of those who follow Him (Heb. 9). Greater obedience is expected of them. Based on a misunderstanding of passages in Hebrews 7-9, many Evangelicals think ordinances were eliminated from the Church at the time of Christ. Paul's praise for the Corinthians, however, shows the error of that notion and the

1. *Reader's Digest Illustrated Encyclopedic Dictionary,* s.v. "ritual."

continued importance of ordinances in the early Church. He said (1 Cor. 11:2):

> Now I praise you, brethren, that ye remember me in all things, and keep the ordinances, as I delivered *them* to you.

Men have always needed public ceremonies or ordinances to mark significant commitments. The marriage ceremony is a perfect example. It is a civil covenant made before witnesses in the hope that it will make a solemn and lasting impression. Evangelicals who deny the necessity of Gospel ordinances have simply invented their own to take the place of those God established, an example being the one described above—the traditional call to the pulpit at the close of a spiritual rally.

Always the perfect example, Christ personally demonstrated each commitment He requires of Men by personally submitting to the ordinances of His Gospel. Those who trust Him will follow His example and make an open commitment to Him by submitting to the ordinances He established, sometimes called *sacraments*. Because they represent a public confession of Christ (Rom. 10:9), these ordinances are a crucial part of the Plan of Salvation

What Shall We Do to Be Saved?

After the Holy Ghost was poured out at Pentecost, Peter initiated the first public sermon given by the Apostles following the Savior's departure. Each of the Jews who had assembled for the Feast heard the words of the Apostles in their native tongue, and many believed. Those whose faith in Christ had thus been engendered asked Peter, "Men *and* brethren, what shall we do?" (Acts 2:37). His answer stands as the quintessential instruction for the salvation of all new believers (Acts 2:37-38, NASB, some emphasis added):

> Now when they heard *this*, they were pierced to the heart, and said to Peter and the rest of the apostles, "Brethren, *what shall we do?*"
>
> And Peter *said* to them, "*Repent*, and let each of you be *baptized in the name of Jesus Christ for the forgiveness of your sins*, and you shall receive *the gift of the Holy Spirit*."

The fact that the Jews asked Peter what they should do reflects their understanding that trusting in Christ means they had to do something. Peter's answer reaffirms that assumption, showing that faith is not a passive requirement of mere intellectual dimension. Notably, Peter did *not* tell the Jews to "do nothing but trust in Christ," and he did *not* ask them to come forward and say a prayer.

He gave them an answer that mentions specific ordinances as the means whereby individuals may obtain salvation. Peter's answer should be carefully examined and understood by all believers as the definitive statement of those acts and ordinances that signify Man's commitment to Christ.

Repentance. The first requirement mentioned by Peter is the first message preached by Christ in Matthew 4:17 "Repent!" (see, also, Mark 1:14-15). Derived from two Greek words, it means literally "to have another mind," the call to repentance is a call for Men to change their minds about the direction of their lives, to turn from the world to the strait gate (Matt. 7:14).

No-lordship Evangelicals claim that repentance means *only* to change one's mind about Christ, *not* "to be sorry for sin or even resolve to turn from sin."[2] These teachers claim that an actual change of behavior is *not* required for salvation, because the word "repent" implies only a change of mental attitude.[3] They teach that "repentance is the root, and change in the conduct is the fruit."[4]

Used in this sense, repentance becomes indistinguishable from the Evangelical definition of faith. Thus, they make the same error with respect to repentance as they do with faith. They believe that one can repent without any change of behavior.

This theology misses the point of the root words entirely. A change of behavior may be a temporary act, purely superficial, wrongly motivated, even hypocritical. For example, one might obey some of Christ's precepts, as the great Indian leader Gandhi did, simply because they are wise counsel, without recognizing Jesus as the Christ.

The change of mind called for in repentance requires much more than this, more than a mere change in behavior. When a believer has faith in Christ he accepts Him as Messiah. The change of mind that necessarily accompanies such faith involves a fundamental redirection of the will. It signifies agreement with Christ and acceptance of His leadership.

---

2. Charles Ryrie, *So Great Salvation* (Wheaton: Victor, 1989), 92, 99.
3. Cocoris, *Lordship Salvation,* 11.
4. *Ibid.*

When a Man thus changes his mind about Christ, he comes around to His way of thinking. Such a change affects every aspect of the penitent believer's lifestyle. It represents an inward commitment to follow Him in all respects. All that is necessary after that is to express this commitment openly.

Lordship Evangelicals also err in their teachings about repentance. Intent upon avoiding any idea that Men's works have even a minuscule impact on their own salvation, John MacArthur claims "[r]epentance is no more a meritorious work than its counterpart, faith."[5] Noting that repentance is an inward change of attitude, Pastor MacArthur glosses over the will that Men must exercise in order to make even that change, let alone the outward confession that must follow. Oddly, he does recognize a *volitional* element in repentance (citing Louis Berkhof's *Systematic Theology*, Grand Rapids: Eerdmans, 1939, p. 486), but neither he nor Berkhof recognize the significance of that element, namely that repentance is a "work" as that term was used by James.

If faith and repentance did not involve effort, Man's struggle to have and exercise faith wouldn't have been described by Paul as a "fight" (1 Tim. 6:12). That term aptly describes the challenge Men face as they decide to change their carnal nature to spirituality. Even when the Spirit of the Lord makes it abhorrent to Men, the flesh often clings to sin. Thus, Men must "fight" to change old habits. That fight is the essence of real repentance.

When Men see their sins in the light God does, being in agreement with Christ, they hate sin (Ps. 45:7; Heb. 1:9) and desire to cease. Thus, true repentance creates a desire for change in behavior. The demand for a change of behavior, which springs from the hearts of those who feel the conviction of sin, is the principle associated with repentance throughout the scriptures. The call to repentance is a call to turn from sin in the present tense (Matt. 3:2, 4:17; Mark 1:15; Acts 17:30; Rev. 2:16; cf. Luke 17:3-4).

What God requires, is that Men bring this inward conviction into fruition through an open commitment. The concept is taught in Romans 10:9 (NASB): "That if you confess with your mouth Jesus *as* Lord, and believe in your heart that God raised Him from the dead, you shall be saved." "Confess" is an ancient and somewhat misleading translation of the Greek

5. MacArthur, *Faith Works,* 75.

word *homologeo*, which literally means "to speak the same thing." The idea is to publicly express one's inward agreement with Christ. A thought-for-thought translation of this verse would read: "If you publicly declare that you agree with Christ, and believe in your heart that God has raised Him from the dead, you shall be saved." The public declaration is accomplished through an ordinance witnessed by others. That ordinance is called baptism (Matt. 3:5-6; Mark 1:5).

Baptism. The next step outlined by Peter in Acts 2:38 is baptism in the name of Jesus Christ for the forgiveness of sins. Baptism appears throughout the New Testament as the first act required of new believers (Acts 2:41; 8:12-13, 36-38; 9:18; 10:47-48; 16:15, 33; 18:8; 19:3-5; 22:16; see also, John 4:1; Rom. 6:3; 1 Cor. 10:1-2; 12:13; Gal. 3:27; Col. 2:12).

Though baptism is the first ordinance mentioned in the Gospel of Jesus Christ, it is of ancient origin, having been practiced by the Jews before Christ's ministry began, as witnessed by the activities of John the Baptist (Matt. 3:1-6). In the centuries prior to John, the Jews had come to require baptism only of proselytes[6], not those born of Jewish parents. John's baptism was new only in the sense that he preached the necessity of that ancient ordinance for *all* Jews

That salvation is the object and effect of baptism is clear from Peter's statement that it is "for the forgiveness of your sins" (Acts 2:38). Forgiveness of past sins is the essence of justification (cf., Col. 1:13-14). As an individual commitment or open confession of Christ, baptism is intended to bring into actual realization the inward desire for obedience that the new convert feels when he first obtains faith in Christ. The event also marks God's justification or forgiveness of the new convert's past sins. Thus, it leaves the believer with a clean slate, standing in perfect holiness before God.

Baptism is performed in the name of the Father, the Son and the Holy Ghost (Matt. 28:19). There is some confusion on this point among non-LDS Bible scholars, because some passages refer to baptism "in the name of Jesus Christ" (Acts 2:38; 8:16; 10:48; and 19:5), while others refer to "the baptism of John" (Matt. 21:25; Mark 11:30; Luke 7:29; 20:4; Acts 1:22; Acts 18:25). The baptism of John simply refers to the rite as performed under the authority of the Levitical Priesthood which John held. John knew that Christ's authority exceeded his own, and willingly

6. *The Interpreter's Dictionary of the Bible,* s.v. "baptism."

transferred the reigns of leadership to Christ (John 3:23-35; Acts 19:4). Thereafter, baptisms were performed by openly citing the authority of Christ (cf., John 4:1). But it was always the same ordinance, performed in the same manner—by immersion, and in the name of the Father, Son and Holy Spirit. John's baptism was perfectly valid, as witnessed by the fact that Christ, Himself, submitted to it.

When the scribes and elders asked Jesus, in Mark 11, by what authority He acted, He brought up the baptism of John and asked them whether or not it was authorized by heavenly authority (Mark 11:27-33). They were afraid and declined to answer. They knew that, if they said it was of heaven, as all the people knew, Christ would close the trap on them by noting that His authority was acknowledged by John to be from the same source.

Contradicting these biblical truths, Evangelicals unitedly reject the doctrine of baptism by water for the remission of sins as an ordinance necessary for salvation. Some teach that baptism is necessary to be a *disciple*, but claim it is not necessary to be a disciple in order to be saved.[7]

The Evangelical position is asserted on the basis of erroneous inferences drawn from the story of the thief on the cross (Luke 23:39-43) and the conversion of Cornelius described in Acts 10. The motivation for these arguments lies in the uncertainty of the Protestant claim to authority for performance of the Gospel ordinances, a subject that will require a book of its own.

One Evangelical argument against the necessity of baptism attempts to explain Peter's instructions as follows:

> Reading this, we see the meaning of baptism *for the purpose of* the remission of our sins. However, this is another instance where examining the translation is necessary for interpretation. The word translated "for" is the Greek preposition *eis*, which in this verse means "because of." We are baptized in the name of Jesus Christ "because of" the remission of our sins.[8]

The translation suggested here is neither accurate nor helpful to the Evangelical argument. Greek scholars do not believe that "because of" is the appropriate translation for the word *eis* in this context. It is not so translated in any respected modern version. "Into" is closest to the correct

7. Cocoris, *Lordship Salvation,* 15-16.
8. Trivanovich, *Speaking the Truth in Love.* 33.

translation of the word.[9] However, both the King James Version and the NASB translate it "*for*."

To be baptized "because of the remission of sins" would not be consistent with other teachings about baptism (see, e.g., Mark 1:4; Luke 3:3). It is particularly incongruous when examined in connection with Ananias' command to Paul, following the latter's conversion. He said, "And now why do you delay? Arise, and be baptized, and wash away your sins, calling on His name" (Acts 22:16, NASB). This statement indicates that the remission, or washing away, of Paul's sins would *follow* his baptism. Ananias never said Paul could be baptized if he felt like it because his sins had *already* been washed away.

The Bible teaches that the removal of sins is the object of baptism, but the remission of sins is neither caused, nor made possible, by baptism. Rather, baptism is the ordinance by which the individual makes the public commitment memorializing his covenant with God, who then declares the believer righteous through the power of Christ's atonement.

From Peter's words and historical evidence in the New Testament, it is clear that Men do not obtain the promised "gift of the Holy Spirit," which constitutes an initial state of salvation, until *after* water baptism (see e.g., Acts 8:14-17). (On this distinction, see also Matt. 3:11; Mark 1:8; and Luke 3:16.) Thus, in a very real a sense, it is water baptism that saves Men (1 Pet. 3:21).

The translation of *eis* suggested by Evangelicals is inconsistent with the symbolic character of the baptismal ordinance. Baptism is symbolic of accepting Christ (Rom. 6:4; Gal. 3:27; Col. 2:12), and hence is actually a corollary to the principle of faith. Men must have faith, i.e., accept Christ, *before* they obtain gifts consistent with salvation. The promise comes from Men first, a commitment to Christ, and from God second, that Men will receive remission of sins. To give the promise before the performance on which it is predicated would leave Man's performance unenforceable and meaningless. That is just the status of water baptism among Evangelicals today—it is thought to be unnecessary (and hence, is unenforceable), and has thereby been stripped of meaning or significance.

Even if Men *were* baptized *because* of the remission of their sins, Peter *commanded* his listeners to be baptized. If it be to have their sins remitted

9. Bauer, *A Greek-English Lexicon of the New Testament and Other Early Christian Literature,* s.v. "*eis*" (and similar root words).

or because their sins have already been remitted, the commandment remains the same. Though the Evangelical interpretation largely vitiates the ordinance, it does not change the fact that the Bible requires Christians to be baptized.[10] Salvation comes only by obedience to God's commandments, which cannot be viewed as optional. Thus, the translation propounded by Evangelicals would not justify their position against the necessity of baptism, even if it were accurate.

The mention of "the gift of the Holy Ghost" in juxtaposition to "baptism" in Acts 2:38 indicates that "baptism" is a different ordinance than that by which the gift of the Holy Spirit is conferred despite the fact that the latter ordinance can be referred to as baptism "with the Holy Ghost, and *with* fire" (Matt. 3:11; Luke 3:16; cf., Mark 1:8; John 1:33; Acts 1:5; and 11:16).

Some Evangelicals teach that when the scriptures speak of baptism being necessary for salvation, the reference is not to *water* baptism but to baptism with the Holy Ghost.[11] But baptism for *remission of sins* was always performed by immersion in water (see, e. g., Matt. 3: 5-6, 13-16; Mark 1:4-5, 9-10; John 3:23; Acts 8:38). Baptism with the Holy Ghost, on the other hand, was often accompanied by the gifts of the Holy Spirit, and involved no immersion in water (Acts 2:1-4; 10:44-46). The Bible does not confuse the two ordinances. Neither should theologians.

Some Evangelicals point to the fact that Paul had a different calling than to baptize as evidence that baptism is not necessary for salvation (1 Cor. 1:17).[12] The Apostles generally had other callings than to perform baptisms (see, Acts 8:5-25), but the function of officers within the organization of Christ's church has nothing to do with the necessity of baptism. Paul, in fact, *did* perform baptisms (e.g., Acts 19:1-6), and, though Christ did not Himself baptize (John 4:2), He commanded His Apostles to baptize all nations (Matt. 28:19), and His disciples baptized more new converts than John (John 4:1).

Still, some scholars erroneously claim that 1 Corinthians 1:17 demonstrates baptism is not part of the Gospel. That verse states in part (NASB), "For Christ did not send me to baptize, but to preach the gospel." The

10. Many Evangelicals encourage baptism despite their theological position regarding its benefits. See, e.g., Cocoris, *Lordship Salvation,* 18-29; MacArthur, *Faith Works,* 207-208.

11. *The Expositor's Bible Commentary,* 8:161.

12. MacArthur, *Faith Works,* 208 (footnote 17).

argument is that this phrase contrasts baptism with the gospel, showing that the two are separate.

That is obviously incorrect. What is contrasted in this phrase is *baptizing* and *preaching*, two separate *ministries* within the Gospel. Paul's assignment required him to do the latter and leave the former to other Church officers. In fact, when the grammar is correctly analyzed, the implication is that baptism was part of the Gospel Paul was sent to preach.

The Household of Cornelius. One of the two most significant prooftexts cited by Evangelicals for the proposition that baptism is not necessary for salvation is the conversion of Cornelius and his household described in Acts 10. Cornelius was a gentile who believed in God, gave alms, and prayed to God continually (Acts 10:2). Because of his righteousness, he and his household were chosen to demonstrate a dramatic new direction for the Church, one which had historic significance as the inauguration of the Age of the Gentiles.

An angel appeared to Cornelius and told him to seek out Peter (Acts 10:3-6), which he did immediately (Acts 10:7-8). At the same time, the Lord gave Peter a vision intended to change his attitude toward taking the Gospel to the Gentiles (Acts 10:9-16). As Peter contemplated the meaning of that vision, Cornelius' messengers arrived, and the Spirit told Peter to go with them (Acts 10:17-23). When they arrived at Cornelius' house, Peter found a large group of friends and relatives assembled to hear God's message (Acts 10:24-27).

Peter then realized the meaning of his vision and asked why they had sent for him (Acts 10:28-29). Cornelius related the vision he received and asked Peter to explain "all that you have been commanded by the Lord" (Acts 10:30-33, NASB). Peter then preached the first Gospel sermon to the Gentiles, bearing witness to the resurrection of Christ and asserting that through Him all who believe may receive forgiveness of sins (Acts 10:34-43).

The Holy Spirit fell upon Cornelius and his entire household (Acts 10:44), as evidenced by their receipt of the gift of tongues and their exultation of God. This manifestation was similar to that experienced with the Jews on the day of Pentecost. It demonstrated to Jewish believers that the Gospel was also to be taken to the Gentiles (Acts 10:45-47).

Evangelicals incorrectly assume that the outpouring of the Holy Ghost on this unique and momentous occasion was equivalent to salvation for those present. Thus, they believe that Cornelius and his family were saved *before* they were baptized and without the laying on of hands by which the gift of the Holy Ghost was always conferred (see, e.g., Acts 8:14-19).

Peter's next words belie that assumption (Acts 10:47-48, NASB, some emphasis added):

> "Surely no one can refuse the water for these to be baptized who have *received the Holy Spirit just as we did*, can he?"
>
> And he *ordered* them to be baptized in the name of Jesus Christ. Then they asked him to stay on for a few days.

When Peter said that Cornelius had "received the Holy Spirit just as we did," he referred to the unique outpouring of the Holy Ghost experienced by the Jews at Pentecost. There was a symmetry between this event and that at Pentecost. The Jews who were converted at the Pentecostal outpouring were not instantly saved without baptism. Peter told them to be baptized for the remission of sins, and that *afterwards* they would receive the "gift of the Holy Ghost" (Acts 2:37-38). In the same manner, Peter ordered all the Gentiles present on this occasion to be baptized (Acts 10:48).[13]

Thus, the requirement of baptism was not abridged in this instance. There is no instance in the Bible where new converts were not baptized, or told that they must immediately be baptized, after they received a conviction that Jesus is the Christ.

The Thief on the Cross. What about the thief on the cross? In Luke 23:39-43, one of the malefactors crucified with Christ acknowledged Him as the sinless Lord and asked to be remembered "when thou comest into thy kingdom." Whether he actually, knew anything about Christ's kingdom or not, he received a very special promise: "And Jesus said unto him, Verily I say unto thee, To day shalt thou be with me in paradise" (Luke 23:43).

Evangelicals assume this was a promise of salvation without baptism, but that isn't what the passage says. The terms of Christ's promise to the thief were quite specific. On *that* day, the thief would be *with* Christ *in* "paradise." To understand this promise it is necessary to determine *where* paradise is, and *what* Christ did there (as a newly disembodied spirit) on the day of His crucifixion.

13. Though not specifically stated in Acts 10, it is certain Cornelius also received the gift of the Holy Ghost by the laying on of hands after he was baptized in response to Peter's command.

The word *paradise* is used only three times in the Bible (Luke 23:43; 2 Cor. 12:4; and Rev. 2:7), and, though these references imply that paradise is a good place, they do not indicate that it is heaven. A close look at the scriptures, in fact, shows that paradise is *not* a place reserved exclusively for saved individuals.

First Peter 3:18-20, reveals that immediately after His death, Christ went to preach the Gospel to those who lived in the days of Noah before the flood. His purpose was to open the work of ministry to the dead (1 Pet. 4:5-6; John 5:25—discussed in Chapter 9.) These souls had been grossly wicked (Gen. 6:5-7, 11-13). They certainly were not in Heaven. If Christ went to paradise the day He died, as his comment to the thief implies, and that place was not Heaven, as 1 Peter 3:18-20 suggests (see, also, Eph. 4:8-10), then Christ's promise to the thief (to be *with* Him *in* "paradise" on *that* day), was definitely *not* one of instant salvation. A more detailed examination of this issue is contained in Chapter 9.

Unchanging Ordinances. The very character of God contradicts the Evangelical position regarding water baptism. Hebrews 13:8 says God is "the same yesterday, and to day, and for ever." He has not changed the requirements for making an open commitment to Him during Man's entire existence on this earth. He changed the Law of Moses, but that Law did *not* bring salvation (Gal. 3:21). It was a "schoolmaster" to bring Israel to Christ (Gal. 3:24), and reached its appropriate end upon its fulfillment in Christ's atoning sacrifice. Baptism was practiced by the Jews, as indicated above, and Christ was baptized "to fulfil all righteousness" (Matt. 3:13-17). All who believed at the preaching of the Apostles were commanded to be baptized (Matt. 28:19-20). The continuity of this requirement spans both the Old and New Testaments.

There remains to this day the requirement that all Men publicly demonstrate that they agree with Christ through the ritual of baptism. The remission of sins, which comes by reason of the atoning sacrifice of Christ, is applied to wash away Man's sins through obedience to that ordinance. This is the sense in which baptism is a saving ordinance.

Peter stated that fact in 1 Peter 3:21 (some emphasis added). After noting that eight persons were saved from the Flood (Noah and his three sons and each of their wives), Peter said that the number eight (8) is:

> The like figure[14] whereunto *even baptism doth also now save us* (not the putting away of the filth of the flesh, but the answer of a good conscience toward God,) by the resurrection of Jesus Christ:

The parenthetical phrase in this verse has presented significant problems for Evangelical exegetes. They erroneously claim that the statement, "not the putting away of the filth of the flesh," means that Man is *not* saved by water baptism. They arrive at this conclusion by assuming that "the filth of the flesh" refers to fleshly sins and "the putting away" refers to water baptism. Thus, Evangelicals would render the passage: "The like figure whereunto even baptism doth also now save us (not water baptism, but the answer of a good conscience toward God,)."

This interpretation is profoundly flawed. It assumes the very concept Peter intended to prove—that water baptism washes away sins—then arrives at a contrary conclusion. To assert that "the putting away of the filth of the flesh" means water baptism, one must accept the idea that water baptism does, in fact, "[put] away" fleshly sins. To do that, and at the same time disclaim the efficacy of water baptism for that very purpose, is a feat of logic that would only be comfortable for a Hellenist. If one assumes that water baptism is the washing away ("the putting away") of sins ("the filth of the flesh"), one must also acknowledge that it is the saving ordinance Peter referred to in this verse.

Actually, the phrase "putting away of the filth of the flesh" in this context is *not* a reference to water baptism, but should be taken literally as washing dirt from the body. The phrase, "the answer of a good conscience toward God," is Peter's allusion to water baptism. What the parenthetical phrase means is that baptism is not the same as taking a bath, it is the answer of the new convert to God's call for Men to commit to Him and obtain a good, or clean, conscience.

Evangelicals say that "the answer of a good conscience toward God" means the baptism of fire, or the gift of the Holy Ghost. But Peter's remarks in Acts 2:38 make it clear that the gift of the Holy Ghost is an answer *from* God *to* the baptized believer. That is, the baptism of fire and the Holy Ghost is *God's* answer, or reward, to Men who have sought a good conscience, and were cleansed by baptism for the remission of sins. It is not *Man's* answer "toward" God.

The NASB translation of 1 Peter 3:21 makes this point clear:

---

14. Mormons believe that "the like figure" (eight), represents the minimum age at which a person may be a candidate for baptism. Baptism is not required of children under that age. Instead, they are cited as the archetype of redeemed saints (Matt. 18:3).

> And corresponding to that, baptism now saves you—not the removal of dirt from the flesh, but an appeal to God for a good conscience–through the resurrection of Jesus Christ.

The ordinance of *water* baptism is an appeal by Men to God for a good (or clean) conscience, washed free of sin and prepared to receive the gift of the Holy Ghost, the baptism of fire. Peter states that this ordinance "now *saves* you . . . through the resurrection of Jesus Christ" (emphasis added).

The word "baptism" here is *baptisma*, meaning to wash or immerse. It is the classical Greek word for bathing, and Peter's effort to clarify his use of that word as a reference to the sacred ordinance, rather than a bath, is understandable in light of the Old Testament's treatment of baptism. The Greek word *baptisma*, of course, does not appear in the Old Testament, but its Hebrew equivalent, the verb "to wash," does Unfortunately, it has several meanings depending on the context. The writers (and translators) of the Old Testament did not use a different word when the context suggested that the ordinance was immersion in water for the remission of sins, as opposed to some other ceremonial washing, or the secular act of bathing. Thus, it is hard to tell when an Old Testament text refers to baptism.

From the context, it appears that baptism is referred to in the following passages where the verb "to wash" has been used in the Old Testament: Psalms 51:2, 7; Proverbs 30:12; Isaiah 1:16; 4:4; Jeremiah 4:14; and Ezekiel 16:9. The same may be true of Exodus 29:4 and Leviticus 8:6, though the washings mentioned in those passages probably refer to a ceremonial washing by the priests before they put on their temple garments (Lev. 16:23-24).

The New Testament is much clearer in its use of *baptisma* as a reference to water baptism. On those few occasions when the scriptures refer to receipt of the Holy Ghost as baptism, the reference always includes a prepositional phrase, e.g., "baptized *with the Holy Ghost*" (Acts 1:5; and 11:16). Whenever the term "baptism" is used alone, as it is in 1 Peter 3:21, it refers to baptism by immersion in water for the remission of sins, as Peter carefully noted in his parenthetical phrase.

Christ taught the efficacy of baptism for salvation in Mark 16:15-16 (NASB):

> And He said to them, "Go into all the world and preach the gospel to all creation.

> "He who has believed and has been baptized shall be saved; but he who has disbelieved shall be condemned."

This passage states two requirements *mutually* necessary for salvation (note the use of "and" in the phrase "He who has believed *and* has been baptized shall be saved"). The language is clear and unequivocal. How, then, do Evangelicals deal with it? Some reject these verses entirely, claiming they were not part of the original gospel written by Mark. That position was discussed in Chapter 1.

Others note that, although the passage states "He who has believed and has been baptized shall be *saved*," it goes on to say, "but he who has disbelieved shall be condemned" (KJV: "he that believeth not shall be damned"). They note that the passage does *not* say "he who has disbelieved *and* has not been baptized shall be condemned." From the absence of any reference to baptism in the second clause of the sentence, Evangelicals argue that even though believers *should* be baptized, they will not be *condemned* for failing to perform that ordinance.[15]

This is, at best, a dangerous way to interpret scripture. Verse 16 may not state specifically what happens to those who believe but are not baptized, but neither does it promise they will be saved. Men might avoid condemnation by believing but not being baptized, but there is certainly no assurance in this passage that they will be saved by following that course of action.

Actually, the Lord, in these closing remarks to His Apostles, is saying that the Gospel includes both *laws* and the *ordinances* that must be followed in order to be saved. If a man believes in Christ, he will follow Christ's instructions for salvation and be baptized. Hence, the phrase "he who has disbelieved" *includes* those who claim to believe but refuse baptism. "He who has believed" in Christ will be baptized. If a person as he commanded wants to be saved, and is not simply trying to see how close he can come to condemnation without being caught in its chains, he will follow Christ's instructions, and (1) *believe*, i.e. accept Christ, His laws, *and* His ordinances, and (2) be *baptized*.

Christ taught Nicodemus this principle at the beginning of His ministry, as recorded in John 3:1-5. He told Nicodemus he had to be "born again" to see the kingdom of God.[16] Nicodemus did not understand, and

---

15. G. Michael Cocoris, *Evangelism: A Biblical Approach* (Chicago: Moody Press, 1984), 29.

complained that a man cannot enter again into his mother's womb (John 3:3-4). Christ did not contradict him on this point. Instead, He indicated to Nicodemus that His words were figurative. In order to be saved, a man who has faith in Him must submit to two ordinances that Christ compared to birth: "Except a man be born of water and *of* the Spirit, he cannot enter into the kingdom of God" (John 3:5).

"Born of water" refers to water baptism, and "born . . . *of* the Spirit" means to receive the gift of the Holy Ghost. No other exegesis of these terms is consistent with hermeneutic principles. These ordinances constitute birth into the kingdom of God, and no one can enter His kingdom without making the commitment they entail. It was precisely from such a lack of commitment that Nicodemus suffered. He believed in Christ, but as a member of the Sanhedrin he wouldn't publicly commit to Him. Hence Christ's confrontation on this subject.

Rather than accept this important message, some Evangelicals argue that the water birth spoken of here is Man's natural birth in the watery womb.[17] If that were true, Christ would have either been ratifying the misunderstanding Nicodemus expressed in John 3:4, or establishing mammalian birth as a condition for salvation. Neither of these options makes sense. Christ was teaching the requirements for entry into *His* kingdom, not the kingdom of this earth.

Other Evangelical teachers claim that the term "water" used in John 3:5 should be translated "spirit."[18] This suggestion is not true to the text. The word translated "water" here is *hudor*, a Greek noun meaning nothing more than "water." In any case, such a translation would result in redundancy. It would render the passage: "Except a man be born of the spirit and of the Spirit, he cannot enter into the kingdom of God." This is obviously poor hermeneutics, and so is every other interpretation of the passage except the one that acknowledges Christ's point in confronting Nicodemus—that Men *must* make a commitment to Him through baptism and the laying on of hands to receive the gift of the Holy Ghost.

The birth to which water baptism is compared in John 3:5 is also viewed as a "death" in the Scriptures. When Men are born into the

16. "Again," in the phrase "born again," is from *anōthen*, and is best translated "born from above," consistent with the Book of Mormon's call to be "born of God" (Mosiah 27:25-26; Alma 5:14; 22:15; 36:5, 23, 24, 26; and 38:6).
17. *The Expositor's Bible Commentary,* 9:47.
18. *Ibid.*

kingdom of God, they simultaneously die to this worldly kingdom. Paul compares water baptism to the symbolic death of the old man and the birth of the new man in Christ (Rom. 6:3-6; Col. 2:12). Thus, total immersion in water, as in a watery grave and a mother's womb, is the only appropriate means for performing the ordinance.

Paul also taught that baptism constitutes entry into the body of Christ. In Galatians 3:27, he said, "For as many of you as have been baptized into Christ have put on Christ." The significance of this statement should be apparent to Evangelical theologians, who believe that the phrase "into Christ" refers to their position of permanent salvation following their conversion to Christ (see Chapter 8). This passage demonstrates that any such position can be obtained only through baptism.

The symbolism in the ritual of baptism has a powerful impact upon converts. Believers are immersed in the water that will be a grave for their old nature. They are lifted out with their sins washed away, reborn into new life as a member of the body of Christ. It is sad that Men have tampered with this powerful ordinance, replacing it with such acts as walking to the front of the congregation in response to an evangelist's call, or saying a prayer prescribed by some modern theologian. God cannot be expected to recognize or accept such substitutes for His sacraments, any more than He can accept the authority of unauthorized volunteers in performing baptisms or other acts in His name (Matt. 7:22-23).

Because they lack biblical authority for performing the ordinance of baptism, the Evangelical attitude toward that ordinance has come to be typified by a new sentiment, expressed in the following statement:

> The true biblical gospel tells us that Christ died for "our sins." 1 John 1:7 says, "the blood of Jesus Christ His Son cleanseth us from all sin." If all my sins are cleansed by His precious blood, if they were borne "in His own body on the tree" (1 Peter 2:24), then how many are left to be cleansed by baptism?[19]

This confused declaration insults (1) Christ, who commanded baptism and was Himself baptized as an example to all Men, (2) Peter, who commanded baptism of the Jews at Pentecost and of the Gentiles at the house of Cornelius, and (3) Paul, who said that baptism is the way Men put on Christ. The answer of all these authorities to the rhetorical question posed in this statement would be an emphatic, "All of them!" The blood of Jesus

---

19. Trivanovich, *Speaking the Truth in Love,* 33.

Christ is the *power* that cleanses sin, but baptism is the *switch* by which Men turn that power on in their lives.

More serious than the misunderstanding expressed in the quotation above is the deception practiced in its second sentence. John did not say "The blood of Jesus Christ His Son cleanseth us from all sin." He said, "But *if* we walk in the light, as he is in the light, . . . the blood of Jesus Christ his Son cleanseth us from all sin" (emphasis added). Thus, John's promise was conditional upon obedience to the very ordinances Evangelicals decry, including the ordinance of baptism, to which Christ, the Exemplar, Himself, submitted.

There is no promise that the blood of Jesus Christ will cleanse Men from sin, *unless* they "walk in the light, as he [Christ] is in the light." Christ was baptized "to fulfil all righteousness" (Matt. 3:15), that is, to show Men how to "walk in the light." If a man is not baptized, he is not walking in the light as Christ did. Such a man will not have fellowship with Christ, and will *not* be cleansed from *any* sins.

Paul taught that Man is saved by baptism through the atonement of Jesus Christ in Titus 3:5:

> Not by works of righteousness which we have done, but according to his mercy he saved us, by the washing of regeneration, and renewing of the Holy Ghost;

The first half of this passage is quoted by Evangelicals to support their misunderstanding of God's Plan of Salvation.[20] But they stop short of acknowledging Paul's mention of baptism in the same verse. According to Paul, there are two ordinances "*by*" which Men are saved "according to his mercy": one is "the washing of regeneration" and the other is "renewing of the Holy Ghost."

The term "washing" is translated from the Greek word *loutron*, which refers to a laver, bath, or washing vessel (see also, Eph. 5:26). Baptism by immersion in water was often performed in such a convenience, which Mormons now call a "baptismal font." Since the word "baptism" means "to wash," and the term "regeneration" means re-creation, or new birth, Paul's metaphoric language, "the washing of regeneration," obviously refers to water baptism.

It would be easy to assume that the phrase "renewing of the Holy Ghost" refers to receiving the gift of the Holy Ghost after baptism.

20. See, e.g., MacArthur, *The Gospel According to Jesus,* 147.

However, the term "renewing" is not entirely consistent with that interpretation. It also suggests something that refreshes or renews the original gift. There is no indication in the Bible that baptism is performed more than once in the life of any believer (except when it was first performed incorrectly by false teachers, as in Acts 19:1-8). Likewise, the gift of the Holy Ghost was conferred only once, following baptism (cf., Acts 8:14-17; 19:2-6). What then is the second ordinance inferred by Paul in Titus 3:5? That question will be examined after a closer look at the gift of the Holy Ghost itself.

The Gift of the Holy Ghost

The "gift of the Holy Ghost [or Holy Spirit]" is not mentioned as a *requirement* in Acts 2:38. Rather, it is a *promise* to the faithful who repent and are baptized. The spiritual gifts that come through the Holy Ghost are many (see, e.g., 1 Cor. 12:8-11), but the promise that a baptized believer will "receive the *gift* of the Holy Ghost" (Acts 2:38 emphasis added) is not the same as a spiritual gift *from* the Holy Ghost.

The gift of the Holy Ghost is a restoration of the believer, who has been saved by repentance and water baptism, to fellowship with a member of the Godhead. Spiritual Death is separation from God. Being granted the right to commune with the Holy Ghost, a member of the Godhead, is a reprieve from that separation, and the beginning of salvation in the presence of God.

This privilege was conferred through the laying on of hands, as indicated in Acts 8:14-17, which tells of the Samaritan saints that were converted by Philip:

> Now when the apostles which were at Jerusalem heard that Samaria had received the word of God, they sent unto them Peter and John:
>
> Who, when they were come down, prayed for them, that they might receive the Holy Ghost:
>
> (For as yet he was fallen upon none of them: only they were baptized in the name of the Lord Jesus.)
>
> Then laid they *their* hands on them, and they received the Holy Ghost.

(Note that verse 14 says they "had received the word of God," while as yet they had only been baptized (verse 16). This indicates that baptism was part of receiving the word of God.)

Christ conferred the gift of the Holy Ghost on his disciples after His resurrection, saying to them "Receive ye the Holy Ghost" (John 20:22). However, the Holy Ghost did not actually come upon them until the day of Pentecost, after Christ's ascension (John 7:38-39, Acts 1:8). As He indicated to His disciples, He had to go so the Holy Ghost could come to them (John 14:26; 15:26; and 16:7).

After Christ's departure, the Holy Ghost was sent to the Jewish disciples in the dramatic Pentecostal outpouring witnessed by multitudes and described in Acts 2:1-13. The promise that the Gentiles could receive the gift of the Holy Ghost was demonstrated by the similar miraculous manifestation at the house of Cornelius (and see, e.g., Acts 19:5-6).

The ordinances of baptism by water and the laying on of hands for the gift of the Holy Ghost were identified as fundamental principles of the doctrine of Christ in Hebrews 6:1-2 (emphasis added):

> Therefore leaving the principles of the doctrine of Christ, let us go on unto perfection; not laying again the foundation of repentance from dead works, and of faith toward God,
>
> *Of the doctrine of baptisms*, and *of laying on of hands*, and of resurrection of the dead, and of eternal judgment.

This passage identifies the "doctrine of baptisms" as part of the "foundation" of the "doctrine of Christ." The word translated "baptisms" here is *baptismos*, not the usual *baptisma. Baptismos* is translated "divers washings" in Hebrews 9:10, and "washing" in Mark 7:4, referring in each case to Jewish ordinances.[21] While these translations would be improper in this context, it is clear that the term "baptisms" does *not* refer to water baptism and baptism with fire and the Holy Ghost.

The "laying on of hands" is mentioned in the next phrase, and refers to the latter ordinance, since it was performed by the laying on of hands.[22] Of course, laying on of hands was employed in many ordinances mentioned in the Bible. E.g., giving blessings (Gen. 48:17-20), conferring authority for a particular calling (Num. 27:23), healing (Matt. 9:18, Mark 6:5, Acts 28:8), appointing officers in the Church (Acts 6:5-6), and giving special

---

21. F.F. Bruce, ed., *The New International Commentary on the New Testament: The Epistle to the Hebrews* (Grand Rapids: Eerdmans, 1964), 115.
22. Evangelicals concur on this point. *The Expositor's Bible Commentary,* 12:53; *The New International Commentary on the New Testament: The Epistle to the Hebrews,* 116-17.

gifts (1 Tim. 4:14). It appears that the author of Hebrews identified all these ordinances, along with conferring the Holy Ghost, as fundamental doctrines of Christ by using a reference to the means by which they were performed–the "laying on of hands."

Though water baptism and the gift of the Holy Ghost are frequently mentioned together (John 3:5; Acts 2:38, 19:1-7), the term "baptisms" in Hebrews 6:2, sometimes translated "ablutions,"[23] probably refers to water baptism and the ordinance, intimated in Titus 3:5 ("the renewing of the Holy Ghost"). What is that ordinance and its significance in connection with Man's salvation? To answer that question, it is necessary first to understand the principal of endurance to the end.

Endurance to the End

The requirement that believers "endure to the end" is usually associated with adversity (Matt. 10:22; Mark 13:13). It reflects the believer's long-term commitment to Christ in the face of trials and persecution. The permanence and reality of commitment becomes evident only as Men continue in their new life-direction to the end of their days.

Man's mind, reflected in his attitudes and beliefs, tends to be unstable and changeable. Varying behavior, sometimes obedient and sometimes not, reflects that changeability. God requires that Men learn to continue in obedience, enduring the trials and temptations of life that affect their attitudes and behavior, until they can be trusted to be obedient in the future as well as the present.

The Savior taught his disciples the necessity of endurance to the end. He did not tell them that if they endured persecution until it stopped (that is, endured to the end of persecution) they would receive a reward. He said, "he that shall endure unto the end, the same shall be *saved*" (Matt. 24:13, emphasis added; see, also, 10:22; and Mark 13:13).

C. I. Scofield claims this passage does not refer to "salvation of the soul of the believer who endures persecution, but to his deliverance by the Lord's return" at the end of "the tribulation."[24] Under this claim, the endurance required in this passage is only that necessary to outlast the persecution to be experienced by believers who live on the earth before the

23. It is so translated in the *Revised Standard Version of the Bible.*

24. *The New Scofield Study Bible,* 1367, 1408 (footnotes to Matt. 24:13 and Mark 13:13).

Second Coming, during the seven-year period Evangelicals call the Great Tribulation.

There are more problems with this interpretation than the fact that nothing in the context of the passage supports it. One of them is Evangelical eschatology (the study of ultimate or last things, such as events in the last days). The popular view today is called "pre-millenialism." In that view, all true Christians will be taken up to heaven in the Rapture, *before* the Great Tribulation.

If that view is correct, only those converted during the Great Tribulation will be on earth to endure the persecution mentioned by Scofield. That means Christ's message on endurance was of no interest to the believers of His day, and of little significance to believers now. None of them will have to endure in the way Christ admonished.

The correct view is demonstrated in the Parable of the Sower, explained by Christ as follows (Mark 4:14-20, NASB):

> "The sower sows the word.
>
> "And these are the ones who are beside the road where the word is sown; and when they hear, immediately Satan comes and takes away the word which has been sown in them.
>
> "And in a similar way these are the ones on whom seed was sown on the rocky *places*, who, when they hear the word, immediately receive it with joy;
>
> and they have no *firm* root in themselves, but are *only* temporary; then, when affliction or persecution arises because of the word, immediately they fall away.
>
> "And others are the ones on whom seed was sown among the thorns; these are the ones who have heard the word,
>
> and the worries of the world, and the deceitfulness of riches, and the desires for other things enter in and choke the word, and it becomes unfruitful.
>
> "And those are the ones on whom seed was sown on the good soil; and they hear the word and accept it, and bear fruit, thirty, sixty, and a hundredfold."

Each group mentioned by the Savior represents different "ones on whom seed was sown." The soils represent the character of the individuals who receive the seed. The importance of enduring to the end is emphasized through Christ's comments on the failure of the second group, who *received* the word with joy (that is, they became true believers), but failed to endure "affliction or persecution . . . because of the word."

In varying degrees *all* believers experience some problem with this kind of affliction or persecution. Thus, Christ's message was directed to all believers to encourage them in the face of tribulation. The ancient saints faced physical persecution as a deterrent to their faith, but the need to endure tests of faith in order to be saved is no less essential for today's Christians.

Once Men have faith, that faith causes them to agree with Christ and view their sins with abhorrence so they turn from them. Then they are ready to receive baptism (Acts 8:34-38; 22:16).[25] When they are baptized, they are clean before God and upon receipt of the gift of the Holy Ghost are saved (at least to a degree). However, as soon as they commit sin, they are no longer worthy of God's presence. They lose that degree of salvation they achieved. If they are to endure to the end, there must be a way to *restore* Men to their association with the Holy Ghost, to *renew* that gift and their state of salvation.

The Sacrament of the Lord's Supper

There are numerous references in the Bible to Man being cleansed through the flesh and blood of Christ. In Romans 5:9, Paul states (NASB, some emphasis added): "Much more then, having now been justified *by His blood*, we shall be *saved* from the wrath *of* God through Him." Likewise, Paul taught the Ephesians about Christ (Eph. 1:7, emphasis added): "In whom we have redemption *through his blood*, the *forgiveness of sins*, according to the riches of his grace;" The author of Hebrews referred to the same concept in Hebrews 13:12 (NASB, emphasis added): "Therefore Jesus also, that He might *sanctify* the people *through His own blood*, suffered outside the gate." Earlier, the same writer states (Heb. 10:19-22, NASB, some emphasis added):

> Since therefore, brethren, we have confidence to *enter the holy place* by the *blood of Jesus*,

25. In the spirit of Paul's warning, "Lay hands suddenly on no man" (1 Tim. 5:22), it is both appropriate and wise for those who are authorized to administer the ordinances of the Gospel to require some evidence of the reality of repentance in the life of the believer before performing these saving ordinances. That is the practice in The Church of Jesus Christ of Latter-day Saints.

> by a new and living way which He inaugurated for us through the veil, that is, *His flesh*,
>
> and since *we have* a great priest over the house of God,
>
> let us draw near with a sincere heart in full assurance of faith, having our hearts *sprinkled clean* from an evil conscience and our bodies *washed with pure water.*

All these passages emphasize that "by His *blood*" Men are justified, redeemed, sanctified, and prepared to enter "the holy place." These references identify every stage of salvation, and suggest that the blood of Christ is involved in Man's salvation throughout the sanctification process, not just at baptism.

In the last verse quoted above, two separate acts are mentioned, one involving the heart and the other, the body. The language is figurative, so the reference to a symbolic washing of the body "with pure water" should be taken as a reference to water baptism. (The waters of baptism are not "pure" because they have been filtered or distilled, but because they purify Men through the forgiveness of their sins.)

In 1 Peter 3:21 (NASB) water baptism is described as "an appeal to God for a good conscience." The reference in Hebrews 10:22 to having "our hearts sprinkled *clean* from an evil conscience" is very similar. Both describe a process by which Men can lose their "evil conscience" and obtain a "good conscience," but, as this verse indicates, the heart is "*sprinkled*," while in 1 Peter the body is "*washed*."

This suggests that sprinkling and washing refer to two different ordinances, each of which comprises an important part of the sanctification process. Men are saved by baptism, a washing, that involves the entire body, but they can fall from that state by committing sin after baptism. That Men's *hearts* can be "sprinkled clean from an evil conscience" suggests there is a saving ordinance that involves a smaller amount of liquid than that required for total immersion, but has the same effect on the soul as water baptism.

Peter speaks of being "sprinkled" in a passage that deals with sanctification (1 Peter 1:1-2, NASB, emphasis added):

> Peter, an apostle of Jesus Christ, to those who reside as aliens, scattered throughout Pontus, Galatia, Cappadocia, Asia, and Bithynia, who are chosen
>
> according to the foreknowledge of God the Father, by the sanctifying work of the Spirit, that you may obey Jesus Christ and be

sprinkled with His blood: May grace and peace be yours in fullest measure.

What is the meaning of these references to being "sprinkled"? Do they relate to the traditional Catholic method of baptism? Are Men to be baptized repeatedly by sprinkling? Revelation 7:13-15 provides further insight as it describes the reward of those who make their robes white in His blood (emphasis added):

> And one of the elders answered, saying unto me, What are these which are arrayed in white robes? and whence came they?
>
> And I said unto him, Sir, thou knowest. And he said to me, These are they which came out of great tribulation, and have washed their robes, *and* made them white in the *blood* of the Lamb.
>
> Therefore are they before the throne of God, and serve him day and night in his temple: and he that sitteth on the throne shall dwell among them.

The reference to washing ("have *washed* their robes") is an obvious allusion to baptism, but what is the significance of the additional phrase, "and made them white in the *blood* of the Lamb"? Is there additional meaning in that phrase, or does it merely explain the result of washing their robes?

Part of the key to all these passages is found in the Savior's words in John 6:48-58 (NASB, some emphasis added):

> "I am the bread of life.
>
> "Your fathers ate the manna in the wilderness, and they died.
>
> "This is the bread which comes down out of heaven, so that one may eat of it and not die.
>
> "I am the living bread that came down out of heaven; if anyone eats of this bread, he shall live forever; and the bread also which I shall give for the life of the world is *My flesh.*"
>
> The Jews therefore *began* to argue with one another, saying, "How can this man give us *His flesh* to eat?"
>
> Jesus therefore said to them, "Truly, truly, I say to you, unless you eat the *flesh of the Son of Man* and drink *His blood*, you have no life in yourselves.
>
> "He who eats *My flesh* and drinks *My blood* has eternal life, and I will raise him up on the last day.
>
> "For *My flesh* is true food, and *My blood* is true drink.

> "He who eats *My flesh* and drinks *My blood* abides in Me, and I in him.
>
> "As the living Father sent Me, and I live because of the Father, so he who eats Me, he also shall live because of Me.
>
> "This is the bread which came down out of heaven; not as the fathers ate, and died, he who eats this bread shall live forever."

Here the Savior refers not only to His blood, but to His flesh, requiring that, in order to have eternal life, Men must "eat" His flesh and "drink" His blood. The Jews were strictly forbidden to drink blood under the Law of Moses (Lev. 17:10-14). Hence, even Christ's own disciples were taken aback by this saying (John 6:60).

Of course, Christ was not promoting cannibalism. The context doesn't suggest a literal interpretation. Even the Catholic position on these verses is too literal for the language employed here (see John 6:63). However, Christ was definitely stating a requirement for salvation, as indicated by His reference to "life" in verse 53, meaning "eternal life," as indicated in the next verse.

Christ did not clarify this figurative language however, until the night before His crucifixion, when He established a ritual that has become known as The Sacrament of the Lord's Supper. It is described in Matthew 26:26-28 (NASB, some emphasis and brackets added) as follows:

> And while they were eating, Jesus took *some* bread, and after a blessing, He broke *it* and gave *it* to the disciples, and said, "Take, eat; *this is My body*." [Luke adds: "do this in remembrance of Me."]
>
> And when He had taken a cup and given thanks, He gave it to them, saying, "Drink from it, all of you;
>
> for *this is My blood* of the covenant, which is poured out *for many for forgiveness of sins*."

See also Mark 14:22-24 and Luke 22:19-20. (Hebrews 13:20 refers to this ordinance when it mentions "the blood of the everlasting covenant.")

This passage provides the figurative meaning for the references to Christ's "body" (or "flesh") and His "blood" in the scriptures cited previously. In the ordinance Christ established, the bread was eaten in remembrance of "His body," and the cup sipped in remembrance of "His blood."[26] The symbolism of these acts is confirmed by Paul's remarks in 1 Corinthians 10:16 (NASB): "Is not the cup of blessing which we bless a sharing in the blood of Christ? Is not the bread which we break a sharing in the body of Christ?"

That the early Church understood this meaning and the importance of this ordinance appears from the fact that the ceremony Christ instituted at the Last Supper was a regular part of their weekly worship services (see, e.g., Acts 2:42; 20:7). It became known as the Sacrament, and was treated with great respect (see 1 Cor. 11:23-34). That the Sacrament is related to salvation is evident from the reference to forgiveness of sins in Matthew 26:28 (and the promise of eternal life in John 6:54).

It follows that, if Men sin after baptism and have need of renewed repentance and justification, they partake of the Sacrament rather than being rebaptized. By this means truly penitent believers can be restored to the state of salvation from which their recent sins dislodged them. The Sacrament refreshes the believer's remembrance of his or her commitment to Christ made at baptism, and thus reestablishes the gift of the Holy Ghost. It follows that Paul's reference to "renewing of the Holy Ghost" in Titus 3:5 includes an allusion to the Sacrament.

Baptism, an *immersion* in liquid, *washes* away Men's sins after belief in Christ and repentance. Partaking of the Sacrament renews the memory of that event through a sip of liquid taken on a weekly basis "in remembrance" of His blood. It is tantamount to being "sprinkled with His blood" (1 Pet. 1:2), and represents the means by which believers are "sprinkled *clean*" (Heb. 10:22, NASB), making their robes "white in the blood of the Lamb" after they have once "washed their robes" in His blood (Rev. 7:14) through baptism.

Conclusion

Baptism is the biblical rite by which repentant believers demonstrate a commitment to Christ and receive justification, that is, forgiveness of their sins. When a man comes out of the waters of baptism, he is washed clean, and, at that moment, is ready to enter the Kingdom of God. Being fit to receive the gift of communion with the Holy Ghost, he is "saved" from Spiritual Death, as Peter used that term in 1 Peter 3:21.

26. "The cup" or "a cup" (from a Greek word meaning "drinking vessel") in the passages establishing the Lord's Supper never indicated the particular fluid contained therein. Though it is presumed to have been wine, the lack of any reference to that libation suggests that the liquid used in the Sacrament of the Lord's Supper is entirely irrelevant. Mormons use water.

The Lord knew that Men would make mistakes after baptism, so He commanded them to endure in the process of sanctification to the end. Given the tendency of the flesh to sin (see Romans 7), all Men are likely to experience some degree of failure while learning perfect obedience. To provide a means for *renewing* their commitment to Him and receiving justification for their *recent* sins without the necessity of rebaptism, Christ instituted the Sacrament. As baptism is a wholesale washing of all sins from the believer's past life, the Sacrament, if partaken of regularly as was the practice in the early Church, is a "sprinkling" of His blood to cleanse the sins of the recent past and to renew the believer's fellowship with the Holy Ghost.

Together, these ordinances provide a divinely instituted plan whereby believers seeking to learn perfect obedience to God through the sanctification process may wash their robes clean in the blood of the Lamb (Rev. 7:14). By making a real commitment to follow the Savior's example, and renewing that commitment weekly, believers can overcome the grasp of bad habits and get ready for full-time residence in God's eternal presence.

Of course, this boon cannot be used for license. It is not available to justify unrelinquished sins week after week. Partaking of the Sacrament under such circumstances will result in condemnation, as Paul made clear in the following warning to the Corinthians (1 Cor. 11:27-30, NASB):

> Therefore whoever eats the bread or drinks the cup of the Lord in an unworthy manner, shall be guilty of the body and the blood of the Lord.
>
> But let a man examine himself, and so let him eat of the bread and drink of the cup.
>
> For he who eats and drinks, eats and drinks judgment to himself, if he does not judge the body rightly.
>
> For this reason many among you are weak and sick, and a number sleep.

Verse 29 indicates that if Men do not "judge the body rightly" they eat and drink condemnation to themselves in partaking of the Sacrament. The original Greek indicates that Men must judge themselves thoroughly in partaking of the Sacrament, or they will be judged by the Lord. What they must decide, and evidence by openly (i.e., publicly) partaking of the Sacrament, is whether or not they are truly *willing* to obey Him. If they are, the atoning grace of Christ is available to restore them to a state of perfection before God. They will remain in that state as long as they continue to obey Him. In time, the duration of their obedience will become greater and greater until it is perfected in permanent obedience, and with that, permanent salvation in the Kingdom of God.

This is the way the Lord has established, using symbolic rituals to aid Men in their struggle along the way to perfection and eternal life. Rather than rejecting those ordinances as unnecessary, simplistic, or too ritualistic, all Men should receive them from His authorized servants, and use them in the manner the Lord intended, openly committing and recommitting themselves to Christ and thereby enjoying continued communion with the Holy Ghost, and eventually with God and Christ.

8

An Assurance of Salvation

Those who enter the strait[1] gate through faith, repentance and baptism, and embark on the narrow way of sanctification through communion with the Holy Ghost, will face a battle Paul described as follows (Rom. 7:24-25, JST[2]):

> And now I see another law, even the commandment of Christ, and it is imprinted in my mind. But my members are warring against the law of my mind, and bringing me into captivity to the law of sin which is in my members.

God knows that Men face a struggle between that which they know in their minds to be good and the habits of their flesh. At first that struggle may seem an impossible battle, but those who persist will find the "fight of faith" (1 Tim. 6:12) gets easier as Men become accustomed to the conflict and learn the taste of victory (2 Tim. 4:7). Still, as Men grow closer to God, they become more perceptive of their sinful nature and more sensitive to what once seemed minor infractions.[3] As a result, the pressures on a believer can, at times, become depressing (see, e.g., Ps. 22:1-6; Jer. 15:10; 20:14-18).

---

1. The word *strait* (not straight) means narrow or restrained, from the Greek *stenos.*

2. Romans 7:14-25 is significantly different in the JST than it is in the KJV or NASB. Principles of textual criticism would suggest that the existing texts of this passage were corrupted in the manner indicated by the JST. They conflict too much with other writings of Paul, in which he frequently displayed himself as an example of correct behavior (e.g., Phil. 3:17; 2 Thess. 3:7). See, also, Acts 24:16; Rom. 15:1; 1 Cor. 16:10; 2 Cor. 11:12; 13:5-6; Phil. 3:4-15; 2 Thess. 3:8-9.

3. This is MacArthur's interpretation of Romans 7:14-25, and if that text is to be accepted as an accurate transcription of Paul's letter to the Romans, it is the only interpretation that provides any resolution of the incongruities cited in the previous note. See, MacArthur, *Faith Works,* 135-136.

Therefore, the Lord has given much encouragement and assurance to Men, indicating that, despite the temptations, trials and tribulations they face, those who persist in the struggle will eventually prevail and enter His kingdom (John 10:27-29; Rom. 8:28, 38-39; 1 Cor. 1:7-9; Phil. 1:6; 1 Thess. 5:23-24; Heb. 13:5; 1 Pet. 1:3-10; 2 Pet. 3:9). Most reassuring of all is the biblical teaching that the Savior is anxiously involved in intercessory efforts on behalf of those who are intent on following Him (John 17:8-26; Heb. 7:25).

Modern Evangelical scholars, however, have taken these encouragements for more assurance than they were intended to convey. Current Evangelical teaching asserts that salvation, once received, is *permanent*.[4] Of course, those who teach Lordship Salvation claim that Men can only be sure they are permanently saved if they have the necessary "*quality*" of faith, that is, if they "*truly*" believe, as demonstrated by their obedience.[5] But the end result is the same: The assurance of salvation is claimed with no regard to the necessity of obedience.

John wrote an entire epistle to dispel this notion (1 John). At the end of that epistle, he said (1 John 5:13, NASB): "These things I have written to you who believe in the name of the Son of God, in order that you may know that you have eternal life." The "things" John had written show unequivocally that when John said "you who believe in the name of the Son of God" he referred only to those who *obey* His commandments (1 John 2:3; 3:6).

> And the one who keeps His commandments abides in Him, and He in him. And we know *by this* that He abides in us, *by the Spirit whom He has given us* (1 John 3:24, NASB, some emphasis added; see also, 1 John 4:13).

If Men obey God's commandments—have faith in him, repent, and are baptized—they will receive the gift spoken of in this verse, "the Spirit whom He has given us," that is, "the gift of the Holy Ghost" (Acts 2:38).

---

4. Some Evangelical teachers disagree with the prevailing position on this issue (e.g., Pastor Raoul Reiss of Calvary Chapel, Golden Springs and Diamond Bar, whose program, "Manna For Today," is heard daily on many Christian radio stations). However, these teachers have made few in-roads against this teaching among today's Evangelical scholars, though this doctrine is not as widely accepted by lay members as among the academia.

5. MacArthur, *Faith Works,* 165 (emphasis in original).

All who have received the gift of the Holy Ghost know when "He abides in [them]." They also know that when they sin, and thereby "grieve the Holy Spirit of God" (Eph. 4:30 to 5:5, NASB), the Holy Spirit leaves. When the Holy Ghost "abides in [a man]," he is saved. If the Holy Ghost departs, that man needs the "renewing of the Holy Ghost" (Titus 3:5), which comes through repentance and worthy partaking of the Sacrament.

God has given passages of encouragement so Men can have hope when they fall, so they will know that they *can* repent and forsake their sins, so they will return to Him and endure forever (1 John 1:9). God has also reminded Men of the seriousness of their sins, to encourage them to persevere in obedience when they are on the strait and narrow way.

At the close of his great epistle on salvation, Paul noted these two aspects of God's admonitions, saying (Romans 15:4, NASB, emphasis added):

> For whatever was written in earlier times was written for our instruction, that through *perseverance* and *the encouragement of the Scriptures* we might have hope.

Not only did God give Men a hope of salvation, He provided a way for them to have absolute assurance about the status of their salvation at all times. If Men have the Holy Ghost with them, they have salvation from Spiritual Death. If they do not, they need to seek salvation as John encouraged the early Church to do (1 John 2:1).

Assurance is not found where Lordship teachers claim, in a list of qualities of the "true believer" against which Men must measure their faith, only to be found wanting.[6] Nor can they assume, as No-lordship teachers do, that, though they continue in sin, they are saved because of their intellectual assent to the fact that Jesus is the Christ.[7] The assurance God promised is found in each individual's personal relationship with God enjoyed through the gift of the Holy Ghost. To maintain that relationship, they must repent every time they fall, until they find in their faith the strengths and qualities John attributed to true believers.

---

6. See MacArthur's explanation of how "true believers" can tell if they are saved in *Faith Works,* 166-172.

7. Hodges, *Absolutely Free!,* 50-51; Bob Wilkin, "Putting the Gospel Debate in Sharper Focus," *The Grace Evangelical Society News* (May 1991), 1 ("one can have firm assurance of salvation and yet walk in sin"); R.T. Kendall, *Once Saved, Always Saved* (Chicago: Moody, 1983), 19, 52-53.

Positionalism

Rather than accept the challenges presented by God's way of salvation, even with His assurance that the way is not grievous, Evangelicals search for ways to reassure themselves that they are saved despite their disobedience. Those who espouse Lordship Salvation look for something special about the quality of their faith. Those who reject Lordship Salvation claim an assurance of salvation based on their intellectual recognition of Christ as Messiah. Neither group recognizes that the Bible never assures salvation to the disobedient, notwithstanding any encouragement God has given to struggling believers.

Those who defend Evangelical claims of security in salvation cite the term "in Christ," used frequently by Paul, to show that once they've had their "moment of faith" and are thereby saved (supposedly without obedience to the laws and ordinances of the Gospel), they have a permanent place reserved in heaven, a *position* "in Christ" out of which they cannot be moved. The term *Positionalism* has been coined to identify this concept of security.

The appeal of Positionalism is strong. All who have been asked whether or not they are saved realize how jealously Evangelicals guard their claim to security in the Lord and look with disdain on those who do not profess a certainty about their place in heaven.[8] Gone is the humble attitude Paul expressed in Philippians 3:12-14 (NASB):

> Not that I have already obtained *it*, or have already become perfect, but I press on in order that I may lay hold of that for which also I was laid hold of by Christ Jesus.
>
> Brethren, I do not regard myself as having laid hold of *it* yet; but one thing *I do:* forgetting what *lies* behind and reaching forward to what *lies* ahead,
>
> I press on toward the goal for the prize of the upward call of God in Christ Jesus.

What then is the effect of disobedience or "backsliding" in Evangelical theology—assuming that the backslider is not one whom Lordship teachers would accuse of never having been saved in the first place? The

8. See, e.g., Charles Hodge, *Systematic Theology,* reprint (Grand Rapids: Eerdmans, 1989), 3:106-107. The attitude of today's militantly saved believers is also decried by Lordship advocates. See, e.g., MacArthur, *Faith Works,* 161-162.

ultimate Evangelical response to questions about the effects of backsliding by saved believers is that they will suffer the consequences of sin in this life, but will not lose their position in the next. That is, they will lose some lesser reward, but not the ultimate reward of eternal salvation.[9]

The response of human nature to this doctrine is predictable. "If I'm going to be saved anyway, I don't much mind losing a few lesser rewards." What inconvenience, what consequence of sin in this life, can compare with salvation? If Men are certain they will be saved, what care they if God should beat them with "a few stripes" (2 Nephi 28:8)? What is the motivation for claiming that salvation is permanent despite disobedience, if it is not to rationalize the commission of sin?

Still, among Evangelicals many well-meaning and intelligent Bible scholars espouse this doctrine, interpreting those passages in which God has provided encouragement to His people (and some that don't go that far—e.g., 1 Tim. 2:4) as if they were unconditional promises of salvation to all who claim belief in Him (or who are "*true* believers"). Do any of these passages afford the security Positionalists claim?

Is Positionalism Biblical?

One of the passages frequently cited in support of Positionalism is John 10:27-29 (NASB):

> "My sheep hear My voice, and I know them, and they follow Me;
>
> and I give eternal life to them, and they shall never perish; and no one shall snatch them out of My hand.
>
> "My Father, who has given *them* to Me, is greater than all; and no one is able to snatch *them* out of the Father's hand."

This is certainly a comforting reassurance—but only to His "*sheep.*" The passage promises *nothing* to those who cannot be so described. Evangelicals claim that "sheep" include all (*true?*) believers, but, in fact, "sheep" do much more than *believe* in the Shepherd, they *hear* His voice and *follow* Him. This passage promises nothing to those who claim to

9. This position is endorsed by MacArthur, who cites Thomas Brooks to that effect. See Thomas Brooks, *Heaven on Earth: A Treatise on Christian Assurance,* reprint, (Edinburgh: Banner of Truth, 1982), 49; and MacArthur, *Faith Works,* 157.

believe in the death, burial and resurrection of Jesus Christ, but do not follow He who is their Shepherd.

Without seriously questioning whether or not they qualify as "sheep," Positionalists take great comfort in God's omnipotent power to hold His sheep safe. They claim that when the passage says they can be snatched from His hand by "no one," that includes the sheep themselves. To them, the Savior's grasp is so firm, it will retain the sheep *against their own will.*

Mormons recognize this doctrine as a tenet of Lucifer in the pre-existence (Moses 4:1-4). It definitely is *not* God's way, and never was. Though His sheep are safe from others, they may always rebel and leave the fold. They may even choose no longer to *be* His "sheep." A just God will not hold Men against their will, nor does this passage contain any suggestion that either Christ or the Father are so inclined.

Positionalists also note that God's hand encompasses the universe, and ask, "Even if the sheep tried to leave His hand, where could they go that He would not be able to save them?"[10] To this reasoning Mormons respond by noting that the universe also encompasses the devil and his angels (who know for certain that Jesus is the Christ), but the Father's hand does not embrace them with such salvation. Neither does His hand clutch believers so tightly they will be saved even when they refuse to follow Him.

The promise of salvation to those who believe is expressed in John 11:25-26 in a manner that fuels Positionalist fervor as follows (NASB):

> Jesus said to her, "I am the resurrection and the life; he who believes in Me shall live even if he dies,
>
> "and everyone who lives and believes in Me shall never die. Do you believe this?"

Obviously, this passage does not refer to Physical Death. Even the saved must die physically, though all will be physically resurrected. Hence, it appears that Christ's promise is of *eternal* life, i.e., salvation from Spiritual Death. But once again this promise is limited to "he who believes in Me" (verse 25) or "everyone who lives and believes in Me" (verse 26), and when reading a passage written by John, it must be remembered that he defined a "believer" as one who *obeys* God.

10. From a statement by David Hocking, on "The Biola Hour," KKLA, in 1990.

That is why the phrases "he who *believes* in Me" and "everyone who *lives and believes* in Me" are used synonymously in these two verses. To live and believe in Him means to live in accordance with a true belief in Him. Yet the same promises are made to he who "believes" (verse 25) as are made to he who "lives and believes" (verse 26). Thust it is clear John intended the two phrases to be viewed as equivalent.

Note also that the term "believes" and the phrase "lives and believes" are both in the present tense. The promise is not to all who "*have* believed in Me," or those who "*will* some day believe in Me." It is to those who *currently* believe in Christ.

Men cannot claim the benefits of a promise unless they fit the description of its promisees. Those who once believed, but have ceased to obey God, do not fit John's description of current believers. Hence, they are not the recipients of this promise.

Another passage frequently cited in support of Positionalism is the statement of Paul in 1 Corinthians 3:11-15; (NASB):

> For no man can lay a foundation other than the one which is laid, which is Jesus Christ.
>
> Now if any man builds upon the foundation with gold, silver, precious stones, wood, hay, straw,
>
> each man's work will become evident; for the day will show it, because it is *to be* revealed with fire; and the fire itself will test the quality of each man's work.
>
> If any man's work which he has built upon it remains, he shall receive a reward.
>
> If any man's work is burned up, he shall suffer loss; but he himself shall be saved, yet so as through fire.

Positionalists feel the phrase "each man's work" in this passage refers to their actions, whether good or bad. They claim this teaches that such actions only affect what *rewards* Men receive, and even if all their works are evil and are burned in the fire of judgment, yet they will be saved.

The problem with this interpretation is it doesn't adequately explain the language. The last phrase, "yet so as through fire," is inseparably connected to the phrase "but he himself shall be saved." This suggests there is yet a condition to the salvation of such a person. Hence, the word "shall" in the latter phrase doesn't express a certainty, but a probability, a conditional assurance. (The translation in the JST is "may.")

The context of the passage is also too narrow for the Positional interpretation. It speaks of those who build a work "upon the foundation." The foundation, of course, is Christ. Therefore, the Men referred to in the passage are those who have already accept Christ and do works based on their testimonies of Him. Some of the works that flow from their faith are of great value (likened to gold, silver and precious stones), while others are of little or no value (wood, hay and straw). They are not identified as good or bad actions. The passage explains that "the day" (judgment day) will reveal the nature of these works.

All Men, even the righteous, must give an accounting of their works in this life. Though a righteous man's works might be burned because they are of little or no value in eternity, he will be saved because he has endured the trials and tribulations of life, which God compares to the fire used to test precious metals "yet so as through fire" (see, also, Zech. 13:9; 1 Pet. 1:7). He may receive a lesser or greater reward in connection with his entry into eternal life, but the passage does not address the issue of security in salvation.

Another passage used by Positionalists is 1 Corinthians 5:1-5. That passage appears as follows in the NASB:

> It is actually reported that there is immorality among you, and immorality of such a kind as does not exist even among the Gentiles, that someone has his father's wife.
>
> And you have become arrogant, and have not mourned instead, in order that the one who had done this deed might be removed from your midst.
>
> For I, on my part, though absent in body but present in spirit, have already judged him who has so committed this, as though I were present.
>
> In the name of our Lord Jesus, when you are assembled, and I with you in spirit, with the power of our Lord Jesus,
>
> *I have decided* to deliver such a one to Satan for the destruction of his flesh, that his spirit may be saved in the day of the Lord Jesus.

This passage deals with the disciplining of a Corinthian believer who committed a heinous sin. The Corinthians erred in not properly subjecting this individual to Church discipline. Positionalists claim verse 5 means that, although Paul "deliver[ed] such a one to Satan for the destruction of his flesh," even this heinous sinner will "be saved in the day of the Lord Jesus."

This interpretation ignores the plain language of the verse. All that can be said from this passage is that Paul *hoped* for such a response to Church discipline. The word used in verse 5 is "may," which indicates uncertainty that this person will be saved at all.

Another passage relied upon by those who preach Positionalism is Romans 8:28 (NASB):

> And we know that God causes all things to work together for good to those who love God, to those who are called according to *His* purpose.

All too often, this passage is quoted in part by those who would use it for the Positionalist theme. John MacArthur relies on it to argue that, if all things work together for Man's good, how can anything work to undo his salvation?[11]

The problem with that reasoning is it fails to take into account the rest of the phrase, which limits its application to "those who love God." Those who love God are those who keep His commandments (John 14:15; 15:10). This passage does not apply to those who do not love God enough to get back up after they fall. To ensure salvation Men must always repent and take up their way again on the narrow path of obedience.

It is unthinkable that continuing in sin will "work together for good." The vicissitudes of life work together for the good of those who obey the Lord, but sin is *never* efficacious. Instead, if Men do not turn from sin, they are removed from the category of those to whom the promise of security was made, i.e., "those who love God."

Sealing. Another approach to Positionalism is made through passages that refer to believers being "sealed" or "sealed up," or having their "calling and election [made] sure." Many of these passages are found in the book of Ephesians. For example, Ephesians 1:13-14 (emphasis added) reads as follows in the NASB

> In Him, you also, after listening to the message of truth, the gospel of your salvation—having also believed, you were *sealed* in Him with the Holy Spirit of promise,

---

11. From John MacArthur's radio program, "Grace to You," KKLA, in December 1991.

> who is given as a pledge of our inheritance, with a view to the redemption of *God's own* possession, to the praise of His glory.

The assumption among Positionalists is that the term "sealed" means a finished transaction that cannot be opened. The Greek word used here, however, is *sphragizo*, which refers to being impressed with a seal, and implies identification. Thus, the Holy Spirit acts as a witness to the "promise" in this passage. In promises like this, called covenants (e.g., the "everlasting covenant," Heb. 13:20), the obligation of God is conditioned upon performance by the promisee. The "seal" only assures that the believer is entitled to the Lord's promise, because the believer has been and is faithful to his or her commitments.

The words "given as a pledge" in verse 14 are consistent with this understanding. The Greek word *arrhabōn*, translated "pledge" here (KJV: "earnest") could also be translated "down payment."[12] The "down payment" is given with a "*view*" to Man's redemption. This wording implies a covenant dependent on continuing performance by the obligee, namely sincere and persistent effort throughout this life to live the laws of God.

The same word, translated "sealed," also appears in Ephesians 4:30 (NASB) as follows: "And do not grieve the Holy Spirit of God, by whom you were sealed for the day of redemption." Again, "sealed" refers to identification of the new convert as a promisee of redemption subject to what lawyers call a "condition subsequent." This is not a guarantee that Men will be redeemed no matter what they do for the rest of their lives. It remains certain because of the continuing performance of the promisee.

Positionalists claim, based on this passage, that if a man sins after he has been "saved," it will merely "grieve the Holy Spirit of God." What they fail to appreciate is the sense in which the Holy Spirit is grieved. Thinking His sorrow has nothing to do with the loss of their salvation, they suppose believers will *remain* "sealed for the day of redemption" in spite of the sins they commit after they receive God's covenant. In truth, the Spirit's grief is expressed by His departure and is prompted by that necessity.

Election. Positionalists seek support for their view in the doctrine of "election," which means, simply, to be chosen by God. They argue that since God has chosen the "elect" for salvation, He won't change His mind. Their idea that salvation is assured once a man is thus chosen is greatly undermined by the following statement in 2 Peter 1:10 (emphasis added):

12. See MacArthur, *Faith Works,* 184.

> Wherefore the rather, brethren, give diligence to make your calling and election *sure:* for if ye *do* these things, ye shall never *fall.*[13]

According to this passage, even the elect must seek to make their election "sure." In 2 Peter 1:5-9, Peter lists the "things" Men must do to accomplish that goal. What he describes is the same as all the other Apostles have taught—Men must obey the commandments of God. Man's "calling and election" is not assured when he has once been saved, otherwise Peter wouldn't have expressed concern that the elect might "fall."

Election to salvation is the beginning of sanctification; making one's "calling and election sure" is the object of that process; ultimate salvation is the end result. Though Christ earnestly prayed for those whom He started on the narrow path, asking that they be "kept" on the way of sanctification until they could be one with God (John 17:11-13, 17-21), the very fact that He was concerned enough to make the request is evidence there is always a danger they could fail.

Losing Salvation or Finding True Security?

In any discussion with Evangelicals on this subject, the greatest resistance is encountered over the idea that Men can lose their salvation. Lordship and No-lordship teachers may differ on whether or not a person is really saved in the first place, but they are equally hard to convince on the issue of "once saved, always saved."[14] Their concern over this issue represents a basic misunderstanding about salvation and the Lord's promises to believers.

Ultimate salvation from sin is reserved until after Man's sojourn on the earth. This life is a probationary period (1 Pet. 1:15-17), and the jury is out until the time for judgment has arrived. Men are given sufficient time in this life to gain *and regain* their salvation (e.g., Rev. 2:21). The sanctification process assumes that salvation *will* be lost and regained frequently as Men grow in spirituality and prepare for life in the Kingdom of God. Christ's institution of the Sacrament as a *weekly* observance shows He knew just how often Men would need to renew the Holy Ghost in their lives.

---

13. Dr. Charles Stanley argues that a sinning believer can only "fall from grace" to another means of salvation—works. But since only Christ was saved by works, such a fall is clearly from salvation.
14. MacArthur, *Faith Works,* 180-183.

The Bible is replete with passages that indicate Man's progress in the way of salvation can be rocky and uncertain. Peter warned the early saints about this prospect in 1 Peter 4:17-19 (NASB):

> For *it is* time for judgment to begin with the household of God; and if *it* begins with us first, what *will* be the outcome for those who do not obey the gospel of God?
>
> And if it is with difficulty that the righteous is saved, what will become of the godless man and the sinner?
>
> Therefore, let those also who suffer according to the will of God entrust their souls to a faithful Creator in doing what is right.

This passage militates against the concept of permanent salvation, even for the "household of God." Peter understood the difficulties Men face in the process of sanctification. Enduring in righteousness through this life is never easy. One must turn again to repentance often in order to stay on the strait and narrow path, and there is always the danger that the righteous will fall into self-righteousness when they become adept at obeying some of God's commandments.

John, too, implies that Men can lose their position in Christ through a lack of enduring obedience, as witnessed by this warning from 2 John 8-9 (NASB):

> Watch yourselves, that you might not lose what we have accomplished, but that you may receive a full reward.
>
> Anyone who goes too far and does not abide in the teaching of Christ, does not have God; the one who abides in the teaching, he has both the Father and the Son.

Positionalists think verse 8 proves disobedience after salvation only brings about a difference in rewards without affecting their ultimate salvation, but that verse cautions that Men may lose their "*full* reward." An understanding of what is meant by that phrase is given in verse 9. If Men go too far and do not maintain their efforts to live Christ's teachings, they may not "*have God.*" "[Having] God" can only mean *living* with Him, having regular access to His presence. This is another way to describe eternal life for *that* is Man's "full reward."

Paul was also concerned that Men not fail in their efforts to work out their own salvation. He frequently spoke of their faith and his efforts for their salvation being "in vain" if believers did not hold fast to the words he preached (see, e.g., 1 Cor. 15:1-2; Phil. 2:12-16; Gal. 4:11; and 1 Thess. 3:5). In 2 Corinthians 13:5 (NASB), he cautioned:

> Test yourselves *to see* if you are in the faith, examine yourselves! Or do you not recognize this about yourselves, that Jesus Christ is in you—unless indeed you fail the test?

If Men can fail this test, and not be found "in the faith," what does that mean about their position "in Christ?" Some Evangelicals claim this passage refers to a test for the determination of whether or not a person is "really saved." They claim only nonbelievers can fail. If this were so, would Paul, an apostle of the Lord, feel the need to test *himself* and his associates? Certainly not! But in the next verse (NASB), he testifies: "But I trust that you will realize that we ourselves do not fail the test."

This statement is in the present tense, signifying that Paul, himself, regularly takes this test and is *currently* approved by it. He goes on, however, to warn the Corinthians that they should "do no wrong" even if it appears he is not passing the test. Paul wanted *them* to be strong (i.e., remain on the path of obedience), even if he proved to be weak. So strong should they be, he says, that they will eventually be made perfect (2 Cor. 13:9 and 11).

John MacArthur tries to give Paul's test mystical significance, suggesting that, "This is the test Paul laid before the Corinthians: Can you see Christ's 'glory' reflected in you—even dimly?"[15] How do Men do this? How do they know if they see Christ's "glory" reflected in themselves, dimly or otherwise? MacArthur doesn't answer this question. Instead, he says "it is that dim reflection of *His glory*—not anything inherent in us—that is the subjective basis for our assurance."[16]

It is good to recognize that the believer's works are "*God's* work in us, not our own accomplishments,"[17] but that is no reason to deny that Man's behavior is the crux of Paul's test.[18] Perfect obedience is the goal of sanctification, and, hence, its measuring rod. To look for Christ's reflection in a man is to see how well he emulates Christ's example. That is the point of Paul's language, and the simple nature of the test he advises. Honestly

15. MacArthur, *Faith Works,* 165.
16. *Ibid.,* emphasis in original.
17. *Ibid.,* emphasis in original.
18. MacArthur emphatically rejects works as a basis for assurance in salvation. MacArthur, *Faith Works,* 162-163.

and humbly, Men must look at whether or not they obey Christ. If they do, they *will* see His glory reflected in themselves. They will also recognize their failures and need for improvement.

In 2 Peter 2, Peter warns of false teachers who will arise promising "freedom" (verse 19) while they themselves are the slaves of sin. Modern Evangelical failures like Jim Bakker fit the description in this verse perfectly. The same is true of some early leaders in the Mormon Church who fell into rebellion and became bitter enemies of the Church. (However, verses 2 and 3 find specific fulfillment in conduct like that exemplified by Bakker's outrageous conduct with Jessica Hahn, and the debacle of his fraudulent conduct regarding Heritage, U.S.A.)

Peter's condemnation of these false teachers addresses the issue under discussion in verses 20-22 (NASB):

> For if after they have escaped the defilements of the world by the knowledge of the Lord and Savior Jesus Christ, they are again entangled in them and are overcome, the last state has become worse for them than the first.
>
> For it would be better for them not to have known the way of righteousness, than having known it, to turn away from the holy commandment delivered to them.
>
> It has happened to them according to the true proverb, "A dog returns to its own vomit," and "A sow, after washing, *returns* to wallowing in the mire."

Verse 14 describes these teachers as "accursed *children*," and verse 1 indicates they will deny the Master "who *bought* them." These references indicate that the passage is directed to persons who were once believers. Indeed, history demonstrates that it is from the community of believers that the greatest traitors and false teachers arise (e.g., Judas Iscariot).

Evangelicals do not want this passage to apply to believers, since that would contradict their theology on the permanency of salvation. Hence, they try various ways to escape its plain meaning. But the phrase "they have escaped the defilements of the world by the knowledge of the Lord and Savior Jesus Christ" indicates that these false teachers once had a saving knowledge of Christ and obtained a remission of their sins. The phrase "to have known the way of righteousness" (verse 21) also implies a knowledge obtained by experience.

The condemnation Peter describes for these false teachers only falls on those who "are again entangled" in "the defilements of the world" and "are overcome." It will not fall on those who become entangled in worldly sin but struggle back to Him, ultimately overcoming the influence of the evil one in their lives.

Men must overcome the snares of worldly sin, or they will be worse off than the heathen who never knew Christ. Those who turn from the path of salvation once they have entered the sanctification process depart from God with what lawyers call "*informed consent.*" This makes theirs a far more serious rebellion than the disobedience of those who never knew God.

The author of Hebrews twice issues the same warning, and in even stronger terms. Hebrews 6:4-8 (NASB) states:

> For in the case of those who have once been enlightened and have tasted of the heavenly gift and have been made partakers of the Holy Spirit,
>
> and have tasted the good word of God and the powers of the age to come,
>
> and *then* have fallen away, it is impossible to renew them again to repentance, since they again crucify to themselves the Son of God, and put Him to open shame.
>
> For ground that drinks the rain which often falls upon it and brings forth vegetation useful to those for whose sake it is also tilled, receives a blessing from God;
>
> but if it yields thorns and thistles, it is worthless and close to being cursed, and it ends up being burned.

Positionalists claim this passage is, also without application to believers. They say those who are described in these verses are investigators who look at the Gospel, but never accept the Savior. While such a person might fit the description given in these verses, it fits believers who have turned from the gospel path especially well.[19] In the Bible, if the shoe fits, it *must* be worn. Believers "have tasted of the heavenly gift and have been made partakers of the Holy Spirit" (if they were baptized and received the

19. H.A. Kent, *The Epistle to the Hebrews: A Commentary* (Grand Rapids: Baker Book House, 1972), 111-112. Kent mentions this interpretation as one of several alternatives, but rejects it on the same basis indicated in the text (though his excellent analysis is more complete and thorough than space here permits).

gift of the Holy Ghost). If they then fall away, they are among those whose fate is described in this passage.

Note again that the condemnation of these verses applies *only* to those who have fallen away so as to be *completely* overcome by the world. Their departure from the way of salvation is so distinct they "again crucify to themselves the Son of God." This does not describe a man who slips from the strait and narrow path temporarily. Those spoken of here have rebelled so they no longer *wish* to return. Rather than being compared to useful vegetation, in their fully ripened state they are "thorns and thistles" worthy only to be burned. (As will be seen in the next chapter, being "burned" is a metaphor referring to destruction in the lake of fire, the ultimate end of the damned.)

Hebrews 10:23-31 (NASB) issues the same warning:

> Let us hold fast the confession of our hope without wavering, for He who promised is faithful;
>
> and let us consider how to stimulate one another to love and good deeds,
>
> not forsaking our own assembling together, as is the habit of some, but encouraging *one another;* and all the more, as you see the day drawing near.
>
> For if we go on sinning willfully after receiving the knowledge of the truth, there no longer remains a sacrifice for sins,
>
> but a certain terrifying expectation of judgment, and the fury of a fire which will consume the adversaries.
>
> Anyone who has set aside the Law of Moses dies without mercy on *the testimony* of two or three witnesses.
>
> How much severer punishment do you think he will deserve who has trampled under foot the Son of God, and has regarded as unclean the blood of the covenant by which he was sanctified, and has insulted the Spirit of grace?
>
> For we know Him who said, "Vengeance is Mine, I will repay." And again, "The Lord will judge His people."
>
> It is a terrifying thing to fall into the hands of the living God.

This passage teaches that, for those who "go on sinning willfully after receiving the knowledge of the truth," the sacrifice of Christ is not available to wash away their sins. This description fits those who know the truth but continue in sin thinking they do not have to obey God in order to be saved. It comes very close to the position of No-lordship advocates, and should be a cause of serious concern for all who think to rely on false assurances of salvation without obedience. Of course, if they repent they can avoid destruction. Otherwise, for them "there no longer remains a sacrifice for sins."

That this passage applies to believers is evident from verse 29. The promise of a "severer punishment" lies in store for he who "has trampled under foot the Son of God, and has regarded as unclean the blood of the covenant *by which he was sanctified*, . . . " (emphasis added). The persons described in these verses definitely accepted Christ at one time, and entered upon the path of sanctification (cf., Acts 26:18).

Paul taught the Galatians the effect of returning to sin after believing and entering the pathway to salvation in Galatians 2:17-18 (NASB):

> "But if, while seeking to be justified in Christ, we ourselves have also been found sinners, is Christ then a minister of sin? May it never be!
>
> "For if I rebuild what I have *once* destroyed, I prove myself to be a transgressor."

Rebuilding what was once destroyed means a return to the slavery of sin from which Men are saved through faith, repentance and baptism. If Men do that, they are "found sinners." But what does Paul mean when he says that, by doing this, a person proves himself "a transgressor?" To be a transgressor is to be in a state of sin (see James 2:8-11). If Men sin after they have once been redeemed, they prove themselves to be in the same position as any other transgressor: they need to be saved from the punishment associated with transgression of the law, through justification.

Christ taught against the theology of Postitionalism in the Parable of the Sower (Matt. 13:3-23; Mark 4:2-20; Luke 8:4-15) quoted in the previous chapter in connection with the principle of endurance. Those who have no endurance, Christ likened to shallow soil. They hear the word and accept (i.e., "receive") it with joy, but "in time of temptation," they "fall away" (Luke 8:13). Such individuals believed, but their salvation wasn't permanent. As the passage says, they "fall."

Positionalists argue that these people never "really believed" in the first place, and hence they did not experience salvation.[20] But the passage does not suggest that those who are compared to "shallow soil" failed to *believe*

20. *The Expositor's Bible Commentary,* 8:907.

in Christ when they accepted the "seed." It focuses on their subsequent *behavior*, which resulted in their "fall."

The Lord's promises of salvation and damnation are *always* conditional. If a man is on his way to Hell, and God says "You will be damned," the promised condemnation can be averted if the man repents and turns from his evil ways (cf., Jonah 3:3-10). Both nations and individuals can lose promised blessings or avoid prophecies of doom, if they cease from righteousness or vice versa (see Jer. 18:7-10).

This point was made with unmistakable clarity by the prophet Ezekiel, who gives the most complete and unequivocal statement on this subject contained anywhere in the Bible. It is as true for Christian believers today as it was for Jewish believers in the day God revealed it, and it is consistent with every passage in the New Testament on this subject. Ezekiel 33:11-20 (NASB) reads as follows (the words "life" and "death" in this passage are references to Eternal Life and Spiritual Death, respectively):

> "Say to them, As I live! declares the Lord GOD, "I take no pleasure in the death of the wicked, but rather that the wicked turn from his way and live. Turn back, turn back from your evil ways! Why then will you die, O house of Israel?'
>
> "And you, son of man, say to your fellow citizens, 'The righteousness of a righteous man will not deliver him in the day of his transgression, and as for the wickedness of the wicked, he will not stumble because of it in the day when he turns from his wickedness; whereas a righteous man will not be able to live by his righteousness on the day when he commits sin.'
>
> "When I say to the righteous he will surely live, and he so trusts in his righteousness that he commits iniquity, none of his righteous deeds will be remembered; but in that same iniquity of his which he has committed he will die.
>
> "But when I say to the wicked, 'You will surely die,' and he turns from his sin and practices justice and righteousness,
>
> *if a* wicked man restores a pledge, pays back what he has taken by robbery, walks by the statutes which ensure life without committing iniquity, he will surely live; he shall not die.
>
> "None of his sins that he has committed will be remembered against him. He has practiced justice and righteousness; he will surely live.

> "Yet your fellow citizens say, 'The way of the Lord is not right,' when it is their own way that is not right.
>
> "When the righteous turns from his righteousness and commits iniquity, then he shall die in it.
>
> "But when the wicked turns from his wickedness and practices justice and righteousness, he will live by them.
>
> "Yet you say, 'The way of the Lord is not right.' O house of Israel, I will judge each of you according to his ways."

The Evangelical concept of Positionalism is that of the righteous man who learns "he will surely live, and he *so* trusts in his righteousness that he commits iniquity" (verse 13). When that happens, as God has witnessed here, "none of his righteous deeds will be remembered." Instead, "he will die." Of course, like any other sinner, if he repents, he can still obtain eternal life. What ultimately matters is that Men learn to walk "by the statutes which ensure life without committing iniquity" (verse 15).

The Jews of Ezekiel's day rejected this doctrine just as Positionalists do today, and for essentially the same reason. They believed they would be saved as children of Abraham irrespective of their obedience. They didn't wish to do His works in order to obtain His promises. But the Lord will judge "each of you according to his *ways*" (verse 20, emphasis added). This word is translated from the Hebrew *derek*, meaning "trodden path." It denotes Man's daily habits of behavior. Thus, the test is a man's regular pattern of obedience. If those "ways" change from good to evil, it will not matter that the man once "accepted Christ," just as it will not matter that disobedient Jews are physical descendants of Abraham (John 8:37).

Conclusion

Positionalism, or any other teaching about assurance in salvation that fails to recognize Men must remain on the strait and narrow path in order to arrive in the kingdom of God, must be rejected. Though Men may stumble and occasionally fall off the path in their effort to learn obedience, God is patient and extremely helpful. The journey is *not* an impossible one, nor in any way grievous, and God judges on the basis of the "trodden path," not the infrequent sidestep.

Men must choose to do something in this life. They can choose to do good as easily as they can choose to do evil. God has provided a way for Men to repent, endure, learn obedience and cleanse their robes in His blood. If they choose humbly to obey His commandments and follow Him, then (and *only* then) will they have the assurance of the Holy Ghost. With that assurance, they may know that they have been saved and will yet obtain their "full reward."

Part III

Mormon Eschatology

9
Salvation for the Dead, Resurrection, and Judgment

The Gospel allows for the salvation of all who take advantage of the opportunities they are given in this life to accept the Savior (Rom. 10:8-15). But what of those who never had the privilege of hearing the Gospel during their lives, or have only been confronted with a false gospel? What provision has God made for their salvation? Have they been pre-judged and condemned to remain in spiritual darkness for eternity? On what principles of justice could that possibly be considered fair?

Some Evangelicals believe that all people receive an opportunity to be saved during their mortal lives. Romans 1:18-20 teaches that God has manifested Himself to all men through the creation, and Romans 2:14-15 indicates that the Gentiles may obey the Law by following their consciences. These passages show that all Men are presented with evidence of God's existence in this life, and are given a basic knowledge of good and evil so they are without excuse if they choose to do wrong in this life.

But in the same book, Paul asks, "how shall they believe in him of whom they have not heard? and how shall they hear without a preacher?" (Rom. 10:14). Men must believe in Christ in order to be saved, and, as Paul testifies, "faith *comes* from hearing" (Rom. 10:17 NASB). It is unrealistic to suppose that every person who has ever lived on earth has heard a preacher tell of Christ. Thus, many, though they know to do good, have been without the basic knowledge essential to their salvation.

Paul implies that the gospel message was taken to the entire inhabited world during his lifetime (Rom. 10:18). Unfortunately, in the two thousand years since and for thousands of years before, whole nations have missed out on the opportunity to hear the true word of God. Vast numbers from every nation have had no "preacher" to teach them a saving knowledge of Jesus Christ.

What happens to all these people—Africans who lived and died without a word about Christ; Chinese who had no contact with the Western world for centuries; aborigines in every part of the globe? According to many Evangelicals these people are lost, condemned forever to the lake of fire and brimstone without so much as a chance to obtain eternal life—all victims of the sovereign election of God.

Apparently, this is so, even if they were eminently obedient to their consciences, since, according to them, God made no provision for these people to hear of and accept Jesus Christ *after death*. Mormons reject the notion that a just God would be so derelict as to omit such measures from His Plan of Salvation.

This chapter will examine the biblical basis for Mormon teachings about God's Plan of Salvation for those who did not have an opportunity to learn the truth during their mortal lives, and it will explore what happens to all Men after death, whether or not salvation is available to them in the grave. In so doing it will demonstrate, contrary to the claims of detractors,[1] that Mormon teachings regarding the nature of eternal punishment, resurrection, the Judgment, and Heaven and Hell constitute the only theological exposition consistent with every detail of biblical eschatology.

The Spirit World

As James 2:26 indicates, the physical body is "dead" when Man's spirit leaves it. After death, that which is still sentient is the spirit.[2] As disembodied spirits, Men "return" to God while their physical bodies return to inanimate physical elements ("dust," see Eccl. 12:7).

"The grave" is the place that spirits stay between death and the physical resurrection of the body. Mormons frequently refer to this abode as the "Spirit World." In the Old Testament, the Spirit World was called *Sheol*, frequently translated "the grave" (see, e.g., Gen. 37:35; 42:38; 44:29, 31;

1. See, e.g., Martin, *The Maze of Mormonism,* 262-264.

2. As note before, those curious about what a spirit looks like should read Luke 24:36-39. In that passage, Christ appeared to the Apostles after His resurrection. They thought He was a spirit. Christ explained that a spirit does not have flesh and bones as He had (having just been resurrected). But the Apostles would not have entertained the thought that He was a Spirit if they had not understood that Man's spirit looks just like his physical body. The only difference was stated by Christ—a spirit is not composed of physical material, i.e., flesh and bones.

Job 14:13; and Ps. 88:3). The Greek equivalent of *Sheol* is *Hades*. That is the word most commonly used in the New Testament to describe the Spirit World, or parts of it (see, e.g., Luke 16:23).

Hades should not be confused with another place for the dead referred to in the Bible under the name "Gehenna." Gehenna was the place in the Valley of the son of Hinnom where human sacrifices were offered anciently (2 Chron. 33:6; Jer. 7:31). Later, rubbish was burned there continuously, producing a distinctive stench. This illustrated for the Jews the nature of judgment on the wicked, "fire and brimstone."[3] Gehenna was the name associated with the ultimate punishment reserved for the wicked—the "lake of fire and brimstone" (Rev. 20:14-15). Christ described Gehenna (translated "hell fire" in the KJV) as the place where "their worm does not die, and the fire is not quenched" (Mark 9:47-48, NASB).

Much of what can be learned from the Bible about conditions in the Spirit World (as they were *before* Christ's resurrection) is contained in a parable told by Jesus in Luke 16:19-31. It reads in pertinent part as follows (NASB):

> "Now there was a certain rich man, and he habitually dressed in purple and fine linen, gaily living in splendor every day.
>
> "And a certain poor man named Lazarus was laid at his gate, covered with sores,
>
> and longing to be fed with the *crumbs* which were falling from the rich man's table; besides, even the dogs were coming and licking his sores.
>
> "Now it came about that the poor man died and he was carried away by the angels to Abraham's bosom; and the rich man also died and was buried.
>
> "And in Hades he lifted up his eyes, being in torment, and saw Abraham far away, and Lazarus in his bosom.
>
> "And he cried out and said "Father Abraham, have mercy on me, and send Lazarus, that he may dip the tip of his finger in water and cool off my tongue; for I am in agony in this flame."
>
> "But Abraham said, 'Child, remember that during your life you received your good things, and likewise Lazarus bad things; but now he is being comforted here, and you are in agony.

3. *The New Scofield Study Bible,* 1325 (footnote to Matt. 5:22). "Brimstone" is sulfur (McConkie, *Mormon Doctrine,* 2d ed., s.v. "Fire and Brimstone").

> 'And besides all this, between us and you there is a great chasm fixed, in order that those who wish to come over from here to you may not be able, and *that* none may cross over from there to us.'"

After death, Lazarus was taken to "Abraham's bosom," obviously a good place. In contrast, the rich man went to a place of torment, described here as "Hades." But the story does *not* say that the protagonists were either believers or non-believers. The rich man is portrayed simply as having been insensitive to the plight of the poor. Implied in Abraham's kindly phrased comments is the fact that it was the rich man's treatment of others that consigned him to torment after death. No other basis for a distinction between the two spirits is given.

The story describes a barrier between the rich man and Lazarus which neither side could cross. The implication is that people from *both* sides may have wanted to, but neither could. That condition made the place of torment a "prison," and it is referred to as such in a number of Bible passages (e.g., Isa. 14:17, KJV). It does not say that either of the two protagonists was judged or resurrected at that time. Hence, the place described could *not* be the ultimate resting place of either. It was the grave, or Spirit World, *not* Heaven or Hell in the ultimate sense.

Hebrews 9:27 (NASB) says: "And inasmuch as it is appointed for men to die once and after this *comes* judgment." The last phrase is not intended to imply immediacy, for Man's ultimate judgment does not come right after death. Indeed, the final judgment will not occur until the *end* of the thousand-year reign of Christ (Rev. 20:6-15). Thus, for "the dead" who will be facing the lake of fire and brimstone, the judgment promised in Hebrews 9:27 will not occur for a very long time, during which they, like the rich man, will remain in the Spirit World (or spirit prison).

If there were no opportunity for the dead to accept the Gospel after death, what would be the necessity for such a long waiting period between death and final judgment? Surely God's kingdom is not like a doctor's office. Souls do not sit in the Spirit World for centuries because of the press of God's business or delays caused by unexpected emergencies.

Most Evangelicals think Judgment and consignment to Heaven or Hell occurs *immediately* after death, but that is a simplification that doesn't accurately reflect the Bible's teachings about life after death. Of course, Judgment and the resurrection *would* follow immediately after death, if God didn't have a good reason for Men to wait in the Spirit World. The existence of a waiting period between death and the resurrection is one of many indications in the Bible that Men can still accept Christ and obey Him after death (though the consequences of *intentionally* waiting to do so are very adverse).

Second Corinthians 5:8 reads as follows: "We are confident, *I say*, and willing rather to be absent from the body, and to be present with the Lord." Some think this means that *believers* are allowed to by-pass the Lord's spiritual waiting room. But the word "with" here is the Greek *pros* which merely denotes locality, without identifying exactly *where* the Lord is waiting to receive believers after death. Since the Lord may be present outside of heaven (see, e.g., Joel 2:27; and John 1:14), one cannot assume that believers will go directly to his kingdom upon their death.

Where Is Paradise?

Christ told the thief on the cross "*to day* shalt thou be with me in paradise" (Luke 23:43). Christ was certainly the archetype of all believers. Where then did *He* go on that fateful day? This passage indicates His destination after death was "paradise," but where is that? Clearly it is not in Heaven, as demonstrated in Chapter 7.

There are only two other references in the Bible to "paradise." The first is Paul's mention of his own visit there in vision (2 Cor. 12:1-4, NASB):

> Boasting is necessary, though it is not profitable; but I will go on to visions and revelations of the Lord.
>
> I know a man in Christ who fourteen years ago—whether in the body I do not know, or out of the body I do not know, God knows—such a man was caught up to the third heaven.
>
> And I know how such a man—whether in the body or apart from the body I do not know, God knows–
>
> was caught up into Paradise, and heard inexpressible words, which a man is not permitted to speak.

In this passage, Paul twice says he was "caught up." In verse 2, he was caught up to "the third heaven," and in verse 4 he describes being caught

4. This is an example of Christian esotericism. The words Paul heard may have been those taught in LDS Temples, which attendees are not permitted to disclose to the world.

5. *The Interpreter's Dictionary of the Bible,* s.v. "paradise", 3:636.

up to "Paradise" and hearing "inexpressible words, which a man is not permitted to speak."[4] The assumption of most Bible scholars is that Paul described a single experience here.[5] However, unless Paul used the term "Paradise" to designate a different location than the one Christ referred to on the cross, this passage relates to two different experiences. Paradise and Heaven could not be the same location (cf, 1 Pet. 3:18-20).

Evangelicals, who assume that "heaven" and "paradise" are synonymous, are as confused as the Jews were at the time of Christ, when there were extensive arguments about the location of *three* paradises. In Jewish thought at the time, the first paradise was Eden, and the third was believed to be the abode of God. The Jews were uncertain as to the second paradise.[6] Mormons believe the third *Heaven*, spoken of by Paul, *is* the abode of God. So, aside from the paradise of Eden, there is but one location referred to as "paradise" in the Bible, and it is *not* Heaven.

That Heaven and Paradise are different locations is indicated, as noted above, by Paul's separate reference to "the third heaven" in verse 2 and "Paradise" in verse 4. That understanding is confirmed by John 20:17, in which Christ, newly risen from the grave, said to Mary, "Touch me not; for I am not yet ascended to my Father." According to Luke 23:43, He had been in Paradise on the day of his death, yet on the morning of his resurrection, He had not yet gone to the abode of His Father.

The conclusion that Heaven and Paradise are different places is also confirmed in the following information provided in Ephesians 4:8-10 (NASB):

> Therefore it says, "When He ascended on high, He led captive a host of captives, And He gave gifts to men."
>
> (Now this *expression*, "He ascended," what does it mean except that He also had descended[7] into the lower parts of the earth?
>
> He who descended is Himself also He who ascended far above all the heavens, that He might fill all things.)

This passage relates to God's plan of salvation for the waiting spirits in prison. It describes Christ's activities in the grave and indicates that He first descended into "the lower parts of the earth." That would have been on the day He died and took the thief with Him to Paradise (Luke 23:43).

---

6. *The Interpreter's Dictionary of the Bible,* s.v. "paradise," 3:655.
7. Some ancient manuscripts say that Christ "had first descended."

Obviously, the phrase "lower parts of the earth" does not describe the third heaven, or the abode of God, but the Spirit Prison.

Verse 8 indicates that He subsequently ascended "on high," leading with Him a "host of captives." Obviously, these captives were spirits who had been imprisoned in the "lower parts of the earth." They left with Christ to go "on high." But where is that? It could not be the same place as that described in verse 10 "far above all the heavens," for that phrase describes the abode of God. If Christ had gone there while in the grave, He would have ascended to His Father, but He didn't do that until after His resurrection and His appearances to the disciples (John 20:17; Acts 1:2-3).

During His post-resurrection visits, Christ gave instruction and evidence of His victory over death to those who believed in Him. Doubtless this was what Paul referred to in verse 8 with the phrase, "He gave gifts to men." One may therefore conclude that the term "on high" does *not* refer to Heaven, but to Paradise, a place *above* the Spirit Prison, but still in the Spirit World.

The last reference in the Bible to "paradise" is in Revelation 2:7. It reads as follows: "He that hath an ear, let him hear what the Spirit saith unto the churches; To him that overcometh will I give to eat of the tree of life, which is in the midst of the paradise of God." This passage gives no indication of where "the paradise of God" is located, only that, wherever it is, "the tree of life" is located there.

The name, "tree of life," suggests something to do with the resurrection. A similar tree was in the Garden of Eden (Gen. 2:9), where its function related to physical immortality (Gen. 3:22). That such a tree is located in Paradise suggests that it is an appropriate place for it. The Spirit World, where the spirits of Men await the resurrection, would be the appropriate place for a tree from which "him that overcometh" can be " [given] to eat"(Rev. 2:7)

Consistent with all these passages, Mormon theology teaches that the good part of the Spirit World is the place called Paradise. The bad part is Spirit Prison, or "Hades" (Luke 16:23), though the latter term may be used to refer to the entire Spirit World. Since *Christ* went to Paradise after He died, and not to the abode of God (the "third heaven"), one must conclude that the experience of *all* Men, even righteous believers, will be the same.[8]

8. Some Evangelicals claim the good part of the Spirit World was eliminated after Christ's resurrection, but there is no biblical evidence for that assumption.

Salvation for the Dead

Evangelicals frequently misunderstand Mormon teachings about salvation for the dead. Though there is no evidence from his writings that he knew more than an inkling about Mormon eschatology, Walter Martin describes Mormonism as a form of "universalism."[9] Like Dr. Martin, many Evangelicals mistake this aspect of Mormonism for a "second chance" doctrine.[10] They assume that Mormonism invites Men to ignore God in this life and repent in the Spirit World, thereby obtaining redemption after a life of sin. Hopefully, the lives of active Latter-day Saints will provide ample evidence that nothing could be farther from the truth (see, Ether 2:15).

It is well-established in the Bible that God gives Men *many* chances to accept Him (2 Pet. 3:9). A time will come, however, when Men will receive no more chances (cf., Rev. 2:20-21). Thus, the real issue is not whether Men get a "second chance," but when are their chances cut off? What is the time when Men will no longer be allowed to repent and accept Christ? Evangelicals say that the cut-off time is physical death, but that leaves them with no explanation for the delay between death and Man's ultimate judgment. The only explanation is this: it is intended to give Men more time *after* death to repent and accept Christ in preparation for their last and final audit.

Christ's Mission to the Dead. The Bible teaches that, following Christ's death, an opportunity for those in the Spirit World to hear the Gospel was initiated by Him. So important was that event it was foretold by Old Testament prophets as well as by Christ. Prior to this event, the Spirit World was truly a prison. Those who died without a saving knowledge of Jesus Christ were in the position of the rich man in Luke 16—confined to hell, entirely unable to cross over to Paradise. Nor could anyone from Paradise cross over to Hades to help the spirits there (Luke 16:26; see, also, Isa. 24:22).

It was foretold by Old Testament prophets that these conditions would change. An example of the prophecies that tell of Christ's mission to the spirits in prison is Isaiah 42:6-7, which reads in the NASB as follows:

---

9. Martin, *Maze of Mormonism,* 248-249.
10. E.g., Trivanovich, *Speaking the Truth In Love,* 43-44.

> "I am the LORD, I have called you in righteousness, I will also hold you by the hand and watch over you, And I will appoint you as a covenant to the people, As a light to the nations,
>
> To open blind eyes, To bring out prisoners from the dungeon, And those who dwell in darkness from the prison."

The language here is metaphorical, as evidenced by the idiomatic reference to the Messiah as "a light to the nations, to open blind eyes." Of course, Christ physically opened the eyes of the blind, but that is not the limit of this phrase. Likewise, the reference in verse 7 is not simply to occupants of a physical prison. "The dungeon" mentioned there is the portion of the Spirit World that constitutes a prison, and those who "dwell in darkness" include the spirits waiting in spiritual darkness for an opportunity to hear the Gospel.

Isaiah here foretells the day when these unfortunates would be brought out of that darkness by the hand of the Lord. See also, Isaiah 49:9; 61:1 (quoted by Christ to the Jews in Nazareth Luke 4:18-21), and Zechariah 9:11.

Christ proclaimed the imminent fulfillment of these prophecies in Luke 4. However, He made the nature and intent of His mission to the Spirit World clear in John 5:25-29 (NASB):

> "Truly, truly, I say to you, an hour is coming and now is, when the dead shall hear the voice of the Son of God; and those who hear shall live.
>
> "For just as the Father has life in Himself, even so He gave to the Son also to have life in Himself;
>
> and He gave Him authority to execute judgment, because He is *the* Son of Man.
>
> "Do not marvel at this; for an hour is coming, in which all who are in the tombs shall hear His voice,
>
> and shall come forth; those who did the good *deeds* to a resurrection of life, those who committed the evil *deeds* to a resurrection of judgment."

While one might suppose that Christ was speaking in verse 25 of the spiritually dead amongst the Jews to whom He was sent, it is clear from verse 28 that He referred also to the *physically* dead in this passage. The promise given is that those who have physically died may yet obtain eternal life if they "hear His voice."

But when did the hour come that those who were in the tombs (KJV: grave) heard His voice? Peter gives the timing of this event in 1 Peter 3:18-20:

> For Christ also hath once suffered for sins, the just for the unjust, that he might bring us to God, being put to death in the flesh, but quickened by the Spirit:
>
> By which also he went and preached unto the spirits in prison;
>
> Which sometime were disobedient, when once the longsuffering of God waited in the days of Noah, while the ark was a preparing, wherein few, that is, eight souls were saved by water.

With the group described in this passage, the thief on the cross was given the opportunity to be saved through the preaching of Christ when a ministry to the dead was opened by Christ's address to the lost who waited in the Spirit World. It was a great boon to the thief to be admitted to that select assemblage, but it was not instant salvation for him or any other spirit in attendance.

Later in the same epistle, Peter explains the efficacy of Christ's preaching to the spirits in prison, confirming the message of John 5:25-29 and the prophecy of Isaiah. He explains (1 Peter 4:6):

> For for this cause was the gospel preached also to them that are dead, that they might be judged according to men in the flesh, but live according to God in the spirit.

Thus, Christ preached to the dead in the Spirit World in order to give them an opportunity to repent and live God's commandments there.

The spirit that goes to the Spirit World is the same one that lived in its physical body here on Earth. If a man was unrepentant here, his spirit will have the same attitudes and desires there. Christ's mission didn't involve forcing these spirits into obedience or to granting them instant salvation. He simply opened the opportunity for them to "live according to God in the spirit."

While this is a great opportunity, the passage also makes it clear that during their *earthly* lives Men must do good rather than evil. As Peter indicates, the spirits in prison will be judged "according to men *in the flesh*," not according to men in the Spirit World. The dead are given the opportunity to repent and accept the Gospel there, receiving justification for their past sins, but their acts while in the flesh will be the major factor in their judgment (see, also, John 5:29). This shows the significance of

Paul's statement about the Gentiles who, though they have never heard of Christ, live according to His laws through the dictates of their God-given conscience (Rom. 2:14-15). How Men view God and treat their fellows is the essence of the test.

In some ways, however, the test continues in the Spirit World. As Paul put it, Men can learn there to "live according to God." This could include learning of Christ and the principles of repentance and obedience. It could even include making a commitment to Christ through baptism for the remission of sins. Clearly, spirits who accept Christ in the Spirit World must be baptized for their past sins, the same as Men on Earth (cf., Rom. 2:16). God has not devised one Gospel for those who hear His servants in this life, and another for those who must wait until the next (Eph. 4:5). But how can a spirit in the Spirit World be baptized in the manner prescribed by Christ, and thereby realize Peter's promise of living according to God in the spirit?

Baptism for the Dead. The answer to that question is found in an illuminating remark made by Paul in 1 Corinthians 15:29 (NASB):

> Otherwise, what will those do who are baptized for the dead? If the dead are not raised at all, why then are they baptized for them?

This verse confirms that God requires baptism for all, even those who accept the Gospel in the Spirit World, and that He has provided a way to accomplish that end. The Greek word translated "for" in this verse is *huper*, which literally means "on behalf of." Thus, the reference in this verse is to "baptism on behalf of the dead." This is a proxy ordinance performed by a living person on behalf of a deceased individual. That is, baptisms may be performed by living believers for spirits in Spirit Prison in the hope that they will repent and seek the benefits of that ordinance.

In the 15th chapter of 1 Corinthians, Paul wrote about the doctrine of resurrection. He makes several arguments to prove that there will be a resurrection of all Men. Baptism for the dead is one of those arguments. It is of such great importance as a confirmation of the resurrection that Paul listed it as one of the foremost proofs in his treatise. He even places it before the testimony of his own behavior, in which he argues that, were it not for the resurrection, he wouldn't risk his life daily for the Gospel's sake (1 Cor. 15:30-32).

The preaching of the Gospel to the dead makes it possible for spirits in the Spirit World to exercise their faith in Christ and make the commitment that will bring remission of their sins. Since baptism is essential for justification, Paul refers to the practice of "baptism for the dead" as a proof of the resurrection. His argument assumes that without baptism there would be no justification. Those who are not justified will only be able to come forth in the Resurrection of the Unjust described later in this chapter. Through baptism for the dead, a person may receive justification in the Spirit World (providing he is otherwise prepared for that blessing), allowing him to take part in the Resurrection of the Just. If there were no resurrection, there would be no reason to perform such baptisms. The dead await their resurrection. Why would any living person perform baptisms on behalf of the spirits of those who are dead if it didn't have an impact on the resurrection of those spirits (see, 1 Cor. 15:40-42)? It follows that the existence of the ordinance of baptism for the dead in the Gospel of Jesus Christ proves that there is a resurrection. This is the essence of Paul's argument.

Paul alludes to those performing baptisms for the dead as "they," indicating that some or all of the Corinthians may not have performed baptisms for the dead. Still, they were sufficiently familiar with the ordinance for Paul to use it as one of his arguments supporting the doctrine of resurrection. Mormon theology teaches that only mature and obedient believers are allowed to perform this ordinance. At the time of Paul's epistle, many Corinthian believers were in a state of great wickedness (1 Cor. 3:1-5). The reference to "they" in this passage suggests that few, if any, of the Corinthians had been given the privilege of performing baptisms for the dead.

Perhaps no other passage in the Bible has caused as much controversy among Evangelicals as 1 Corinthians 15:29. It was the catalyst, in fact, for the conversion of the author's father, formerly a student minister, who at first thought the verse was unique to "Mormon Bibles." There are as many different Evangelical interpretations of this passage as there are commentaries, and they only agree on one point—that the Mormon interpretation is false, despite the fact that it is faithful to the text and the only exegesis of the passage consistent with other Bible passages that teach salvation for the dead.

An example of Evangelical exposition on this passage, is the following commentary by C. I. Scofield:

> Paul is not here speaking of baptizing living believers in place of either believers or unbelievers who have died. There is no

> assignment of saving efficacy to baptism. The argument is: Of what value is it for one to trust Christ and be baptized in the ranks left vacant by the believing dead, if there is no resurrection for believers? Why place life in jeopardy and forfeit the benefits of this life, if there is no life after death?[11]

Scofield appears to recognize the plain meaning of the passage, but in this explanation, he rejects it. He then tries to read into it some alternative meaning. Unfortunately, his explanation is much more than a paraphrase of the passage, it is a complete revision, an excellent example of eisegesis. Further, he refrains from giving a single reference to biblical authority for his conclusions. This is strictly his opinion, and it misses the essential character of Paul's argument altogether. Paul wasn't trying to prove "life after death," as Scofield puts it, but that the dead will be resurrected.

"Baptism for the dead," according to Scofield, is baptism into a spot in "the ranks left vacant" by a believer who has died. At one time, variations on this explanation of 1 Corinthians 15:29 were quite popular. The problem is that they suggest believers were only baptized when other believers died. There is no indication in the Bible that, before baptism, anyone ever inquired as to whether or not another believer had died. Instead, every account of a conversion is accompanied by some indication that the baptism was performed immediately.

Scofield's explanation is no longer the most popular eisegesis of this passage among Evangelicals. The most common theory is that the ordinance of baptism for the dead was a false practice, probably not even a practice among the Corinthians (because of the reference to "they" in 1 Cor. 15:29). It is thought that Paul pointed to this "false" practice (notably *without* identifying it as such) to argue, in essence, that those who engaged in baptism for the dead believed in the resurrection more than the Corinthians did.

Not only does this interpretation strain the language of the passage, it does a gross disservice to Paul. If baptism for the dead were a false or pagan practice rather than an essential part of God's plan of salvation, what possible connection could it have to the true doctrine of resurrection, of which Paul was testifying in chapter 15? Unless baptism for the dead were a true Gospel ordinance effectually connected to the resurrection, as

11. *The New Scofield Study Bible,* 1634 (footnote to 1 Cor. 15:29).

indicated by Paul's argument, he would never have raised the subject, except to condemn the practice.

But Paul never identifies baptism for the dead as either false or pagan. In other addresses and letters where Paul refers to pagan beliefs and sources, he identifie them as such (see, e.g., Acts 17:22-23; Titus 1:12). Not a disparaging word is said against baptism for the dead in the Bible, rather the practice *itself* is held up as *evidence* of the resurrection. Would a teacher of truth use a false or pagan practice to prove a true doctrine? The notion is beyond reason and without parallel in inspired writ.

Another Evangelical complaint about this passage is that baptism for the dead is mentioned only once in the Bible—in this single verse. Some see this as a violation of God's requirement that everything must be established in the mouths of two or three witnesses (2 Cor. 13:1). That instruction however is directed to the establishment of *Man's* testimony, not *God's* (Matt. 18:16; 1 Tim. 5:19; Heb. 10:28). In dealing with Men, God frequently provides many witnesses, but God's testimony needs only one witness—His! In fact, a number of doctrines are taught in only one place in the Bible, the most notable being that which Evangelicals identify as the *core of the Gospel*. It is specifically identified in only one passage—1 Corinthians 15:1-5.

There is no reasonable alternative explanation of 1 Corinthians 15:29. That is a fact the author's father had to face, and every honest scholar of the Bible does likewise. It is not enough to say that this is an obscure passage, and dismiss the inability of Evangelical theologians to explain it on that basis. This is a significant doctrine, an essential element in God's Plan of Salvation for the dead. It stands out as a pivotal inadequacy in Evangelical teaching. For many, this inadequacy has been the turning point in their tolerance for Evangelical theology.

Procrastinated Repentance. A word of caution is in order before leaving the subject of salvation for the dead. Those who accept Christ in the Spirit World on the same terms as those who accept Him while in the flesh will receive the same blessings, for Christ is "no respecter of persons" (Acts 10:34). But if a man makes no effort to do good rather than evil in his mortal life, he will have failed the crucial element of the test this life administers, and will not qualify for the same rewards as those who learned to choose good over evil in mortality.

Therefore, though biblical teachings about salvation for the dead give reassurance that loved ones who were lost before they could accept or reject Christ will have that opportunity, the living who are exposed to the truth have no business waiting for a "second chance" after death. Mormon theology contains no reassurances for those who thus procrastinate the day of their repentance (Alma 34:33-35). Men cannot knowingly resist God until the end and expect the same results as will be enjoyed by those who obey the Gospel in this life (or who follow their conscience, and obey the law without hearing the Gospel, as in Rom. 2:14-15). Men cannot expect to enjoy eternal life with God after spending their lives in rebellion to His message (see, Eph. 5:3-7).

Eternal Punishment

In his book, *The Maze of Mormonism*, Walter Martin claims that "[t]he largest cult embracing universalism in the United States today is the Mormon Church."[12] He defines Universalism as "the theory that at the final consummation of the ages God will punish in a *remedial* way the souls of men who have rejected Jesus Christ as Lord and Savior, reconciling them to Himself after a proper period of chastisement."[13] This misunderstanding is consistent with Dr. Martin's general lack of accurate information about Mormonism, and his habit of applying labels to its doctrines.

Universalism teaches some doctrines that are similar to Mormonism, hence, in Dr. Martin's mind, Mormonism is a universalist religion. In fact, however, Mormon eschatology differs materially from Universalism, and is in strict harmony with the Bible.

One object of Dr. Martin's criticism and much negative Evangelical comment, is the concept of "eternal punishment" in Mormon theology. Mormons teach that *eternal* punishment is a reference to *God's* punishment just as *eternal* life is a reference to *God's* life or lifestyle (see John 17:3; 2 Thess. 1:9; and D&C 19:4-12). The use of the word "eternal" to identify the punishment that awaits the ungodly raises issues regarding the *duration* of such punishment, and the *persons* who will be required to suffer it.

Evangelicals assume that the word "eternal" means it will last forever. Mormons believe that this is not the sense in which the language was intended. God's punishment may not last forever in the case of every person who must experience it. Instead, it will fit the crime, varying

12. Martin, *Maze of Mormonism,* 248.
13. *Ibid.,* emphasis in original.

according to that which is appropriate under the circumstances (Heb. 10:28-31). In fact, God is always more merciful than Men deserve (Ezra 9:13). However, Mormon's teach that eternal punishment will be suffered more broadly than Evangelicals suppose. Even those who *profess* belief in Christ but fail to *do* His works (Matt. 7:22-23) will be required to suffer a measure of His wrath.

Psalms 103:9 gives some information about the issue as follows: "He will not always chide: neither will he keep *his anger* for ever." This verse teaches that God will not always chasten Men. That is not an entirely positive promise. God chastises those whom He loves so they will repent and be saved (see, Deut. 8:5; Ps. 94:12; Prov. 13:24). But in the context of this verse, the Psalmist reassures Men that their punishment need not last "for ever."

An important point in this regard may be adduced from the suffering of Christ. He suffered for *all* the sins of Mankind so that, if any will repent, they need not suffer as He did. God "laid on him the iniquity of us all" (Isa. 53:6). Yet Christ's suffering did not last forever. In terms of temporal duration, it lasted no more than three days and three nights (from Gethsemane to the Resurrection). It appears, therefore, that it is not the *duration* of eternal punishment that distinquishes it, but its quality, its nature and source. It is God's punishment, for God is eternal (1 Tim. 1:17), and His punishment is terrible no matter how long it lasts (Heb. 10:31).

Dr. Martin claims that "Mormon theology cannot conceive of eternally punishing the infinite sin of rejecting His Son."[14] In fact, however, Mormonism teaches that this is the very sin for which eternal punishment *will* last forever. To demonstrate this point, the entire issue of Man's ultimate punishment and reward must be examined in greater detail than Dr. Martin attempts in his *Maze of Mormonism.* This will show that Mormon eschatology provides the only satisfactory explanation of all the Bible's teachings about Judgment, the Resurrection, and Man's ultimate place in the Heavens (or the alternative).

The Accountability of All Men

The Bible makes it clear *all* Men will be judged at some point in time, both the righteous and the wicked (Eccl. 3:17). Paul's incontrovertible testimony is that those guilty of gross sin cannot have an inheritance in the

14. Martin, *Maze of Mormonism,* 257.

kingdom of Christ and of God (Gal. 5:19-21; Eph. 5:3-7; see, also, D&C 76:103-105). That believers too will be judged, is clear from the teachings of Paul to the Romans (Rom. 14:10-12, NASB):

> But you, why do you judge your brother? Or you again, why do you regard your brother with contempt? For we shall all stand before the judgment seat of God.
>
> For it is written, "As I live, says the Lord, every knee shall bow to Me, And every tongue shall give praise to God."
>
> So then each one of us shall give account of himself to God.

Note that Paul included *himself* in this passage by use of the first person plural "we" in verse 10, and "us" in the statement "each one of us shall give account of himself to God" in verse 12. This is consistent with Peter's statement that judgment begins with the "household of God" (1 Pet. 4:17). Likewise, according to Ezekiel 33:20, (NASB), God will judge *all* Men "according to [their] *ways*."

How does one prepare for such an audit? John admonished the saints to abide in perfect love. Since love is the sum and substance of all the laws of God, John knew that if Men would concentrate on that attribute they would follow all the laws of God. So he promised that if a man's love is perfect, he will have confidence before God in the day of Judgment (1 John 4:17-18, NASB):

> By this, love is perfected with us, that we may have confidence in the day of judgment; because as He is, so also are we in this world.
>
> There is no fear in love; but perfect love casts out fear, because fear involves punishment, and the one who fears is not perfected in love.

If Men are "perfected in love," they will be like God, obeying His laws perfectly. They will have no fear of punishment or the loss of any reward, if they have "perfect love."

In 2 Corinthians 5:9-10 (NASB) Paul indicates how he prepared for the judgment of God:

> Therefore also we have as our ambition, whether at home or absent, to be pleasing to Him.

> For we must all appear before the judgment seat of Christ, that each one may be recompensed for his deeds in the body, according to what he has done, whether good or bad.

It was Paul's "*ambition*" to please God. With such an ambition, He could rest assured that his accounting to the Lord would be pleasing. Paul's statement demonstrates that it will be hard to enter the kingdom of God if Men work easy, but easy if they work hard.

Verse 9 refers to pleasing God "whether at home or absent." In the context of 2 Corinthians 5:6-10 the word "absent" refers to the spirit being absent from the body and present with God in Paradise. Thus, Paul recognized that, in addition to pleasing God in this life ("at home"), Men would have some opportunity to please God after death (when they are "absent"). However, the importance of doing good in *this life* is reiterated by Paul in his statement that each person will be "recompensed for his deeds *in the body*."

The Greek word translated "judgment seat" in Romans 14:10 and 2 Corinthians 5:10 is *bema*. That word refers to the judgment or "mercy seat" of Christ before whom believers, like Paul, will be brought to give their accounting. This is the seat from which those who have part in the first resurrection will be judged.

Exactly when judgment will occur for any particular believer is not stated in the Bible. Many saints that died were raised immediately after Christ's resurrection (Matt. 27:52). There will be a significant resurrection of the righteous at Christ's Second Coming (1 Thess. 4:17). Other than that, the *bema* Judgment will most likely occur concurrently with the individual's resurrection, since the individual believer's resurrected state is determined at that Judgment (cf., 1 Cor. 15:42). Judgment will doubtless take place whenever the individual is ready to be resurrected, though the time will not be later than the end of the Millennium, at which time the Final Judgment takes place (Rev. 20:5).

The word translated "throne" in Revelation 20, speaking of the Final Judgment at the end of the Millennium is *thronos*, referring to the Great White Throne of God (Rev. 20:11). The Judgment associated with the Second Resurrection will take place in front of this throne. There is a significant difference between the *thronos* and the *bema* Judgments. The *bema* Judgment focuses on Eternal Life as its reward, while the *thronos* Judgment focuses on the Second Death as its punishment. Naturally, there will be some who do not merit eternal life at the *bema*, and correspondingly, some who do not deserve the Second Death at the *thronos*.

The fact that believers appear before the *bema* rather than the *thronos* should not be viewed as an assurance of their salvation in the Kingdom of God, as Evangelicals suppose. Believers are equally accountable for their actions on earth. In 2 Corinthians 5:10 the recompense promised at the *bema* includes both good and *bad*. Some believers will be disappointed to find that they are unworthy of the reward they thought they had permanently appropriated.

Note the great similarity between the *bema* Judgment described by Paul above and the *thronos* Judgment described by John in Revelation 20:12 (NASB):

> And I saw the dead, the great and the small, standing before the throne [KJV: "stand before God"], and books were opened; and another book was opened, which is *the book* of life; and the dead were judged from the things which were written in the books, according to their deeds.

The basis of both judgments is the same: Man's *deeds* "in the body." This is the standard indicated in 1 Peter 4:6 and the other passages discussed above. *All* Men are judged on this basis, whether they accept the Gospel in mortality or in the Spirit World. Every person will be asked, "What did you do during your life on earth?" Those who sought to do good in this life, rather than evil, will be asked that question at the *bema*. Those who chose evil will be asked the same question at the *thronos*.

The Records. Revelation 20:12 indicates the Lord keeps records (a "book") of all that Men do. As to sins truly repented of, the Lord has promised to remember them no more (Jer. 31:34). The writer of Hebrews reiterated that promise as follows (Heb. 8:10-12):

> For this *is* the covenant that I will make with the house of Israel after those days, saith the Lord; I will put my laws into their mind, and write them in their hearts: and I will be to them a God, and they shall be to me a people:
>
> And they shall not teach every man his neighbour, and every man his brother, saying, Know the Lord: for all shall know me, from the least to the greatest.
>
> For I will be merciful to their unrighteousness, and their sins and their iniquities will I remember no more.

If the Lord remembers sins no more, that implies Men's sins are erased from the record of them kept by the Lord. In fact, however, His notation process is just the opposite. Revelation 20:12 mentions "another book," called the Book of Life. Because of its importance in the Judgment, a brief review of scriptures relating to this book, the Lamb's Book of Life, will show the approach the Lord uses in His record keeping.

The Book of Life

The Book of Life is first mentioned in Exodus 32:31-34 (NASB, emphasis added) in the following exchange between Moses and the Lord:

> Then Moses returned to the LORD, and said, "Alas, this people has committed a great sin, and they have made a god of gold for themselves.
>
> "But now, if Thou wilt, forgive their sin—and if not, please *blot me out* from Thy book which Thou hast written!"
>
> And the LORD said to Moses, "Whoever has sinned against Me, I will blot him out of My book.
>
> "But go now, lead the people where I told you. Behold, My angel shall go before you; nevertheless in the day when I punish, I will punish them for their sin."

"Thy book," referred to in this passage, is the Lamb's Book of Life. Moses, as the leader of rebellious Israel, felt to take personal responsibility for their sins and asked the Lord to "blot [him] out" of the Book He had written, along with Israel. In response to his plea, the Lord indicated that Israel will be judged on an individual basis, not vicariously through the punishment of Moses, their leader. "Whoever has sinned against Me, I will blot *him* out of My book" (emphasis added).

Being "[blotted] out" of the Book of Life was a punishment David requested for his enemies in Psalm 69:28 (NASB): "May they be blotted out of the book of life, And may they not be recorded with the righteous." "The righteous," as used here by David, means those who "walk in the statutes of life, without committing iniquity" (Ezek. 33:15).

From these passages, it appears that a man may have his name "blotted out" of the Book of Life if he cannot be included among the "righteous." The Lord's record keeping is done from the positive direction. Men start out with their names in the Book, but through wrongdoing they can have their names removed. This suggests Man starts this life with a clean slate with their names already in The Book of Life Indeed, it is called the Book of *Life* because it contains a continuously updated and current list of all who are entitled to receive eternal life.

Consistent with that understanding, Revelation 3:5 (NASB, emphasis added) explains how Men avoid having their names blotted out of the Lamb's Book of Life:

> He who *overcomes* shall thus be clothed in white garments; and I will not *erase* his name from the book of life, and I will confess his name before My Father, and before His angels.

The Greek word translated "overcomes" means to "gain the victory." Since it is unrighteousness, or sin, that results in a man's name being blotted out of the Book of Life, it is obviously sin over which Men must be victorious in order to keep their names from being taken out of that record.

Men overcome sin in their lives through justification, and learn to maintain righteousness through the process of sanctification (see Chapters 6 and 7). Consistent with Mormon soteriology, it is much easier to get in the Book, than it is to stay there. Those who gain victory over sin, whose names will not be blotted out of the Lamb's Book of Life, are those who learn to obey the laws and ordinances of the Gospel and do His will.

Universal Resurrection

The Bible indicates that resurrection involves not simply the restoration of a Man's spirit to an immortal body, but a determination of the fate to which that resurrected body will be consigned. The distinction between receiving a resurrected body that is immortal but consigned to the Resurrection of the Unjust, for example, and receiving a body that will be gloriously resurrected to eternal life with God, is very significant, but somehow it has escaped the Evangelical critics of Mormonism. Because they misunderstand this point, some Evangelicals reject the idea of a universal physical resurrection altogether. Their view is expressed as follows:

> Satan is deceiving the Latter-day Saints to think that salvation by grace constitutes a general resurrection for all; "that which comes to all men irrespective of belief in Christ" (Doctrines of Salvation 1:134).
>
> It is true that Christ died to provide a sacrifice through His blood for "all" men, and His sacrifice is sufficient for the sins of

> "all" men, but the justification of life to all men was supplied only on the condition of acceptance of the Lord Jesus Christ as Savior. John 3 explains that God "gave His only begotten Son" so that "the world through Him might be saved." Therefore he who accepts this sacrifice has "everlasting life" while he who does not believe "shall not see life; but the wrath of God abideth on him."[15]

It is not Mormons, but their critics who are deceived by Satan on this point. The Bible clearly teaches a physical resurrection of *all* Men. Some are resurrected to good, while others receive a resurrection of damnation. On this point, even that lion of Mormon criticism, Dr. Walter Martin, agrees. Though he seems entirely unaware that his teachings are in harmony with Mormon theology, he interprets 1 Corinthians 15:22 in *The Maze of Mormonism* as follows:

> The context is clearly one of resurrection—physical resurrection for judgment. To capture the sense of the Greek properly it should be rendered, "As in Adam all die, so in Christ all shall be raised to life, or resurrected." This we know to be true, because there will be a resurrection of the just and of the unjust (Acts 24:15).[16]

Paul's earlier remarks in 1 Corinthians 15 support this conclusion. He taught that physical resurrection from the grave (salvation from Physical Death) is a "free gift" to all (Rom. 5:14-15), and that all Men will be resurrected regardless of their spiritual condition. Paul includes both believers and unbelievers when he refers to "the dead" in 1 Corinthians 15:16-18 as follows:

> For if the dead rise not, then is not Christ raised:
> And if Christ be not raised, your faith is vain; ye are yet in your sins.
> Then they also which are fallen asleep in Christ are perished.

In this passage, Paul states unequivocally that all Men who pass from this life ("the dead"), both good and evil, will be resurrected. He emphasizes this point by arguing that, if the resurrection were not universal,

---

15. Trivanovich, *Speaking the Truth in Love,* 44.
16. Martin, *Maze of Mormonism,* 256.

Christ would not have been raised. (Why? Because in this respect He is like all other Men—a spirit child of God the Father.) Then Paul reasons that, if Christ were not raised, Christianity would be false (verse 17), and all who have died in reliance on Him would be lost (verse 18). Thus, the gift of salvation from Physical Death must come to *all* Men, or there is *no* salvation in Christ.

Mormonism teaches there will be a Resurrection of all Men. But being resurrected is *not* the same as enjoying eternal life with God. Even the terminally wicked, who will be cast into the "lake of fire," will be resurrected, but their resurrection will be to eternal *death, not* eternal *life* (see Alma 41:2-6, contrasting these two ends of the judgment spectrum).

Judgment and Resurrection

While judgment is left to the Son (John 5:22), the Bible provides a clear indication of its outcome, lest any man complain that he was surprised at the last day. Nevertheless, few teachers outside The Church of Jesus Christ of Latter-day Saints have analyzed the Bible's message about this all-important subject. Most think only in terms of Heaven and Hell, even when they understand that there are two separate Judgments (*bema* and *thronos*).

Dr. Walter Martin, for example, in his *Maze of Mormonism* supplies a chart entitled "Mormon Plan of Eternal Progression," which he describes as a " 'revelation' of the Mormon prophets."[17] Actually, the chart is nothing more than a Sunday School teaching aid intended to give investigators and new members a summary overview of an enormous body of knowledge, the history of Man from his pre-existence through the Final Judgment.

No attempt is made by Dr. Martin to analyze the chart or any of the issues it raises. (In fact, he falsely alleges that Mormons view the position of African-Americans on the chart as somehow different from that of other children of God, though not a word on the chart or in any official Mormon Doctrine, implies any such distinction.) Having thus failed to examine Mormon eschatology, even in summary, as depicted in the chart, Dr. Martin declares that Mormon theology on "judgment, and everlasting

17. Martin, *Maze of Mormonism,* 262-263.
18. Martin, *Maze of Mormonism*, 264.

life (universalism) has been examined in the light of the Holy Bible and found sadly wanting."[18]

What is really wanting, however, is a complete and rational analysis by Evangelicals of Bible teachings on the Judgment and the Resurrection. In his book, *Essential Christianity*, Dr. Martin categorizes and numbers various "judgments" referred to in the scriptures.[19] Though he identifies both the *bema* and *thronos* Judgments,[20] Dr. Martin does not even acknowledge the fact that the *bema* Judgment has the potential of both a good and a bad outcome (2 Cor. 5:10). Accordingly, the most obvious of conclusions seems to escape him, as it has other Evangelical scholars, namely that the Judgment must result in Men being divided into *four* major categories, two established in the *bema* Judgment and two at the *thronos* Judgment, *not* the traditional *two* (Heaven and Hell).

In the analysis of Bible passages about judgment and the Resurrection that follows, reference will occasionally be made to passages in D&C 76, which provides the definitive statement of Mormon eschatology regarding the Judgment and Resurrection. These references demonstrate that Mormonism contains the only systematic teaching that agree fully with all the teachings of the Bible on this subject.

The Resurrection of the Unjust. Paul mentions the Resurrection of the Unjust in Acts 24:15 (NASB) as follows:

> having a hope in God, which these men cherish themselves, that there shall certainly be a resurrection of both the righteous [KJV: "just"] and the wicked [KJV: "unjust"].

The terms "righteous" (KJV: "just") and "wicked" (KJV: "unjust") are from the Greek *dikaios*, which, as *dikaioo*" is translated "justify" in the Bible. Thus, the Resurrection of the Unjust, the *thronos* Judgment, involves a division between those who have been justified and those who have not.

The unjustified do not appear in the Lamb's Book of Life, and hence, cannot live with God eternally. But, by the end of the Millennium, when the *thronos* Judgment occurs, the justified will include, not only those who heard the Gospel on earth and accepted it, but spirits who learned to live like God in the Spirit World, the dead who, through faith in Jesus Christ,

19. Martin, *Essential Christianity,* 109-113.
20. Martin, *Essential Christianity,* 110.

real repentance, and baptism by proxy, receive justification after their physical death.

It is clear, from all the passages regarding salvation for the dead, that during Man's sojourn in the Spirit World, the test of this life will continue in some respects. Even those who were evil all their days on earth will have an opportunity to repent and receive remission of their sins in the Spirit World. As noted before, however, repentance in the Spirit World after a life of evil will not make a man worthy of eternal life (Gal. 5:19-21; Eph. 5:3-7; D&C 76:103-105). Of what value is it then? Paul's description quoted above indicates that it will save the penitant from ultimate punishment in the Resurrection of the Unjust.

The ultimate punishment associated with the final Resurrection will only be meted out to those so profoundly depraved that they have done evil and resisted Christ's message of salvation *both* in this life and in the Spirit World. Though God is more patient than Evangelicals suppose, the ultimate condemnation *will be meted out to* those who commit the ultimate sin. That sin is the very one Dr. Martin identifies as "the infinite sin of rejecting His Son."[21]

The scriptures speak of the "son of perdition" (see, John 17:12; 2 Thess. 2:3) being bound for this punishment, which is also referred to as "perdition" (1 Tim. 6:9; Heb. 10:39; 2 Pet.3:7). Those men who truly resolve to choose Satan over Christ, including, those mentioned in Hebrews 6:4-6, will be subjected to the ultimate punishment in the Resurrection of the Unjust. With Satan and his angels, they will suffer the unquenchable fire of the Second Death *forever* (Rev. 20:10-15; D&C 76:32-38).

Since the Final Judgment, and with it the Resurrection of the Unjust, is reserved for the very end of the Millennium (Rev. 20:5), those bound for it are utterly without excuse, having received every opportunity to choose Christ, both here and in the Spirit World. This Resurrection is identified in Mormon theology as the *Second Resurrection.* It is so named because it occurs after the resurrection associated with the *bema* Judgment, which is called the *First Resurrection.*

How many Men will be condemned in the Second Resurrection is a matter of pure conjecture. Some believe that, in view of the opportunity to be justified in the Spirit World, the number of those who will be subjected to the Second Death forever will be few. Certainly that would be

21. Martin, *Maze of Mormonism,* 257.

consistent with God's desire for His children as expressed in 2 Peter 3:9. But no one can be sure how Men will react to the Gospel message in the Spirit World after their lives have been spent in evil, and, if they had a sufficient opportunity in this life to accept the Gospel, they may not be given another chance in the Spirit World (see Rev. 2:21). Only God has sufficient knowledge to make these determinations.

Those who face this Judgment and Resurrection are described by Paul in Ephesians 5:3-6, and by other prophets similarly. All who have done evil while on earth will face the *thronos* Judgment and will be in danger of the Second Death. God will judge their hearts at the last day, and those who have not turned from evil to Christ, whether in this life or in the next, *will* receive a punishment appropriate for the rebellious. For God has decreed that every knee shall bow and every tongue shall confess Christ (Rom. 14:11; Phil. 2:10).

Permanent consignment to the Second Death is only one possible outcome of the last, or Final Judgment, however. There are other possibilities. Not everyone who is subject to the Resurrection of the Unjust belongs in the same category as the Sons of Perdition and the Devil and his angels. Some Men may have done evil in this life, but accepted Christ, repented, and received a remission of their sins through baptism for the dead while in the Spirit World. Others may have chosen good in this life, but stubbornly refused to accept Christ even in the Spirit World. Then there is the issue of how well those who have accepted Christ actually learned to obey His commandments.

Clearly, there are individuals who may not end up permanently consigned to the Second Death at the *thronos* Judgment, but who are precluded from receiving eternal life with God and Christ (see, e.g., Eph. 5:5). This is the most poorly defined group in the scriptures because God has focused on the two extremes in His dealings with Men: eternal life as the goal, and the Second Death as the antigoal. He gives some information about those who miss eternal life, so Men won't be deceived and fall short of that goal, but the Bible contains no definitive discussion of how Men may be wicked but not quite bad enough to spend eternity with Satan and his hosts. Still, it is clear that many who have been evil on this earth will not suffer the same wrath as the Devil and his angels in the Resurrection of the Unjust.

The Resurrection of the Just. The Resurrection of the Just involves righteous believers in this life and those who followed their consciences, behaving righteously in the flesh even without the law, i.e., those who show "the work of the law written in their hearts" (Rom. 2:14-15). The latter group will have the same opportunity to receive Christ and be saved "to the uttermost" (Heb. 7:25) as those who accept the Gospel and learn to obey God in this life. All these individuals will receive eternal life, the greatest reward of all, and become like God (1 John 3:2; 2 Cor. 3:18; see Chapter 4).

They will receive this Resurrection at the *bema* Judgment. However, as noted above, that Judgment also has a downside. That downside will be felt by among others, those spirits whom Christ will reject because they cried "Lord, Lord" but did not *do* the will of the Father (Matt. 7:21). They will include those whom Christ rejects at "that day," saying "I never knew you," despite their protestations of wondrous works in His name (Matt. 7:22-23). "That day" refers to the Judgment, but not the Judgment of the wicked, for the wicked do not make such protestations. Matthew 7:21-23 describes an appearance at the *bema* Judgment.

The Men described in Matthew 7:21-23 obviously think they led good lives. They openly profess belief in Christ and their opinion that they worked for Him. When they learn that they acted without His knowledge or authorization and that the extra effort necessary to learn obedience to God's commandments was crucial, they will be at the mercy seat of Christ. Those who give only lip service to righteousness, who profess to love Christ but do not follow in His footsteps, who are not valiant as a result of their testimonies of Him, will all know the downside of the *bema* Judgment, (see D&C 76:71-80).

Three Degrees of Glory. Christ said there are many different rewards in His Father's house (John 14:2). As revealed by the discussion above, everyone will fall into one of *four* main categories depending on whether they pass or fail one of the two judgments mentioned. In 1 Corinthians 15:36-42, Paul teaches that *three of these* categories will be degrees of glory. He describes these three "glories" by comparing them to different types of bodies:

> *Thou* fool, that which thou sowest is not quickened, except it die:
>
> And that which thou sowest, thou sowest not that body that shall be, but bare grain, it may chance of wheat or of some other *grain:*

> But God giveth it a body as it hath pleased him, and to every seed his own body.
>
> All flesh is not the same flesh: but *there* is one *kind of* flesh of men, another flesh of beasts, another of fishes, *and* another of birds.
>
> *There are* also celestial [NASB: "heavenly"] bodies, and bodies terrestrial [NASB: "earthly"]: but the glory of the celestial [NASB: "heavenly"] *is* one, and the *glory* of the terrestrial [NASB: "earthly"] *is* another.
>
> *There is* one glory of the sun, and another glory of the moon, and another glory of the stars: for *one* star differeth from *another* star in glory.
>
> So also *is* the resurrection of the dead.

After his analogies in verses 36-39 (and no matter how the terms are translated in verse 40), Paul indicates in verse 41 that the resurrection will involve one glory comparable to the Sun, another comparable to the Moon, and a third comparable to the Stars (in which he specifically notes vast diversity). That he is speaking only of those who will not be permanently consigned to the Second Death is evident from the fact that he uses the term "glory" in identifying these divisions. The Sons of Perdition will receive nothing that could be described as "glory." Theirs is the fourth, the lowest category.

At the bottom end of Paul's spectrum of glories are those whose ignominy was insufficient to justify permanent consignment to the Second Death. These individuals obviously were not all bad on earth, or they made some major improvements in the Spirit World so as to avoid becoming Sons of Perdition. They will receive a "glory" which Paul compared to the object of lowest magnitude in the heavens—the stars. Mormons refer to this "glory" as the Telestial Kingdom.

At the other end of the "glory" spectrum are those who have done good and overcome sin so that their names remain written in the Lamb's Book of Life. These are they who will enjoy eternal life with God and Christ (John 17:3). This "exceeding great reward" (Gen. 15:1) is compared to the object of greatest magnitude in the heavens—the Sun. This is the ultimate salvation of Man, and is synonymous with the Kingdom of Heaven or the Kingdom of God. Mormons refer to this "glory" as the Celestial Kingdom.

Those who receive the "glory of the Moon" lost their full reward at the *bema* Judgment. Strictly speaking, these souls do not come forth in the Resurrection of the Just, for, having failed the *bema* Judgment, they are not found to be justified.[22] They will pay a price for their brand of wickedness, as indicated below. But there is more good in them than in those who chose evil in this life and only repented in the Spirit World, so they will receive a greater glory. Mormons refer to their "glory" as the Terrestrial Kingdom.

The Resurrection of Life. John testifies of the resurrection also. John 5:28-29, quoted above in regard to salvation for the dead, contains John's description of the resurrection as follows (emphasis added):

> Marvel not at this: for the hour is coming, in the which *all* that are in the graves shall hear his voice,
>
> And shall come forth; they that have done good, unto the resurrection of *life;* and they that have done evil, unto the resurrection of *damnation.*

While Paul focuses on justification, referring to the Resurrection of the Just. (Acts 24:15; see, also, Luke 14:14) at one end of the spectrum and the Unjust (Acts 24:15) at the other, John's description looks at Resurrection from a different perspective. He focuses on the attainment of eternal life as the ultimate reward and refers first to the Resurrection of Life. All other resurrections are part of what he calls the Resurrection of Damnation. "Damnation" is translated from the Greek word *krisis*, which means "judgment." The implication is that the resurrection of all who do not receive eternal life will involve some element of judgment or condemnation.

The Resurrection of Life refers to the ultimate salvation of Men who are resurrected to eternal life with God and Christ. It is the same as the Resurrection of the Just, the glory Paul describes as comparable to the Sun. John includes the other glories, along with permanent consignment to the Second Death, as the Resurrection of Damnation.

In Revelation 20:4-6, John calls the Resurrection of Life the "first resurrection," and describes it (with some emphasis added) as follows:

> And I saw thrones, and they sat upon them, and judgment was given unto them: and I *saw* the souls of them that were beheaded

22. D&C 76:50-65 describes the resurrection of those who receive the Celestial Kingdom and specifically refers to it as "the resurrection of the just."

> for the witness of Jesus, and for the word of God, and which had not worshipped the beast, neither his image, neither had received *his* mark upon their foreheads, or in their hands; *and they lived* and reigned with Christ a thousand years.
>
> But the rest of the dead *lived not again* until the thousand years were finished. This *is* the first resurrection.
>
> Blessed and holy *is* he that hath part in the first resurrection: on such the second death hath no power, but they shall be priests of God and of Christ, and shall reign with him a thousand years.

The statement in verse 5 that the rest of the dead "lived not again" means they are *not* resurrected during the Millennium. The reference in verse 4, "and they lived," referring to those described in that verse, means these individuals *are* resurrected during the Millennium. Thus, the statement in verse 5, "This *is* the first resurrection," refers to those who are found worthy of eternal life at the *bema* Judgment. They will be resurrected first, i.e., while that judgment is on-going during the Millennium. All who are not so rewarded must await the Second Resurrection which occurs in connection with the Final Judgment.

The Resurrection of Damnation. All who are subject to any form of condemnation receive what John describes as the Resurrection of Damnation. This includes those who fail the *bema* Judgment and receive the glory of the Moon. The rest of Mankind will take part in the Final or *thronos* Judgment. They consist of the Sons of Perdition, and those who are not permanently condemned, but receive the glory of the Stars.

Revelation 20:10 states:

> And the devil that deceived them was cast into the lake of fire and brimstone, where the beast and the false prophet *are,* and shall be tormented day and night for ever and ever.

This passage indicates that Satan, and all who have followed him, either in pre-mortality (Rev. 12:4), or on Earth, will be consigned to the lake of fire and brimstone permanently. However, Revelation 20 mentions another group in connection with the Second Resurrection who are called "the dead" (Rev. 20:12-14). The righteous will have been resurrected by the time the *thronos* Judgment occurs. So they will not be among "the dead" when these events occur. "The dead" will include all other Men, namely: 1) the Sons of Perdition, 2) those who receive the glory of the Stars and 3) those who failed the *bema* Judgment.

Of this group, Revelation 20:12-13 (with some emphasis added) says:

> And I saw *the dead,* small and great, stand before God; and the books were opened, and another book *was* opened, which is *the book* of life; and *the dead* were judged out of those things which were written in the books, according to their works.
>
> And the sea gave up *the dead* which were in it; and death and hell delivered up *the dead* which were in them: and they were judged every man according to their works.

Revelation 20:14 states that "*death and hell* were cast into the lake of fire." "Hell" can only refer to those who have associated themselves with Satan and his minions—the Sons of Perdition. "Death," therefore, must refer to the other two categories—those who receive the glory of the Moon, and those destined for the glory of the Stars.

Revelation 20:15 says that "whosoever was not found written in the book of life was cast into the lake of fire." That includes *everyone* who does not come forth in the Resurrection of Life. So it is clear that those who come to the *thronos* Judgment, along with those who failed the *bema* Judgment, will *all* be cast into the lake of fire for some duration (cf., D&C 76:103-105, and 36-39).

Revelation 20:10, states that the devil and his followers (the Sons of Perdition), will be cast into the lake of fire *forever.* The same is *not* said of "the dead" generally (see Rev. 20:14-15). The inescapable conclusion is that those who receive the glories of the Moon and of the Stars must expect to spend some lesser time in hell fire.

Revelation 21:7-8 supports this conclusion as follows:

> He that overcometh shall inherit all things; and I will be his God, and he shall be my son.
>
> But the fearful, and unbelieving, and the abominable, and murderers, and whoremongers, and sorcerers, and idolaters, and all liars, shall have their part in the lake which burneth with fire and brimstone: which is the second death.

"He that overcometh" (verse 7) refers to those who are found worthy of eternal life. In contrast, John describes several very different types of people in verse 8. He includes the "fearful," from the Greek, *deilos,* meaning "timid" (those who have been timid or hesitant about accepting Christ), and the "unbelieving," from the Greek, *apistos,* meaning "disobedient," or "not faithful." He also lists specific groups of more wicked individuals. All of these will have "their *part*" (Greek: *meros,* meaning "division") in "the second death."

This passage confirms that there will be different "divisions" in the Second Death. Revelation 20:10 refers to one such division (the Sons of Perdition), and specifically states that those consigned to that division will remain subject to the second death forever. It follows that the other divisions will not be subject to the same duration of punishment.[23]

Those Evangelicals who teach only of Heaven and Hell have failed to discern the more complex outcome described by the Bible. Since there will be two major Judgments associated with the two Resurrections described in scripture, there must, of necessity, be *four* major divisions in the Resurrection, corresponding to those who pass and those who fail each of the two Judgments discussed.

For those who wish to compare these teachings to the chart in Dr. Martin's book,[24] Mormons call the three higher divisions the Celestial Kingdom, the Terrestrial Kingdom, and the Telestial Kingdom (the three degrees of glory). The lowest division is the Second Death which refers to the place where the Sons of Perdition, with Satan and his angels, will be consigned permanently.

Conclusion

The Lord gives all Men who live upon the earth an opportunity to know good from evil, either through the teachings of His prophets or through the promptings of their consciences. Likewise, He will give all Men the opportunity to hear the Gospel and receive justification, either in this life or in the Spirit World. But all Men will be judged according to their deeds *in the flesh.* Hence, they must learn to do good rather than evil *in this life.*

The Spirit World provides an opportunity for Men to turn to Christ and have their sins forgiven and forgotten by the Lord. The extent to which the Lord will grant this opportunity lies in His wisdom and knowledge, but there is strong reason to believe He is generous and patient with Men in this regard. Many, however, who think they are saved, will be turned away from the Resurrection of Life because they refuse to accept the necessity of obedience to God's commandments.

In the *bema* judgment (associated with the First Resurrection), the Lord will decide whether or not *believers* are prepared to receive the gift of

23. On this point, compare D&C 76:103-105 to Rev. 21:7-8; and see, D&C 76:36-39.
24. Martin, *Maze of Mormonism,* 263.

eternal life, the glory Paul compared to the Sun. Those who are will live with God and become like Him. Those who are not, will receive a glory comparable to the Moon.

The wicked, who are not in the running for eternal life, will face the *thronos* Judgment. At that, the Final Judgment, God will decide whether the dead who remain subject to this most terrifying of audits receive permanent consignment to the lake of fire and brimstone, the Second Death, or come forth, after some finite time, to the glory of the Stars. Even those who fail the *bema* Judgment, whose glory is compared to the Moon, will be consigned to the Second Death for a time.

Thus, Mormons do *not* teach that Men will be punished *until* they accept Christ, as some Evangelicals claim.[25] Rather, they teach that Men will receive the punishment of God after they have demonstrated whether they will refuse to accept Christ or will follow His teachings. God's punishment is based on their deeds in the flesh, with due consideration given to whether or not they accept Him in the Spirit World before the end of the Millennium.

God has made it clear throughout the scriptures that all of Man's deeds on Earth are accounted for in the Judgment. Those who reject the Gospel, who choose to do evil instead of obey God's commandments, *no matter what they profess to believe,* must suffer the most dire of consequences for at least a finite time.

The punishment Men will endure if they do not repent is described by Christ in the most sobering of terms as follows (D&C 19:15-20):

> Therefore I command you to repent—repent, lest I smite you by the rod of my mouth, and by my wrath, and by my anger, and your sufferings be sore—how sore you know not, how exquisite you know not, yea, how hard to bear you know not.
>
> For behold, I, God, have suffered these things for all, that they might not suffer if they would repent;
>
> But if they would not repent they must suffer even as I;
>
> Which suffering caused myself, even God, the greatest of all, to tremble because of pain, and to bleed at every pore, and to suffer both body and spirit—and would that I might not drink the bitter cup, and shrink—

25. Martin, *Maze of Mormonism,* 255.

> Nevertheless, glory be to the Father, and I partook and finished my preparations unto the children of men.
>
> Wherefore, I command you again to repent, lest I humble you with my almighty power; and that you confess your sins, lest you suffer these punishments of which I have spoken, of which in the smallest, yea, even in the least degree you have tasted at the time I withdrew my Spirit.

Mormons sincerely pray that all who hear the biblical truths taught by The Church of Jesus Christ of Latter-day Saints will repent of their sins and seek justification through faith, repentance, and baptism by those having authority to administer that saving ordinance. Those who do, and who seek to remain on the strait and narrow path, can be assured that they will be saved from the lake of fire and brimstone which is the Second Death, and will abide forever in the Kingdom of God. All who currently teach or believe otherwise are invited to reconsider, and turn to the righteousness taught in biblical Mormonism.

Appendix A

An Overview of External Evidence for the Accuracy of Old and New Testament Texts

The tedious process of higher criticism employed to review Old and New Testament texts is not appropriate for inclusion in this work. (It is also fraught with much controversy, the nature of which need not concern the beginning student.) Reference may be had to the works cited in Chapter 1 for further information on textual criticism of the Bible. This Appendix will explore the external evidence for the texts of the Old and New Testaments that is available to Bible scholars today. A basic familiarity with this material will give the Mormon apologist an essential foundation for Bible-based discussions.

The Old Testament

So exact was the process used by the Masoretic scribes to copy Old Testament texts that, for example, some words in the manuscript have odd marks over them which are not understood by any scholar. These are possibly the result of an accidental splutter of the pen by some long dead copyist, which is now faithfully repeated in every copy. Even the size and placement of letters in the text is copied precisely, without regard to the fact that such variations have no effect on the meaning of the text.

The texts have been critically examined over the years, and a few errors have been noted. But even known errors in the text are copied, with the corrections appearing only in marginal notes or through the insertion of vowels. The vowels were not considered part of the Hebrew text itself. Therefore, the insertion of vowels was not considered tampering with the text. If a word in the text was considered superfluous, it was copied, but was not supplied with vowels; if a word was to be inserted, its vowels were written without consonants; and if a word was changed, the consonants were left in tact, but were provided with the vowels of the word to be substituted.

In addition to the texts themselves, there are huge collections of Masoretic notes that deal with such matters as how often each letter of the Hebrew alphabet occurs in the Old Testament, how many verses contain all the letters of the alphabet, and the number of words in the text and the middle word. All this minutia attests to the care used by the Jews in copying the Old Testament texts.[1]

The Masoretic tradition did not allow any text of the Old Testament to remain until it was so worn by use that it could not be accurately deciphered. Once copied, older versions were destroyed. Hence, until the Dead Sea Scrolls were discovered in Qumran in 1947, there were no texts of the Old Testament, or any portions thereof, from a date earlier than 916 A.D.

The accuracy of current Old Testament texts was confirmed by discoveries in the Dead Sea Scrolls. The Scrolls include fragments from every book of the Old Testament except Esther. Comparison of the Isaiah scrolls (c. 200 B.C.) to the Masoretic text indicates that deviations are minor, even after 1100 years of copying![2]

However, comparisons with the Book of Samuel suggest that the Qumran texts followed the Septuagint version ("the LXX") rather than the Masoretic texts. The LXX is a Greek version of the Old Testament compiled by seventy-two Jewish scholars at Alexandria in approximately 285-275 B.C. By the time of Christ, Hebrew had ceased to be a spoken language. (It was largely lost during the Babylonian captivity.) Aramaic and Greek were the dialects of the day, and the Septuagint was written in Greek for common use. Most New Testament quotations of the Old Testament are from the LXX.

The LXX is highly regarded, but modern critics note that it contains many Greco-Egyptian words; that the five books of Moses (the Pentateuch) are translated with greater accuracy than the other books; that the Book of Job, the Psalms and the Prophets, especially Isaiah and Daniel, are believed to be inferior; and that the historical books are often translated inaccurately. The use of the Masoretic text, on which scholars are almost entirely dependent for the purity of the Hebrew original, in the Qumran text of Isaiah confirms some of these

1. This information is provided in Angus, *The Bible Handbook,* 24-35.

2. Lewis M. Rogers, "The Significance of the Scrolls and a Word of Caution" in *Progress in Archaeology: An Anthology,* Ross T. Christensen, ed. (Provo: Brigham Young University, 1963), 46-47.

criticisms. However, the closeness of the Qumran text of Samuel to the LXX suggests that a slightly different, and possibly older, Hebrew text than the one finally adopted by the Jews in the Masoretic text may have been available to the translators of the LXX.

The New Testament

The existing Greek manuscripts of the New Testament are divided into two principle categories, *uncial* and *cursive*. Uncial manuscripts are older, written entirely in capital (*majuscule*) letters. Later documents were written in the smaller script popular in commerce. These are the cursive (or *minuscule*) manuscripts. There are a total of 101 uncial manuscripts of the four Gospels (127 if smaller fragments are counted); 22 of Acts and the non-Pauline Epistles; 27 of the Pauline Epistles; and six of Revelation.[3] Of the cursive manuscripts, there are 1,420 of the Gospels; 450 of Acts and the non-Pauline Epistles; 520 of the Pauline Epistles; and 194 of Revelation.[4]

All the important manuscripts, besides being specifically named, are designated by a letter or symbol. The chief uncial manuscripts are as follows:

Aleph (first letter of the Hebrew alphabet), or *Codex Sinaiticus,* was discovered in the Convent of St. Catherine on Mount Sinai in 1859 in a waste basket. It dates from the fourth century, and contains the apostolic epistles, the prophecies of Jonah, and the fifth book of Moses. It is written in coptic.

A, or *Codex Alexandrinus,* dates from the middle or end of the fifth century. It contains the Old Testament in Greek, and the New Testament beginning with Matthew 25:6, omitting John 6:50-8:52, and 2 Corinthians 4:15-12:6. It also contains the First Epistle of Clement of Rome and a small portion of the Second.

B, or *Codex Vaticanus,* dates from the fourth century. It contains the Old Testament in Greek (with omissions), and the New Testament down to Heb. 9:14. It also contains the General Epistles, but does not contain the Pastoral Epistles of Paul, Philemon, or Revelation.

C, or *Codex Ephraemi,* contains twelfth-century copies over an older text. Fortunately, the ink of the later scribe proved less durable than that of

3. Angus, *The Bible Handbook,* p. 50.
4. Angus, *The Bible Handbook,* p. 51.

the earlier copyist, who wrote in the fifth century, probably in Egypt. *C* contains fragments of the Old Testament, and all the books of the New Testament (with large omissions), except 2 Thessalonians and 2 John.

D, known as *Codex Cantabrigiensis* or *Codex Bezae,* was probably written near the beginning of the sixth century in Greek and Latin parallel columns. It contains the Gospels and Acts (with omissions), and is remarkable for its deviations from the ordinary text and for its additions.

D2, or *Codex Claromontanus,* was written in the sixth century, approx. 550 A.D., and is also in Greek and Latin. It adds to *D* the Pauline Epistles (with omissions) and the Epistle to the Hebrews.

In addition to the foregoing, there are about 170 papyrus uncial fragments dating from the second through the seventh century. The cursive manuscripts date from the ninth to the sixteen century. Three-quarters of these texts contain only the Gospels and one third of those are fragmentary. The vast majority of these manuscripts comprise the Byzantine Texts from which the KJV was derived.

In addition there are about 1,678 *lectionaries*. These are collections of the Gospels and the Epistles which were used for reading in the Greek Church. They were copied with extreme care and in large clear characters.

It is interesting to note that, except for a fragment not much larger than a postage stamp, there is not a single text dating from the early second century. Many texts of other historical documents from that era are still available to scholars, so one must wonder why there are no New Testament texts that old. Notably, it was during the second century that most of the events identified by Mormons with the Great Apostacy took place.[5]

The texts are divided into three classes according to the locale in which they were popular. The Western Texts are so called because they contain the form of text found in the writings of the early Church Fathers at Rome, especially Irenaeus, Tertullian, Cyprian, and Augustine. The most important manuscripts of the Western Text available today are *D* and *D2.* Two other documents of importance in regard to the Western Texts are the Old Latin and Old Syriac versions of the New Testament.

The next category is the Alexandrian Texts, which contain the version used by Origen and the other early Church Fathers who lived at

5. See Hopkins, *How Greek Philosophy Corrupted the Christian Concept of God*, Part II.

Alexandria. The most important texts of this class are *Aleph* and *B*. The NASB was derived from a text that relies heavily on these, the oldest texts.

The remaining texts, which constitute the vast majority available today, are the Byzantine Texts. They contain the Greek New Testament in general use throughout the greater part of the Byzantine Period (312-1453 A.D.) This was the text of the Greek or Eastern Orthodox Church, and for three centuries after the Protestant Reformation this text was used by the entire Protestant movement.

The Byzantine Texts are generally designated with the letter *K* (Common) and variations to designate individual families of texts. The *Kl* class contain the earliest forms of the Byzantine Text, of which *Omega* (eighth century), *V* (9th century), and *S* (tenth century) are the best examples. The *Kr* class of texts are considered to be revisions of the *K* texts made in the eleventh and twelfth centuries to exhibit the scripture lessons that were read in Greek Church services. The *Kx* class contain miscellaneous manuscripts, the *x* indicating that the small differences that distinguish them from each other have not been thoroughly studied.[6]

While the older texts, *Aleph* and *B,* are preferred by most scholars, Dr. Edward F. Hills makes a convincing argument in favor of the Byzantine Texts in his book *The King James Version Defended!* (Des Moines: The Christian Research Press, 1956). He indicates that the second and third centuries were not favorable to the accurate transmission of New Testament texts. This was due, in part, to the extreme persecution of the early Church by Rome.[7] That persecution began in the reign of Nero (64-68 A.D.), which resulted in the martyrdoms of Paul and Peter at Rome, and continued in the second officially sanctioned persecution of Christians during the reign of Domitian (c. 93 A. D.). John was banished to the isle of Patmos during the latter persecution. There were additional persecutions under Trajan (98-117 A.D.), Marcus Aurelius (161-180 A.D.), Severus (193-211 A.D.), Maximin (235-238 A.D.), and Decius (249-251 A.D.).

The most widespread Roman persecution of Christians occurred under the reign of Diocletian (284-305 A.D.). This persecution was so extensive it was believed to have resulted in the entire annihilation of the Christian

6. Information on the Byzantine Texts is from Hills, *The King James Version Defended!*

7. It should be noted however, that Roman persecution did not generally involve book burning until the third century.

religion. Most significantly for the New Testament texts, Diocletian ordered a general destruction of Christian books and decreed the death penalty for any who kept such works in their possession.[8]

During this period of Roman persecution, numerous errors crept into the few copies of the New Testament that survived in Rome. Many arose through carelessness, but some variant readings were introduced by editors and revisors (readily apparent in *D* and *D2,* as noted above). The rewritten text became popular in the early Roman Church. It is generally regarded as inferior, however, containing many additions, deletions and errors.

An extensive effort was made during the third century in Alexandria to correct the errors of the Western Texts using techniques of textual criticism that were in vogue at the library there. In their zeal to delete spurious additions, however, these early textual critics omitted much that was genuine from the Western Texts.

Fortunately, most of the original *autographa* of the New Testament books were kept at the Church in Antioch, in Asia Minor, which was somewhat removed from the influence of Rome and Alexandria, and was even a little antagonistic to those regions (because of an early controversy over the date of Easter–the Quartodeciman controversy during the last half of the second century). Having the originals, they were not dependent upon importing their texts from distant regions, and were doubtless more careful in copying them.

Beginning in the fourth century, the texts from the Asia Minor region came to be preferred over the Western and Alexandrian texts. They were read and copied so frequently they wore to tatters and were lost, but not before they spawned a host of fresh and highly accurate copies.

Thus, according to Dr. Hills, the fact that there are no old copies of the Byzantine Texts is a reflection of their accuracy. Being recognized as the most accurate texts, they were worn out by use, but not before true and accurate copies were made, from which, ultimately, the majority of remaining texts are derived. This argument implies that the reason *Aleph* and *B* survived to the present day is that they were not in active use and may have been regarded as inferior. Thus, it was no wonder to Dr. Hills that *Aleph* was found in a waste basket!

---

8. James E. Talmage, *The Great Apostasy: Considered in the Light of Scriptural and Secular History,* (Salt Lake City: Deseret News Press, n.d.), 67-75.

However compelling this theory, even Dr. Hills recognizes that over the centuries some errors crept into the Byzantine Texts. Using other texts as well, such errors were largely corrected by Erasmus in his compilation of the *Textus Receptus*. All the texts are useful in arriving at the most accurate text possible since the same errors are not found in every text. For good reason, the oldest texts, *Aleph* and *B,* are highly regarded by modern scholars, though they too are not without problems. It is the combination, the number of different texts, that makes the difference. This wealth of textual evidence suggests that LDS scholars may be confident the current text accepted by most scholars today is extremely close to the original.

Appendix B
Lost Scripture

Evangelical theology denies the possibility that any of God's revelations to Man has ever been lost. Their position is stated thus:

> To say that there are scriptures missing is to claim that Christ lied when He said, 'Till heaven and earth pass, one jot or one tittle shall in no wise pass from the law, till all be fulfilled. (Matt. 5:18).[1]

This analysis presents a grossly flawed interpretation of Matthew 5:18, which has nothing to do with the canon of scripture. The Bible was not even compiled at the time the Gospel of Matthew was written. Matthew 5:18 relates to "the law," the Law of Moses, and Christ's fulfillment thereof. The Law of Moses was contained in the Pentateuch, the first five books of the Bible. Thus, if the Evangelical position on Matthew 5:18 were correct, it would require them to limit their scriptures to the Pentateuch (a view that may have been adopted by the ancient Sadducees and certainly by the Samaritans[2]).

What Christ says in Matthew 5:18 is that not one dot of an "i" or cross of a "t" in the Law of Moses would be changed until it was all fulfilled by Him. Far from teaching that the Law would never change, it is implicit in this statement that the law would "pass" once it was fulfilled. The Law of Moses was fulfilled by Christ, and *did* pass away (Heb. 7:18).

The Evangelical interpretation of Matthew 5:18 is based on an assumption not specifically identified in their exegesis, namely that the word "scripture" is the same as the word "law" in that verse. That interpretation can be tested using the hermeneutic device of substitution. The passage should have the same meaning if the word "scripture" is substituted for the word "law" in the text. In fact, however, such a substitution changes the entire meaning of the passage. Clearly, Matthew 5:18 does *not* teach that there have been no lost scriptures, and cannot be used as a basis for that thesis.

---

1. Trivanovich, *Speaking the Truth in Love,* 13.
2. Angus, *The Bible Handbook,* 17.

There are a number of references in the Bible to works that have apparently been lost, or at least they are not available in any recognizable form today. Table 2, Lost Scripture, below, lists these works. The context of the references indicates that many, if not all, were inspired. Of course, Evangelicals earnestly deny this possibility.

Instead, their argument is, "The Bible does not say that these are scriptures."[3] While that may be so, the Bible rarely says that any of its respective books are scripture. The canon of scripture is not self-identified. It should also be noted that Christ didn't always say that the writings of Isaiah, for example, from which He quoted extensively, were scripture (see, e.g., Matt. 13:14-15).

Nevertheless, in support of their argument Evangelicals note that sacred writers have occasionally cited non-sacred works. Paul quotes a Cretan identified in the passage as "a prophet of their own" in Titus 1:12. The problem with that argument is that Paul makes it perfectly clear in the same verse that he is not citing scripture. He specifically identifies his source as secular. See also, Acts 17:23, 28. There are no similar indications in any of the references listed in Table 2.

The reference in Matthew 2:23 has proven particularly thorny for Evangelicals. Matthew 2:23 (NASB) explains that Christ and His family went to Galilee,

> and came and resided in a city called Nazareth, that what was spoken through the prophets might be fulfilled, "He shall be called a Nazarene."

Here Matthew quotes from a prophetic work available to the Jews of his time but not included in the Masoretic Text (not a surprise considering how accurately this text identifies Jesus as the Messiah). His quotation from "the prophets" is recognized by most Bible scholars as being of unknown origin.

C.I. Scofield argues that it may have come from Isaiah 11:1, which prophesies that Christ will be a "shoot [Hebrew: *netzer*] . . . from the stem of Jesse."[4] While the Hebrew word *netzer* may be vaguely similar to the word "Nazarene," the citation in Isaiah hardly contains the language, "He

3. Trivanovich, *Speaking the Truth in Love,* 13.
4. *The New Scofield Study Bible,* 1320 (footnote to Matt. 2:23).

shall be called a Nazarene," quoted by Matthew. Hence, this stretch of hermeneutic imagination is questionable at best.

However, an alternative theological context in which these "lost scriptures" may be viewed is suggested by Dr. Angus. He states:

> A book may have had *a long literary history* before its admission into the Canon. This is perhaps most obvious in regard to the Book of Psalms. Many of those inspired songs were certainly held to be of Divine authority before all were written, and therefore before the Psalter as a whole was 'canonized.' In other books we may clearly discern the inclusion of fragmentary material, venerable for its antiquity.
>
> In the Pentateuch are embedded separate codes of Law which in all probability are older than the books in which they appear. A store of national religious poetry is indicated by the Song of Deborah, the Song of Moses and the Children of Israel after the crossing of the Red Sea, the Dirge of David over Saul. The titles of two such collections are preserved in 'The Book of the Wars of the Lord,' Num. 21:14 and 'The Book of Jasher' (the Upright) Jos 10:13, 2 Sa 1:18. History was preserved in the same way: the historical books contain references to such earlier chronicles as 'The history of Samuel the seer and the history of Nathan the prophet and the history of Gad the seer' 1 Ch 29:29 R.V.: 'The Book of the Acts of Solomon' 1 Ki 11:41, 'The histories of Shemaiah the prophet and of Iddo the seer' 2 Ch 12:15, and others. The prophetical books, again, are obviously collections of utterances separately spoken and separately preserved. Behind the books of the Old Testament we may frequently discern an earlier literature, the primitive records in song, law, history, prophecy, of the nation's life and the nation's faith. And we may recognize in the making of an Old Testament book the three stages—the primitive material, the editing into present literary form, and the canonization or final acceptance as Scripture. It need hardly be added that to acknowledge this principle of literary growth neither impairs the Divine authority of the books nor involves the extravagant analysis of some modern imaginative criticism.[5]

---

5. Angus, *The Bible Handbook,* 18-19.

Mormons should be familiar with the process described above. It is similar to that used by the ancient American prophet Mormon in abridging the Book of Mormon (see, e.g., The Words of Mormon 3-11). It is also reminiscent of the process by which additions have been made to the modern canon of scripture during the history of The Church of Jesus Christ of Latter-day Saints, as witnessed by the addition of Sections 137 and 138 to the Doctrine and Covenants. These new sections contain inspired writings that have, over the years, become recognized by the Church as inspired revelations.

The fact that inspired works that are part of today's canon may have been based upon earlier inspired works should instill confidence in the accuracy and importance of the final product.

The significance of the records listed in Table 2 is not that they represent some deficiency in God's word as contained in the Bible. Rather, they are supporting evidence for the process by which inspired writing has in the past, and may in the future, become part of the scriptural canon.

Table 2
Lost Scripture

Reference:	Lost Scripture:
Numbers 21:14	The Book of the Wars of the Lord
Joshua 10:13 & 2 Samuel 1:18	The Book of Jasher (the real one, not the apocryphal version we have today.)
1 Samuel 10:25	Another Book of Samuel
1 Chronicles 29:29 & 2 Chronicles 2:29	The Book of Nathan the Prophet and The Book of Gad the Seer
1 Kings 11:41	The Book of the Acts of Solomon
2 Chronicles 9:29 & 2 Chronicles 13:22	The prophecy of Abijah the Shilonite and the visions of Iddo the Seer
2 Chronicles 12:15	The Book of Shemaiah the Prophet and the Book of Iddo the Seer
2 Chronicles 20:34	The Book of Jehu
2 Chronicles 33:19	The Sayings of the Seers (NASB The Records of the Hozai)
Matthew 2:23	The book containing the prophecy that Christ would be called a "Nazarene."
1 Corinthians 5:9	Another epistle to the Corinthians
Colossians 4:16	Paul's epistle to Laodicea
Jude 3	Another epistle from Jude
Jude 14-1	The book from which Jude quotes the writings of Enoch.

Bibliography

Angus, Joseph. *The Bible Handbook: An Introduction to the Study of Sacred Scripture.* Rev. by Samuel G. Green. New York: Fleming H. Revel Company, n.d.

Bauer, Walter. *A Greek-English Lexicon of the New Testament and Other Early Christian Literature,* 4th ed. Trans. William F. Arndt and F. Wilbur Gingrich. Chicago: University of Chicago Press, 1957.

Berkhof, Louis. *Systematic Theology.* Grand Rapids: Eerdmans, 1939.

Bickersteth, Edward. *The Trinity.* Grand Rapids: Kregel Publications, 1957.

Bleicher, Josef. *Contemporary Hermeneutics: Hermeneutics as Method, Philosophy and Critique.* London: Routledge & Kegan Paul Ltd, 1980.

Bloesch, Donald. *Essentials of Evangelical Theology: Volume 1, God, Authority, and Salvation.* San Francisco: Harper & Row, Publishers, 1978.

Brooks, Thomas. *Heaven on Earth: A Treatise on Christian Assurance, reprint.* Edinburgh: Banner of Truth, 1982.

Chafer, Lewis Sperry. *Dispensationalism,* rev. ed. Dallas: Dallas Seminary Press, 1951.

Cocoris, G. Michael. *Evangelism: A Biblical Approach.* Chicago: Moody Press, 1984.

___ Letter to the author. November 3, 1989

___ *Lordship Salvation: Is it Biblical?* Dallas: Redención Viva, 1983.

The Concise Evangelical Dictionary of Theology. Walter Elwell, ed., abridged by Peter Toon. Grand Rapids: Baker Book House, 1991.

Emmons, Steve. "The Mystery of Memory," *Los Angeles Times.* Tuesday, January 11, 1994, Section E.

Encyclopaedia Britannica, 1960 ed. Chicago: William Benton, 1960.

The Expositor's Bible Commentary, 12 vols. Frank E. Gaebelein, ed. Grand Rapids: Zondervan, 1984.

Geisler, Norman. "The Battle for the Resurrection," *Christian Research*

Newsletter 5, no. 1. Irvine: Christian Research Institute, 1992.

Gifis, Steven H. *Law Dictionary.* Woodbury: Barron's Educational Series, Inc., 1975.

Hills, Edward F. *The King James Version Defended!: A Christian View of the New Testament Manuscripts.* Des Moines: The Christian Research Press, 1956.

Hocking, David. *Grace and Good Works: A Study of Titus* 2:11-15. La Mirada: Biola Hour Ministries, 1989.

Hodge, Charles. *Systematic Theology,* reprint. Grand Rapids: Eerdmans, 1989.

Hodges, Zane. *Absolutely Free!* Grand Rapids: Zondervan, 1989.

The Holy Bible, Authorized King James Version. Salt Lake City: The Church of Jesus Christ of Latter-day Saints, 1979.

The Interpreter's Dictionary of the Bible: An Illustrated Encyclopedia, 4 vols. George A. Buttrick, ed. New York: Abingdon Press, 1962.

Kendall, R.T. *Once Saved, Always Saved.* Chicago: Moody, 1983.

Kent, H.A. *The Epistle to the Hebrews: A Commentary.* Grand Rapids: Baker Book House, 1972.

Larkin, Clarence. *Dispensational Truth.* Philadelphia: Larkin, 1918.

Luther, Martin. "Table Talk," *Luther's Works,* 55 vols. Ed. Helmut T. Lehman, trans. Theodore G. Tappert. Philadelphia: Fortress, 1967.

Maas, Paul. *Textual Criticism.* Trans. Barbara Flower. Oxford: University Press, 1967.

MacArthur, John F., Jr. *Faith Works: The Gospel According to the Apostles.* Dallas: Word Publishing, 1993.

___ *The Gospel According to Jesus.* Panorama City: Word of Grace, 1988.

Martin, Walter. Essential Christianity. Ventura: Regal Books, 1980.

___ *The Maze of Mormonism.* Ventura: Regal Books, 1978.

Metzger, Bruce M. *The Canon of the New Testament.* Oxford: Clarendon Press, 1987.

McConkie, Bruce R. *Mormon Doctrine,* 2nd ed. Salt Lake City: Bookcraft, 1966.

McDowell, Josh. *Evidence That Demands a Verdict.* San Bernadino: Here's Life Publishers, 1979.

Morey, Robert. *Battle of the Gods.* Southbridge: Crown Publications, 1989.

Mormonism: *The Mormon Concept of Gods,* 4 audiotapes. A debate between Robert Morey and Richard Hopkins. Irvine: Christian Research Institute, 1992.

The New International Commentary on the New Testament: The Epistle to the Hebrews. F.F. Bruce, ed. Grand Rapids: Eerdmans, 1964.

New Scofield Study Bible: New American Standard, rev. 1967. C.I. Scofield, ed., consultants Paul S. Karleen and Glenn R. Goss. New York: Oxford University Press, 1988.

Reader's Digest Illustrated Encyclopedia Dictionary. Pleasantville: The Reader's Digest Assn., 1987.

Rogers, Lewis M. "The Significance of the Scrolls and a Word of Caution," *Progress in Archaeology: An Anthology.* Ross T. Christensen, ed. Provo: Brigham Young University, 1963.

Ryrie, Charles. *So Great Salvation.* Wheaton: Victor, 1989.

Schaff, Philip. *The Creeds of Christendom,* 6th ed., 3 vols. Grand Rapids: Baker Book House, 1983.

Smith, Joseph, Jr. *History of The Church of Jesus Christ of Latter-day Saints,* 2nd ed. rev., 7 vols. Salt Lake City: Deseret Book Company, 1978.

___ *The Holy Scriptures: Inspired Version.* Independence: Herald Publishing House, 1974.

___ "Lecture First," A Compilation Containing the Lectures on Faith. Comp. N.B. Lundwald. Salt Lake City: Bookcraft, Inc., n.d.

___ *Teachings of the Prophet Joseph Smith.* Comp. Joseph Fielding Smith, 1970 reprint. Salt Lake City: Deseret Book Company, 1938.

Standard Dictionary of the English Language: Combined with Britannica World Language Dictionary, international ed. New York: Funk & Wagnals Company, 1960.

Talmage, James E. *The Great Apostasy: Considered in the Light of Scriptural and Secular History.* Salt Lake City: Deseret News Press, n.d.

Terry, Milton S. *Biblical Hermeneutics: A Treatise on the Interpretation of the Old and New Testaments.* Grand Rapids: Zondervan, n.d.

Trivanovich, Cary. "Speaking the Truth in Love" (Ephesians 4:15) *What Every Mormon Should Know.* Orange: Promise Publishing Company, 1988.

Webster's Ninth New Collegiate Dictionary. A. Merriam-Webster, ed. Springfield: Merriam-Webster, Inc., 1987.

Wilkin, Bob. "Putting the Gospel Debate in Sharper Focus," *The Grace Evangelical Society News.* May 1991.

Scripture Index

Old Testament

New Testament

Book of Mormon

Doctrine And Covenants

Pearl of Great Price

Subject Index

A

B

F

G

H

I

J

L

M

O

P

R

S

T

V

W